Maximum Climbing

"For anyone interested in learning more about how the mind works and how important psychological factors are in determining the quality of our experience and performance, *Maximum Climbing* is a useful and fascinating read. In this powerful text, Hörst presents an impressive collection of mental training techniques, practice exercises, and insights for climbers at all levels of ability."

—Lynn Hill, first woman to climb 5.14

"There are volumes of books on how to train your body for climbing, but *Maximum Climbing* teaches you how to climb better by flexing the most critical muscle—the three-pound one between your ears. Using a highly detailed step-by-step process that is clearly presented for beginner to expert climbers, Eric Hörst instructs on mental training. His book runs that gamut from A to Z, but my favorites include how to manage fear, build confidence, and focus—three areas all of us need to work on but, until now, didn't even know where to begin."

—Duane Raleigh, Publisher/Editor-in-Chief of *Rock and Ice*

"Eric Hörst's new book, *Maximum Climbing*, provides climbers with a clear path to athletic mastery. As a climber and performance coach, I've sought out every piece of information I could find on improving athletic performance. Use the methods put forth in this book, and you will improve; not just as a climber, but as a human being."

—Steve Bechtel, CSCC, Elemental Training Center

"Eric Hörst's *Maximum Climbing* fills a deep need for a training book that explores the broad array of elements that make a climber and fully integrates the physical, technical, mental, and spiritual. This is a book as much about soul as grit, as inspiring as it is educational."

—Susan E. B. Schwartz,
author of *Into the Unknown: The Remarkable Life of Hans Kraus*

"Dissolving the illusion of mind/body separation, Eric Hörst's *Maximum Climbing* shows the way to achieve what I like to call one's Vertical Path: a completely holistic state of being in which the spirit—the essence of climbing—is woven into the tapestries of our lives."

—John Gill, legendary boulderer and master of rock

"I've been climbing forty years and studying it as long, yet a great deal of this book was new and, even better, helpful to me personally. *Maximum Climbing* is in part the author's personal manifesto, and it is worth reading on that basis alone."

—Dr. Mark Robinson, veteran climber
and doctor to the climbing stars

"In this fascinating work, Eric Hörst reveals many of the secrets to rock climbing your best by tapping into the vast potential of the human brain. Soundly based in scientific research, *Maximum Climbing* is both user-friendly and interactive, drawing the reader into the book's ideas and concepts through self-tests and exercises. I will strongly recommend this groundbreaking work to every one of my climbing students."

—Alli Rainey, professional climber,
writer, and climbing coach

"Do you really want to be the best climber that you can be? Then read all of Eric Hörst's how-to books and, in particular, read *Maximum Climbing*! Get out your highlighter for this powerful book. I did!"

—Hans Florine,
El Cap speed climbing record holder and
author of FalconGuide's *Speed Climbing*

"As both a neuroscientist and avid climber, I can't help but love this book! I found *Maximum Climbing* to be a fascinating amalgamation of both the intellectual and athletic parts of my life. As a result, not only do I now look at climbing differently, but surprisingly, I now look at neuroscience at bit differently as well. *Maximum Climbing* is a profound text that will revolutionize how you think about climbing, how you train for climbing, how you experience climbing—and perform—whether in the gym, or out at the crags!"

—Courtney Behnke, Cognitive Neuroscience
Lab manager, University of Michigan

"As someone who has spent a lot of time and energy with mental training, I can say with confidence that *Maximum Climbing* is your best tool for taking control of your most powerful asset as a climber: your mind."

—Kevin Jorgeson, highball sendmaster

"Eric Hörst is one of those exceptional individuals who radiates positive energy virtually wherever he goes. Just to be in his presence recently I felt the urge to train again, to go up to the rock and once again try to conform my hands and fingers to the holds."

—Pat Ament,
legendary climber, poet, and author of
Master of Rock: The Biography of John Gill

Maximum
Climbing

Mental Training for Peak Performance and Optimal Experience

Eric J. Hörst

Foreword by Richard Fleming, PhD

FALCONGUIDES

GUILFORD, CONNECTICUT
HELENA, MONTANA

AN IMPRINT OF GLOBE PEQUOT PRESS

FALCONGUIDES®

FalconGuides is an imprint of Globe Pequot Press.

Falcon, FalconGuides, and Outfit Your Mind are registered trademarks of Morris Book Publishing, LLC.

Text and layout designer: Casey Shain
Project manager: John Burbidge

Library of Congress Cataloging-in-Publication Data
Hörst, Eric J.
  Maximum climbing : mental training for peak performance and optimal experience
/ Eric J. Hörst.
      p. cm.
  Includes bibliographical references and index.
  ISBN 978-0-7627-5532-5
  1. Mountaineering. I. Title.
  GV200.H67 2010
  796.52'2—dc22

                                                                    2009044393

Printed in China
10 9 8 7 6 5 4 3 2 1

To Todd Skinner, one of my greatest climbing influences. And to my parents, Bob and Ethel Hörst, for their unconditional love and support.

Kevin Jorgeson in a precarious position whilst headpointing Gaia (E8 6c) at Black Rocks, Derbyshire, UK. A slip from here would lead to a serious and unforgiving ground fall.
DAVID SIMMONITE

Contents

Foreword

The book you hold in your hands is a first. Sure, other climbing authors have delved into the psychology of rock climbing and have offered credible programs for improving climbing performance. What's different here is that Eric Hörst has gone many steps deeper than his predecessors to give us a comprehensive and up-to-date guide on how we can apply the findings from research on brain science and human performance to our own rock climbing (and life) pursuits.

Mental training may well be the final frontier for climbers, as physical limits are reached. But it's a relatively new frontier. Whereas many cognitive-behavioral performance improvement strategies have been validated, much research is still needed on the underlying psychology of brain–behavior relationships, and on the practical approaches that will come from that research. *Maximum Climbing* represents a solid starting point for teaching us in depth about what is known about the psychology of performance applied to climbing, and for exploring and interpreting "works in progress" in the area of brain and behavior science.

Eric Hörst has climbed at a high level for thirty years, and he has written authoritatively on the sport for nearly as long. Eric penned his first article on mental training for *Rock and Ice* in 1988, and in 1990 he wrote a series of three articles on developing "mental muscle" for *Climbing.* If you've read some of the many books he's written since, including *Training for Climbing, How to Climb 5.12, Learning to Climb Indoors,* and *Conditioning for Climbing,* you'll probably agree that when it comes to mental and physical training, Eric Hörst is climbing's most authoritative author.

I, too, am a longtime student and researcher of climbing performance with a focused interest in the psychology of human performance. I began climbing in 1974 and spent the late 1970s as a full-time climbing instructor based in North Conway, New Hampshire. In 1980 I was pleased to do the FFA of *Heather* (5.12b) on Cathedral Ledge, one of the first 5.12s in the northeastern United States. Shortly after, I took an eight-year hiatus from climbing, during which I went to grad school, got married, launched an academic career, and had two beautiful daughters. When I returned to the game, sport climbing, sticky rubber, and climbing gyms had livened things up, and bouldering was soon to flourish again. I got re-addicted and, as a psychologist, also became fascinated with the mental and behavioral aspects of climbing and training—in recent years I came to engage Eric in numerous discussions and collaborations relating to physical and mental training for climbing.

Before returning to talk about *Maximum Climbing,* I want to share a current and relevant psychological perspective on the development of expert or elite-level performance. It concerns yet another chapter in the age-old debate over nature versus nurture, and it goes like this: While genes certainly play a role in what individuals can achieve, when you look more objectively it is hours of deliberate practice that actually distinguishes top experts from otherwise reasonably accomplished performers. Deliberate practice refers to a persistent (many hours), structured, and disciplined approach (goals, monitoring, and feedback) to engaging in the full range of mental and physical activities needed to improve performance in a certain area. The power of deliberate practice has been shown to apply to music, art, and a host of sports. It is transferable to rock climbing, and indeed supports much of what Eric offers in *Maximum Climbing*. In short, while spending many hours engaged in climbing is important, at the higher levels it is not the mere volume of effort that matters most; it is how we configure our climbing and training activities that will lead to the maximum result. Training deliberately, in a manner that fully engages our brain–behavior system, is what will see us through to the next level. Throughout *Maximum Climbing* you will find well-reasoned, scientific information that will guide you to plan, think, and act deliberately in your quest to improve your performance.

Maximum Climbing proceeds from the premise that "we climb with our minds." While it's true that external environmental events such as peer pressure and competition can influence our climbing, for better or worse, it's how we come to understand and command our internal environment—our thoughts, feelings, and emotions—that sends us on the path to our biggest breakthroughs as climbers. Eric brings us on a trek that begins in the brain. We learn about complex neurodevelopmental processes that underlie and, reciprocally, are affected by the acquisition of complex action. There are plenty of practical tips on how to train for optimal brain development, so science and practice are nicely melded. Eric then moves on to present a highly engaging discourse on the cognitive, emotional, and behavioral factors that influence our performance, again supported throughout with a full complement of practical strategies from sport psychology that we can use to take charge of our own personal climbing trajectories. Finally, Eric serves up three basic programs, so we can each find our place on the novice-to-expert continuum. Once you have established and tailored your program, you will find that *Maximum Climbing* will be your "go-to" resource as you advance and find even greater enjoyment in this amazing world of climbing.

RICHARD FLEMING, PHD
Associate Professor in Psychiatry
University of Massachusetts Medical School

Acknowledgments

I've been thinking about writing this book for more than twenty years. In fact, I remember drafting a brief outline for a book on mental-fitness training while on a road trip out West in 1990. In the preceding years I had read several books on sports psychology, and I felt that I had recently broken some personal barriers via mental training. And while I went on to write a trilogy of articles on mental training for *Climbing* magazine that summer, I really had no idea how to write a book, nor did I have the subject figured out well enough to write a comprehensive how-to guide.

You could say that I spent much of the next two decades learning how to write a book and researching and experimenting with methods of mental training. However, it was not until an illness shut me down for most of a year that I had the time—and felt the urgency—to solidify my ideas into words on a page. Today you are holding the final product of this arduous year (of writing and getting well) and a twenty-plus-year inward journey!

This book integrates a vast array of information that I've gathered through my extensive studies and by way of conversations with many climbers as well as professionals in the field of psychology and human performance. Most important, in recent years, has been time spent climbing and discussing all things performance with Rick Fleming, a PhD psychologist and researcher with University of Massachusetts Medical School, and neuropsychologist Dr. Jim Sullivan. Add in dialogue with motor learning and performance researcher Dr. Richard Schmidt, and you can see that I have been blessed with three excellent "consultants" during this multiyear writing endeavor. I am also fortunate to have numerous veteran climbers, both rock stars and climbing coaches, who reviewed the manuscript to provide feedback and advanced reviews, including Pat Ament, Courtney Behnke, Steve Bechtel, Han Florine, John Gill, Lynn Hill, Kevin Jorgeson, Dougald McDonald, Alli Rainey, Duane Raleigh, Mark Robinson, and Susan E. B. Schwartz. So it is with deep gratitude that I thank the aforementioned friends of mine, as well as the countless climbers with whom I've talked training over the years.

After the writing is done, my manuscript was crafted into this nifty book by the good people at FalconGuides and Globe Pequot Press. Therefore, I'd like to extend a sincere thank-you to Scott Adams, John Burbidge, Laura Jorstad, Casey Shain, and all others of the Falcon team. I must also thank the photographers whose fantastic imagery adds another inspirational dimension to the book. Kudos to Danno Brayack, Jimmy Chin, Bill Hatcher, Keith Ladzinski, Andy Mann, Celin Serbo, David Simmonite, Eric McCallister, and Jorge Visser for the great pix! Finally, I am grateful for the climbing companies that continue to support me and my many projects, including Nicros, La Sportiva, Verve, and Sterling Ropes.

Many thanks to my small circle of close friends and family who provide aid and comfort and, most important, tolerate my obsessive tendencies toward work, working out, writing, and climbing. In particular I must acknowledge my parents, Bob and Ethel, my wife, Lisa Ann, and my sons, Cameron and Jonathan, for supporting me and sharing in the activities that I'm so passionate about. I love each of you more than words can express.

Finally, I thank all the readers of my previous books who have written to me, or communicated in person, about their successes and breakthroughs both on and off the rock. Such feedback, expressing how my work enhances a reader's climbing and life, helps me justify spending so much time writing about an activity that could be viewed as meaningless and self-centered. Of course, we all know the truth—climbing is a rich, magical activity that shapes our characters, strengthens our minds and bodies, and allows us to experience nature's wonder . . . and occasionally even touch the sky. Given this perspective, it's my hope that you will find this book to be educational, inspirational, and beneficial in all your endeavors in the mountains and beyond. I welcome your correspondence via my Web site TrainingForClimbing.com.

Part One

In Pursuit of Maximum Climbing

Ethan Pringle climbing Five-Year Plan, a 5.13+ roof crack on Dinosaur Mountain in the Flatirons, Boulder, Colorado.
ANDY MANN

Introduction

As physical as climbing is, it is even more mental. Being technically sound and physically honed is not enough to navigate a highball boulder problem, personal-best lead, intimidating big wall, or treacherous mountain. Ultimately, we climb with our minds—our hands and feet are simply extensions of our thoughts and will. Becoming a master climber, then, requires that we first become a master of our mind.

Actually, this book is about more than mental training—it's about brain training. From the three pounds of brain matter between your ears emanate not only your thoughts, but also all motor skills, muscular recruitment, and the mystical forces of intuition and willpower. Given this broad purview it becomes clear that the brain is the epicenter of all aspects of climbing performance and that brain training is of paramount importance to participants in all climbing subdisciplines. No matter if your preference is bouldering, sport climbing, traditional climbing, or mountaineering, the quality of your performance and experience arises

The brain is the epicenter of all aspects of climbing performance, and therefore mental training is the ultimate—and most powerful—method of training for climbing.

from the hundreds of billions of neurons and synapses in your brain. Consequently, the brains of master climbers (of every kind) run a most complex "software" that facilitates execution of highly refined motor and mental skills, and gives rise to the intangible psychic forces of intuition and willpower. You might consider *Maximum Climbing*, then, to be your user's guide to the software of your brain.

The prospect of brain training may initially trigger some thoughts of apprehension and perhaps even skepticism. After all, you've made it this far in climbing by way of your current program of climbing and training, so why venture into the unknown of Hörst's brain-training program? The answer should be self-evident given a bit more thought. First, consider that breaking barriers and performing at a higher level demands that you not only train differently, but also learn to think and act more effectively. Furthermore, why do you choose to venture up an unknown climb? Because you wish to partake in a novel experience and in doing so explore your potential to achieve. These are the very reasons you must embark on a brain-training program—to discover a new level of life experience and to realize your true potential to perform and achieve.

I've arranged this book in four distinct parts that make up the full scope of what I call brain training. After chapter 1, which sets the stage for your maximum climbing journey, part two begins with a study of brain physiology and the fascinating process of neuroplasticity (how your brain physically changes as a result of your thoughts, actions, and experiences) in chapter 2. Given this basic knowledge of brain function, chapter 3 delves into the specific processes by which the brain assimilates, learns, and directs skilled movements. No matter how skilled or technically sound you are right now, I guarantee that you can improve your technique and efficiency of movement by applying the material in this chapter. Chapter 4 goes on to explore how the brain governs the recruitment of the muscles and in doing so grossly restricts your maximum level of strength and stamina as a protective mechanism. The powerful implication of this overprotective "central governor" is that you can recalibrate (upward) the maximum threshold via specialized training techniques to enhance strength, power, muscular endurance, and stamina.

Part three ventures into the cognitive realm of thoughts, fears, concentration, habits, strategy, and much more. Master climbers think vastly differently from the mass of climbers. Elevating your performance and maximizing experience thus demands that you elevate all aspects of your mental game. Chapter 5 begins the mental-training process with instruction on improving self-awareness. In climbing, the pinnacle of self-awareness is an acute on-demand monitoring of your internal climate and outward efficacy. Given this high level of self-awareness, you are

I n the past I trained like a fiend. I could do something like 150 fingertip pull-ups in five minutes, and as a gymnast I preceded that with all sorts of hollow-back presses off the floor. They tell me I invented the one-arm mantel—a skill I applied to a few actual boulder problems.

So maybe I know a little about training and climbing. That was all a long time ago, however. We live in a new age, and climbers more and more transcend our modest achievements of the past. To get to the new levels, the new generation employs secret methods. I mean, some have almost literally mastered the art of levitation. In my day it was simply our weak arms and fingers against the world. We expended all sorts of energy in the wrong ways. We wasted effort, and there was more we didn't know than what we did.

Maximum Climbing is full of novel ideas and how-to instruction to empower climbers to achieve the next level and beyond, while at the same time it speaks about other important values, such as how to love life and celebrate good friendships. Eric Hörst shows us ways to better direct whatever level of focus we have, to make it a more productive focus, not simply work out, not merely to do mindless numbers of pull-ups. One of the goals is to find certain freedoms—in terms of strength—that involve mental control.

Maximum Climbing presents what one might call the new philosophy, the way to best bring mind, body, and spirit together to enhance both performance and experience. This book will help climbers go far beyond what they could do simply by hook or crook, as did the old guard. It will show eager hearts and minds some of the key skills, and enable them. All that much quicker they will be able to get to the most intense experience they can imagine. The climber who wants to push the limits will, in these pages, gain the training tools to be a Greek god, to conquer the world, and then move on.

—Pat Ament, author of
Master of Rock: The Biography of John Gill

empowered to make tiny course corrections on the fly that will maximize your chances of completing the climb. Toward this end, chapter 6 provides numerous self-regulation strategies for optimizing your mental, physical, and emotional states.

In chapter 7 the process of organizing and focusing your psychic energy moves on to goal setting and goal pursuit. Get ready to be engaged by a hands-on process of identifying your values, establishing some compelling goals, and analyzing what step you can take today to move closer to those goals. And since any worthy goal is likely to challenge you in unexpected ways, chapter 8 will arm you with ten indispensable strategies for overcoming adversity and problem solving. In exposing yourself to challenging situations, you must also come prepared with the mental skills needed to maintain concentration and manage fear in the face of technical difficulty, physical stress, and unexpected adversity. To aid your journey, chapter 9 serves up twelve powerful strategies for improving concentration and focus, while chapter 10 provides fourteen must-know techniques for managing fear. Perhaps nothing is more elemental to climbing than fear; learning to control fear (instead of letting it control you) is essential to performing your best. Part three then concludes with chapter 11's broad study of mind-programming and behavior-modification techniques for improving conscious and unconscious brain function. By learning and steadfastly applying these techniques, you will come to perform and achieve—in climbing and beyond—at a level that you can hardly imagine today!

Part four of *Maximum Climbing* dovetails the many topics covered in parts two and three into a complete mental-training program. Chapter 12 details three stages of mental training that roughly correspond to beginner, intermediate, and elite levels of experience and commitment to climbing. While you will certainly need to develop a personalized mental-training program to address specific goals and constraints, the three program stages that I outline will serve as a robust template to build upon. The book then comes to a close with what I hope will be inspiring sections on finding your own path in the sport of climbing, becoming a climber for life, and sharing your climbing power with the world.

Into this book I've folded three decades of experience, study, and experimentation, as well as countless discussions with climbers (and minds) that are far greater than I. *Maximum Climbing* is thus a content-rich text with enormous information flow, and it has the astonishing potential to change and serve you in new ways as you change in the years to come. I encourage you to frequently reference this text, and perhaps even re-read it annually, in search of new distinctions and strategies to help you prevail over evolving challenges and reach for higher goals.

Ultimately, it's your dedication to learn and apply the individual mental-training exercises that will determine how great an impact *Maximum Climbing* will have on your future. Knowing this, I hope you will begin a consistent, disciplined mental-training program and strive to exert greater mental control in all you do. Persist patiently in your training, and trust that the long-term cumulative effects of your efforts will yield a seismic shift in who you are and what you will accomplish and experience in the future.

The journey starts now!

CHAPTER ONE

The Maximum Climbing Program

All climbers share a love of recreating in the vertical world, whether they are ascending a 10-foot boulder problem or 8,000-meter peak. In deviating from the flatlands of everyday existence, we take life to another dimension that bonds mind and body in a highly distinct way. Our senses and emotions are amplified as we experience the acute pains and pleasures, and heightened awareness unique to our crucible of the vertical world. But this outward journey is led by a profound inward journey of mind and spirit that only the master climber comes to fully understand and leverage.

The premise of this book, then, is that we climb with our minds—our hands and feet are simply extensions of our thoughts and will. And thus the pursuit of maximum climbing is ultimately an inward journey to gain mastery of the mind. In essence, becoming a master climber requires that we first become masters of our minds.

This journey toward mastery of the mind is arduous and never-ending. You must trust, however, that through disciplined training you will develop powerful mental

Maximum climbing is born from the will and skill of the brain, and in spite of our physical limitations.

skills that few climbers possess. Unlike physical capabilities that plateau with middle age and degrade thereafter, disciplines of the mind offer unlimited potential for growth throughout your lifetime. With regular "mental exercise" you will gradually discover a higher level of consciousness in which you climb with single-pointed focus, detachment from concerns about results, and unstoppable confidence and willpower. This rare state will give birth to experiences that transcend the ordinary and reveal your true potential to do great things. Like wielding a sword with empty hands, your mind will lead your body to new summits. The profound experience that unfolds—in which thought and action merge in a powerful and transcending union—is what maximum climbing is all about.

Chris Sharma working on his revolutionary 250-foot overhanging route on Clark Mountain, California. After more than a year-and-a-half of working on and training for the climb, Chris established Jumbo Love *(5.15b) on September 11, 2008, perhaps the world's hardest rock climb.* JORGE VISSER

Upcoming in this chapter, you'll learn the basics of the maximum climbing program, discover the infinite power of brain-centered training, and ponder the far reaches of your own climbing potential. The chapter concludes with a ten-part self-assessment questionnaire to score your current command of brain-based skills.

An Overview of the Maximum Climbing Program

Next time you visit a crowded crag or climbing gym, invest some time in observing the climbers around you. Imagine that you are a TV sports analyst and mentally break down their game. Take note of their preclimb rituals and demeanor; assess their quality of movement and confidence; gauge their attitude and emotions when challenged with a crux or a fall; assess their level of physical conditioning and how effective they are at utilizing their energy reserves. Perform this analysis on as many climbers of varying experience levels as possible.

Given a large enough sample of climbers (say, a dozen or more), you will discover a quality-of-movement continuum ranging from coarse, hesitant, and lumbering at one extreme to smooth, decisive, and flowing at the other. This continuum is the ultimate metric by which we should gauge climbing prowess. It's quite easy to subjectively assess quality of movement in others—we all know an efficient and elegant climber when we see one. Unfortunately, it's often difficult to assess our own level of movement quality, and there's no easy way to measure these attributes empirically (although fast climbers who touch the fewest holds tend to exhibit high movement quality).

What sets great climbers apart from others is not their physical prowess (amazing as it may be), but their brains.

By contrast, physical aptitude, including strength, power, and endurance, is easier to measure. Consequently, many climbers are quick to compare their physical capacity with others', and there's a strong tendency to train obsessively to improve these parameters as if they were the ultimate secret to climbing. While proper physical conditioning (which I have written about extensively in previous books) certainly is a central component of climbing, the point here is that a singularly body-centered paradigm to improving performance represents a gross handicap. In fact such a narrow approach is the antithesis of the maximum climbing program outlined in this book.

Let's return for a moment to your analysis of the various climbers you observed at the gym or crags. Chances are you will identify a person who climbs harder than you despite the fact that she appears to possess a lower level of physical fitness. Assuming that this climber does possess less absolute strength, power, and endurance than you, then what are the reasons she climbs harder? The answer lies in the many, often subtle, skills of the mind. Actually, it's the brain we should credit for her prowess, since it directs all motor skills and technical movement, in addition to yielding all thoughts, mental skills, intuition, and willpower. From this perspective it should be clear that the purview of brain-based skills is broad (see table 1.1), and that a brain-training program is the most practical approach to improving climbing performance.

The bottom line: What sets great climbers apart from others is not their physical prowess (amazing as it may be), but their brains. The same is true for you, me, and every other climber. Whatever our physical strengths and limitations, maximum climbing is born from the will and skill of the brain.

Table 1.1 Purview of Brain-Based Skills

Motor Skill and Movement Control	Cognitive Processes
• Skill development	• Self-awareness and arousal control
• Technique improvement	• Goal setting and strategy development
• Muscle recruitment	• Problem solving and memory
• Motor control	• Concentration and focus
• Unconscious and preconscious movement	• Fear control and confidence
• Intuitive movement control	• Behavioral modification and skill programming
	• Risk management and intuition

A Definition of Maximum Climbing

I've mentioned the concept maximum climbing a couple of times already, and since it is the title of the book I feel it's important to expound further, rather than risk misinterpretation of this unique pursuit.

For some climbers, the goal is to climb as difficult a grade as possible. While I admit to having owned this perspective on a few occasions, I have come to discover that the very best climbers—and the happiest, as well—do not possess this as a primary intention. Certainly great pleasure can be gained by achieving a rare, difficult climb. In making this your sole intention, however, you diminish the experience and quite possibly set yourself up for failure.

One of the greatest ironies of the performing arts—and one that all climbers should recognize—is that the mind-set of needing to succeed at a difficult task and the mind-set required to effectively undertake that endeavor are mutually exclusive. Climbing your best, then, comes only by replacing outcome-oriented thinking with a focus on the process of climbing, an enjoyment of the dance, and a becoming one with the experience.

Master climbers, past and present, tend overwhelmingly to emphasize quality of experience, self-discovery, and attaining oneness with the climb and nature over pure difficulty of achievement and an absolute need for success. Consider these quotes:

- *Your achievements in climbing are a lot less relevant than what you learn in the process.*
  —Lynn Hill
- *For me climbing is moving meditation. To focus so single-pointedly that the self melts away, and pure awareness, energy, and emotion are the only things left remaining.*
  —Chris Sharma

- *On certain routes I achieved a mind/no mind state of mystical connection to the mountain. I was not affected by gravity. I became the mountain.*

  —Mark Twight

- *In the lessons of the vertical lie the power of conscious connection to spirit—in the rock, air, water, trees, and each other.*

  —Ron Kauk

- *Climbing is so magical, but it's so easy to lose that and get caught up in the numbers game . . . climb because you love it.*

  —Katie Brown

- *The goal with climbing is to keep it fun; and to make sure that it continues to be a game. When I climb my best, it's because I'm in that state of mind.*

  —Robyn Erbesfield-Raboutou

- *Climbing transports you to the realm of a truly human experience . . . the lacerating familiarity under your fingers doesn't matter because the adrenaline and joyfulness compress it into the experience.*

  —Kevin Jorgeson

- *The unity of mind and body is one reason why climbing is so compelling . . . the powerful integration of thought and action, emotion and performance.*

  —Mark Robinson

- *Mastery lies not in the capturing of a summit, but in a oneness with each detail of the experience.*

  —John Gill

- *Climbing has shown me the existence of force beyond the seen world.*

  —Steph Davis

- *The best climber in the world is the one having the most fun!*

  —Alex Lowe

Take these masters' words and internalize them with the new high-held belief that it is better to focus on self-development and accumulating experiences than a pursuit of maximum difficulty. This process of accumulating experiences will reward you with many valuable lessons and keepsake memories in addition to your share of difficult ascents along the way, whereas the MO of focusing only on climbing difficulty will provide a far more shallow experience. Don't you agree that climbing solely for the pursuit of absolute difficulty reduces climbing to little more than a quest to break your record at some meaningless race?

Let's examine this concept further considering the physical, mental, and spiritual dimensions in which we engage the world. In the physical world, we have definite limitations; we are only so strong and can endure only so long, as set by our

DNA, nutritional habits, and training practices. Therefore by primarily focusing on development and achievement in the physical realm, we naturally approach a ceiling in ability and unknowingly limit our potential for experience and self-exploration. Conversely, the mental and spiritual realms have no limits. Our ability to learn, imagine, and discover is essentially infinite; the only limitations are self-imposed. So, what can you imagine yourself climbing, achieving, and experiencing? These are important questions to answer, because you—and only you—are the designer of your future!

Of course, to live only in the mental realm is to be a dreamer, not a doer. Our volition to act on a dream is what transmutes a mental image into a physical reality. Masters in sports, science, and the arts live and learn in both in the mental and physical realms, and their would-be creations and achievements are leavened in the spiritual realm. So while modern culture worships physical image and possessions, masters know that great things are born in the infinite realm of the mind and spirit. Therefore the pursuit of maximum climbing can be aided by dismissing the trappings of modern culture.

The mind–set of needing to succeed at a difficult task and the mind–set required to effectively undertake that endeavor are mutually exclusive.

Surely the master climbers quoted earlier eschew many aspects of popular culture, in particular things that might quell their mental and spiritual growth.

In summary, the maximum climber is not the one who climbs the hardest. He is instead the climber most engaged in the moment, most open to gaining a deeper understanding of his present situation, and most willing to embrace each experience—whatever it may be—knowing that it is the stuff of life.

In the mountains climbers can discover the Truth, when beauty, danger, and a rich, novel experience combine to etch our souls in a way that will last a lifetime. This is maximum climbing.

The History of Mental Training for Climbers

While Olympians in ancient Greece were probably the first athletes to ponder the cognitive aspects of physical performance, it was the Russians who first researched and applied formal mental-training protocols in the 1950s. Along with leading-edge physical-training techniques and performance-enhancing drugs, disciplined mental training enabled the Eastern Bloc countries to dominate the Olympics from 1956 through 1980.

In the early 1970s Thomas Tutko, the father of American sports psychology, famously observed that American athletes were "physically overeducated and emotionally undereducated." Tutko went on to develop and popularize mental training, as used increasingly among collegiate and professional athletes, and the field of sports psychology began to gain traction across America during the 1980s. For climbers, however, mental training remained a mainly self-directed matter of forging the essential mental skills via the red-hot experiences of the vertical world.

Among climbers, the first widely read texts on the mental domain were Carlos Castaneda's series of books on the teachings of Don Juan. Viewed by academics to be mainly fictional tales, these books describe Castaneda's experiences under the tutelage of a Yaqui Indian named Don Juan. Aided by psychotropic plants and harrowing desert journeys, Castaneda gained heightened awareness and gleaned wisdom and truth amid the sandy, rocky landscapes along the Mexico–Arizona border. Interestingly, the hardman climbers of the 1970s found some value in the lessons of Don Juan—a few of that era's greatest Yosemite climbs even bear the names of Castaneda books—and reading these books became somewhat of a rite of passage for an aspiring hardman during the 1970s and early 1980s.

Fortunately, the 1980s bought a growing body of athlete-oriented, cognitive-behavior research and the release several excellent books. Then, in my second decade as a climber and after years of rigorous physical training, I read my first few books on sports psychology. While I had read the Castaneda books years earlier, it was these more scientific, sport-oriented books that connected with me and opened my mind to the limitless potential of mental training. In May 1988 I wrote what was perhaps the first climbing magazine article on mental training for *Rock and Ice;* two years later I wrote a trilogy of articles on "mental muscle" for *Climbing* magazine. Based on feedback from these articles, as well as my own successes in pushing out personal limits via mental training, I continued to study and write on the subject. My 1994 book, *Flash Training,* included a full chapter on mental training, and my follow-up books, *How to Climb 5.12* (1997) and *Training for Climbing* (2002), included ever-expanding treatments that have ultimately given birth to this book.

The first full-length book on mental training for climbers, Arno Ilgner's *The Rock Warrior's Way,* was published in 2003. Ilgner's book presents a Castaneda-inspired, awareness-based examination of the psychology of climbing—the tome is recommended reading for every serious climber. In writing *Maximum Climbing,* then, it was my goal to provide an innovative new perspective that not only incorporates the latest in sport and exercise psychology, but also adapts powerful concepts from the exciting fields of neuropsychology, motor learning and performance, and total quality management.

It seems that future climbing breakthroughs—technical and experiential—will be more mental than physical. Thus I imagine a not-so-distant future when avid climbers engage in as much mental training as they do physical workouts. It's my hope that this book will help lead the way by instructing and inspiring all climbers to leverage their brain power for peak performance and optimal experience, both on and off the rock!

What Is Brain Training?

The late, great Wolfgang Güllich was fond of saying that "the brain is the most important muscle for climbing." Nearly twenty years ago Wolfgang piqued my interest in the subject; much study and exploration ensued, and I am now gratified to present climbers with this book on brain training, which was in small part inspired by my discussions with Wolfgang. But what exactly is "brain training" and how does it relate to "mental training"?

The Difference Between Brain Skills and Mental Skills

In this text I divide the broad subject of brain training into two highly distinct, yet not completely independent, areas that require targeted training.

- Brain activity that controls involuntary body functions such as heart rate, temperature regulation, and other vital protective mechanisms, as well as conscious and unconscious brain functions that direct motor control and skilled movement via the central and peripheral nervous systems. These important topics—largely overlooked by climbers—will be covered in the breakthrough chapters on brain training upcoming in part two.

- Cognitive, emotional, and volitional states of consciousness that spring forth from the brain. These are the common areas of traditional mental training that include increasing self-awareness, improving thought control, and modifying behavior, among other things. These disciplines of the mind will be explored in great depth in part three.

Given this purview, it should be clear that nothing is more fundamental to enhancing performance and maximizing experience than improving the "fitness" of the three pounds of gray matter between your ears! In the pages and chapters to follow, you will learn numerous methods for training your brain to improve climbing movement, as well as dozens of mental-training techniques to improve self-awareness, increase confidence, manage fear, control your emotions, and more. So while many climbers—and the majority of flatlanders—let their brain run on an autopilot programmed by past experience, negative life events, peers, and popular culture, you will be empowered to direct the show. Train the brain and your body will follow!

The Stages of Brain Development

In this section we'll examine the general stages of brain-based motor learning and cognitive development that a climber would experience over many years (and not the literal neurobiological stages of brain growth).

For many climbers, brain-directed motor skills are rough and inefficient, and mental control ebbs and flows with little notice or control. The result is inconsistent performance and a relatively poor experience on the rock. The goal, of course, is to constantly improve in both areas of brain development—in fact, the combined effects of increasing mastery of technical motor skills and mental attributes can yield a remarkable advance in climbing ability in a single season. Let's examine the three stages of brain-skill development.

Beginners naturally lack the motor programs needed to execute many climbing moves, while cognitive focus centers mainly on dealing with fear and basic risk management. During this stage motor skills tend to develop quickly, especially when the climber emphasizes learning of proper technique over simply struggling sloppily up a climb. Rate of cognitive-skill development tends to lag in many cases, perhaps influenced by global factors of self-concept and personality, in addition to lack of instruction on mental aspects of the game.

Table 1.2 Summary of Benefits and Methods of Brain and Mental Training

Brain Training (see Part Two)	Mental Training (see Part Three)
• **Accelerate learning of motor skills.** Use practice drills to accelerate skill development and coordination.	• **Increase self-awareness and quality of action.** Engage in regular metacognition and self-coaching to optimize effectiveness of goal-directed actions.
• **Facilitate performance of novel moves on-sight.** Broaden skill sets and vary practice conditions to develop motor programs and schema.	• **Improve thought control, focus, and volition.** Take control of self-talk and use cue words to improve focus and initiative.
• **Improve "feel" and quality of movement.** Foster awareness of proprioceptive cues to aid development of optimal climbing technique.	• **Modify behaviors.** Train to reduce bad habits and forge new habits and rituals that enhance performance.
• **Develop intuitive sense.** Solidify and deepen experience base by broadening outdoor climbing horizons.	• **Manage fears and risk.** Learn to assess whether fears are legitimate or bogus. Take action to mitigate real fears and dispel bogus fears.
• **Boost strength and power.** Employ reactive training to recruit high-threshold motor units and synchronize motor unit firing.	• **Increase mental toughness.** Develop coping skills that empower you to persevere in adverse situations.
• **Improve neuromuscular efficiency.** Train to reduce tension in antagonist muscles to facilitate smoother, more economical movement.	• **Boost motivation and confidence.** Manage physiology and thoughts to elevate mood and confidence.
• **Elevate fatigue-signaling thresholds.** Train the brain to allow for physical performance output nearer absolute limit.	• **Preprogram the brain for ideal outcomes.** Use visualization and other programming techniques to prepare the brain and body for performance.

Intermediate-level climbers exhibit increasingly smooth, more efficient movement and a calmer, more confident demeanor. Motor programs are refined and expanded as a function of hours invested in practicing skills and exploring new types of climbing (crack climbing, overhanging terrain, and the like). Cognitive abilities also exhibit remarkable growth, particularly in individuals who begin to engage in lead climbing. Whereas toprope climbing allows for safe, low-pressure ascents, the risks and challenge of the sharp end better develop and stretch cognitive abilities. There is value and enjoyment in both styles of climbing, but the intermediate will develop valuable cognitive skills more quickly via the crucible of the sharp end.

The hallmark of the advanced climber is mastery of many styles of climbing and the ability to climb confidently on-sight. Some gifted individuals may reach this advanced stage in just a few years, while others may require a decade of more of dedicated effort to achieve this level of prowess. Undoubtedly many advanced climbers exhibit impressive physical attributes, yet it's their brain development that's ultimately to credit for their prowess on the rock. Mental agility, masterful on-sight intuition of severe sequences, and awesome physical strength are all born of a long-term conscious effort to develop capabilities without prejudice and to train up weaknesses, be they mental, technical, or physical. Clearly, developing such a high skill level takes effort, discipline, and, at the highest ability levels, much sacrifice. The very best climbers are able to push out boundaries only by identifying and breaking free from things—both mental and material attachments—that limit dedication and divert focus from training and climbing.

This book on brain training, then, strives to lead you on a more direct journey through these stages of development. Simply reading this book, however, will do nothing for you. It is in understanding and applying the material that you will accelerate your rate of improvement above that of the common trial-and-error approach of learning to climb. What's more, by integrating daily mental training and a never-ending pursuit of technical mastery with intelligent physical training, you will discover a profound new level of experience and unknown potential, which I guarantee is far greater than you can imagine.

Pursuing Your Limitless Potential

I believe that human beings are "success machines" that possess unlimited potential to create and do. By leveraging our endowments of imagination and intelligence, and through consistent disciplined application of free will, we can achieve truly remarkable things. Consider the once-thought-impossible ascents of Mount Everest without oxygen or free climbing El Capitan. Or look up at the night sky and imagine man flying to the moon and scrambling over those remote lunar mountain ranges—this feat was achieved over forty years ago, and it still boggles the mind! Each of these "impossible" feats became possible because a human being dared to dream big, and then conceived and executed a plan with intelligence and the power of will. You, too, can do great things—perhaps greater than you can even imagine right now—if you embrace a brain-centered approach to training and performance.

In this section you will learn about the Law of Imperfection, the maximum climbing training model, and the X-Factor behind all great climbing achievements.

The Law of Imperfection

Despite having an nearly unlimited potential, humans do possess physical limitations, and we are in fact inherently imperfect in all we do—this is the essence of the Law of Imperfection. The human body has obvious physical constraints: We can only run so fast and lift so much before our flesh and bones fail us. Thus, our ability to create and achieve new things is largely a matter of the limitlessness of our mind. While it's a myth that "the average person only uses 10 percent of his brain" (functional brain MRIs of healthy individuals have shown that brain function is not localized or limited in this way), it is true that we often fail to use our minds in the most effective ways. Common bad habits of thought, such as pondering failure, making excuses, and engaging in critical self-talk, wield a powerful negative influence over our physical abilities and potential to achieve.

Similarly, our imperfect technical execution of physical skills robs us of strength, endurance, and energy reserves. For example, the seemingly simple skill of running—something we all learn to do by age two—is in fact an activity executed with much inefficiency by many runners. A good running coach can quickly point out speed- and energy-robbing flaws of stride, foot strike, knee lift, hip position, posture, arm swing, and breathing in the average runner. So, despite the popular belief that becoming an elite running machine is simply a matter of proper training and good genetics, the less obvious and absolutely essential requirement is the development of superb running technique. The bottom line: A person of average genetics can become an elite runner given the development of exceptional technique and a highly effective physical-training program.

The same is true in rock climbing. In fact, the diverse terrain and novel challenges of the vertical world (compared with running on flat ground) mean that skill development and efficient movement are of even greater importance. And since these technical abilities are all brain-directed, we return to the idea that the brain is the most important muscle for climbing! Surely we do need to maintain and develop our bodies to the fullest extent—after all, the body is a vehicle for physical achievement—but it's the motor skills and cognitive skills of the brain that represent both the greatest constraints and the infinite potential to improve.

Let's distill the aforementioned distinctions into three powerful laws of imperfection. The laws are adapted from a manufacturing performance improvement discipline called total quality management. They were first set forth by my father, Robert L. Hörst, an engineer and proponent of Six Sigma performance analysis and an inventor with more than twenty-five patents. I've taken the liberty of reworking these laws to the world of climbing, and I trust that you'll find them instructive and perhaps even inspiring.

- **First Law of Imperfection.** While perfection is the goal in every climbing endeavor, "zero defects" in technical and cognitive performance is never achieved. First, consider that the world's best climber is an imperfect climber. Now consider: What does that mean for you and me? Obviously, then, there is always room for improvement—and for many climbers it's the biggest room in the world! Even if you've reached an apparent plateau or ceiling in performance, believe in the message of the First Law that you can always reduce defects and thus enhance performance.

- **Second Law of Imperfection.** Perfection is not required to achieve a world-class performance or a maximum climbing experience. You don't need to climb perfectly to send your hardest-ever route—you simply need to have fewer performance defects than in previous failed attempts. In such a performance setting, it's somewhat ironic that you will climb your best and maximize experience by detaching from outcome-oriented thoughts and the pursuit of perfection. The optimal mind-set when climbing for performance is one in which you embrace and enjoy each moment of climbing and simply let the experience unfold without expectation. Reserve the mind-set of striving to reduce climbing defects for your workouts and practice climbs. Thus, it's essential that you always distinguish between climbing for practice versus climbing for performance.

- **Third Law of Imperfection.** Gross defects in technical and cognitive performance are often tolerated by individuals resigned to climbing well below their potential, whereas a would-be peak performer will strive to reduce defects and grow capabilities. Climbers with lackluster technique and poor mental control can continue to get by with these handicaps as long as they are satisfied climbing within their current ability level. A climber wanting to grow his capabilities and pursue his ultimate potential, however, must engage in targeted training to remove limiting physical constraints and reduce mental and technical defects.

Training for Maximum Climbing

In my book *Training for Climbing*, I presented a training model based on the idea that climbing performance is roughly one-third mental, one-third technical, and one-third physical ability (see figure 1.1, "The Climbing Performance Pie"). An effective training program would target all three aspects, rather than focus on a single aspect such as physical training. And since many climbers develop their abilities disproportionately, a most effective program would identify the weakest aspect and invest more time in training it up, with less time being spent on the stronger aspects.

From the perspective of this brain-training book, I'm compelled to modify this training model to depict the full scope of the brain's influence over training and performance (see figure 1.2). Here we see that neurodevelopment, mental skills, emotions, and behaviors surround the technical and physical aspects of performance. This new model best reflects the fact that every climbing move or training exercise is brain-directed by our thoughts and motor skills. So whether you are climbing economically or sloppily, or are using your physical energy effectively or ineffectively, is a direct result of your cognitive and brain-directed motor skills.

Your quest for maximum climbing, then, must focus first and foremost on training your brain. The scope of such brain training is vast, hence the many aspects of motor skill and cognitive development covered in this book. Your journey is one of developing technical and physical abilities, while reducing performance defects that rob you of energy or steer you off course from your goals. Self-awareness of action and thought quality (metacognition) are at the heart of the matter— ultimately you must learn to take control of your thoughts during all your waking hours, consciously directing effective action toward your goals and self-correcting

Figure 1.1 *The Climbing Performance Pie*

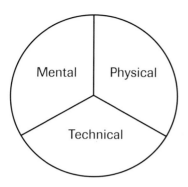

Figure 1.2 *Pie Amendment*

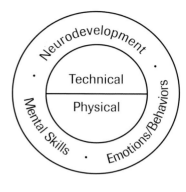

when you veer off course. To this end, the chapters that follow will reveal a wealth of powerful brain and mental-training techniques that are the true secret to peak performance in all you do. Apply them with discipline and you will be on the path to achieving and experiencing without limit.

The X-Factor—The Power of Will and Imagination

Achieving the next grade or doing the "impossible" is a battle fought more in the mind than the body. Consider Todd Skinner and Paul Piana free climbing El Capitan in 1988 (when four-day aid ascents were the norm), Reinhold Messner's and Peter Habeler's 1978 ascent of Mount Everest without oxygen, John Gill bouldering V9/5.13 in 1959 (when the hardest climbing moves on a rope were at best 5.10), and even Alex Honnold's mind-bending free solo of the *Northwest Face* of Half Dome. All these once-thought-impossible achievements are the result of coupling indomitable willpower with unbridled imagination. These remarkable achievements, then, are sterling examples of limitless willpower of the mind winning over the limitations of the body, as well as unleashed imagination yielding a paradigm shift that shattered a prevailing belief system. This is the X-Factor that separates the best from the rest, in any endeavor.

Similarly, your potential to create and achieve things, big or small, is a function of your imagination and willpower. More than your genetics, age, financial resources, or current situation, it's your ability to unleash your imagination and tap into your gift of willpower that determines what you can or cannot do. Lynn Hill expresses her support of this belief by stating that "you have to be strong to accomplish what you imagine, but you have to imagine it first before you can accomplish it physically."

The individuals named above were all "common" folks who achieved uncommonly great things because they dared to imagine audacious goals, developed novel ways of thinking and acting, and persevered through adversity and criticism with enormous willpower and belief in the endgame. In this way you, too, must learn to leverage all the powers of your mind, and like the above-named individuals step out of the din of the crowd and act in your own ways toward your personal cause or goals.

While you may think it so, growing your mental prowess is not difficult. Simply apply a few of the exercises in this book in the morning, before you work out and climb, and before going to sleep at night. The fields of your mind are fertile and waiting for you to plant the seeds that will yield remarkable new abilities, greater confidence, and higher achievement. Daily mental training integrated over weeks, months, and years will give rise to a spectacular new way of experiencing life that you can't even imagine today. Toward this end, let's take a deeper look at just what will is, and examine three areas in which it's vitally important to leverage your willpower.

Achieving the next grade or doing the "impossible" is a battle fought more in the mind than the body.

Willed Training

Will is the ability to make choices, decide on a course of action, and act resolutely. Will is a human endowment that empowers us to be proactive and self-directed, whereas animals are reactive and operate mainly on instinct. The force of will can therefore be used to influence all human action, including the things you do in the name of "training."

You can leverage willpower to grow stronger through execution of appropriate exercises and to improve your technique through focused practice of climbing skills. Through the power of will, you can crank out one more repetition, one more move, or one more training burn, if that's what it takes to grow stronger. It also takes willpower, however, to not train when injured or fully exhausted, to consume the right foods for accelerated recovery, and to take adequate numbers of rest days between workouts.

The essence of will in training is to proactively manage exactly what and how you train so that you get the greatest results for a given training input. In the setting of a commercial climbing gym, it can take significant willpower to follow through with your workout plan instead of being swayed by another person's agenda or affinity for socializing. Whether you have two hours or twenty hours per week to train, you must make the right training choices and engage in the proper course of action, no matter what other climbers say or do.

Willed Climbing

In climbing, you can exploit the power of will in a number of ways that can instantly improve your maximum ability and enable you to send your projects more quickly! Through willpower you can direct more focus on footwork, increase your "attack" and speed of ascent (or slow things down) as needed to be most economical in your movement, and direct relaxation and optimal use of rest positions in order to maximize the effectiveness of your ascent. Most dramatically, will is a causal force in critical moments when the specter of failure arises. It's in these instances that strength of will, manifest as single-pointed focus and the volition to continue on, can lift you upward to successful completion despite pain, fatigue, and the weight of past failures.

An important distinction, however, is that successful application of the will in extreme situations requires a self-defined endpoint to the challenge. Whether it's a rest stance or gear placement you are gunning for, a given number of pull-ups you intent to crank out, the finishing jug on a max boulder problem you are about to throw to, or the top of a PR redpoint or alpine wall, your awareness of the endpoint and your willpower in the present moment will sustain progress until the endpoint is reached. Embodiment of this process is known as willing yourself up a climb—a state in which you persevere beyond previous limits or beyond what others view as possible. A common hallmark of long willed ascents (or descents) is collapsing on the summit (or in base camp).

Finally, like a mental muscle that gains tone through use, your willpower—and the confidence to apply it—grows each time you marshal this mystical force in an intense effort that surpasses what you were previously capable of. So in exercising your willpower, you make it stronger!

Willed Living

To fully leverage willpower in your climbing life, it's essential that you progressively develop an MO of willed living. All the nonclimbing areas of your life—friends and family, school and career, relationships, possessions, and other obligations and life goals—exert an influence over your climbing ability and potential to achieve, although it's often happening in unseen ways. Your trajectory as a climber is massively influenced by your ways of thinking and acting during your nonclimbing hours. Exercising your willpower in all these areas—with your climbing and life goals in mind—is tantamount to directing the flow of your life, as opposed to the more common MO of going with the flow.

Your willpower—and the confidence to apply it—grows each time you marshal this mystical force in an intense effort that surpasses what you were previously capable of.

Let me wax philosophical for a bit. Each moment of our life—climbing, working, thinking, or whatever—has two potentially controlling forces: determinism and free will.

Determinism is the way of the physical world, as ruled by cause and effect. Everything comes from things before it and gives rise to other things outside our control. In essence, we are but puppets in the hands of genetic, environmental, or experiential forces.

Willpower, on the other hand, is neither matter nor energy; it exists outside space and time and is not measurable. It's a mystical causal force of unlimited power—a human endowment from our creator. Exerting free will, then, is a spiritual act that empowers us to take control of our lives.

Without willpower we are doomed to the forces of strict determinism. And sadly, many individuals exercise little will in their life, thus serving as puppets of others and living in the flow of determinism. With the power of will, however, you take hold of the reins of your life and can transmute original acts of the mind (imagination) into material inventions, novel activity, and unique achievements. Willpower is the secret behind remarkable individuals including Albert Einstein, Mother Teresa, Nelson Mandela, and, in the sports world, Roger Bannister, Lance Armstrong, Ed Viesturs, and Lynn Hill. Willpower, of course, can be utilized in negative ways, as objectified by murderers, tyrants, and anyone with evil intentions put into action. The power of free will is in your hands to use as you choose to affect the material world.

Any climber who has sat on a belay ledge or summit basking in the transcending glow of life has in fact experienced the spiritual realm. So regardless of whether you consider yourself religious, it's essential that you acknowledge and embrace the spiritual realm—and exercise the power of will—to maximize performance and life experience.

Self-Assessment of Brain and Mental Skills

The following ten-part self-assessment isolates many of the critical areas of brain training to be covered in upcoming chapters. Each part consists of five questions totaling a maximum of twenty-five points. In taking this assessment, it's best to read each question once and then immediately select an answer based on recent experience. Don't overanalyze the questions, and resist the common tendency to cheat up on your scores. Circle the answer that most accurately describes your current modus operandi in climbing, training, and everyday living.

Willpower and Self-Concept

If necessary for success in training or climbing, I can push myself to an extreme level of fatigue and pain.
1—seldom or never, 2—occasionally, 3—about half the time, 4—often, 5—always

I push myself through a long, scary runout between bolts or gear when I know either that the gear will hold a big fall, or that I'm capable of climbing the section without falling.
1—seldom or never, 2—occasionally, 3—about half the time, 4—often, 5—always

I march to my own drummer and possess the confidence to step away from the crowd and follow my own path.
1—seldom or never, 2—occasionally, 3—about half the time, 4—often, 5—always

I get down on myself and question my abilities and worth when I struggle on a climb or have an off day.
1—almost always, 2—often, 3—about half the time, 4—seldom, 5—never

When the chips are down, I can perform up near my maximum ability and throw all I've got at a climb or goal.
1—seldom or never, 2—occasionally, 3—about half the time, 4—often, 5—always

Add up your scores for each question and record the total here: _____.
See chapters 1 and 5 for discussions of these topics.

Motor Learning and Technique Training

I think about, experiment with, and strive to discover ways to become a more efficient climber.
1—seldom or never, 2—occasionally, 3—about half the time, 4—often, 5—always

When climbing, I concentrate on the feelings of my body and strive to use this information to improve my performance. (Examples of this include paying attention to which muscles are tense/relaxed, and feeling your center of gravity and knowing how to best position it in relation to your hand and foot positions.)
1—seldom or never, 2—occasionally, 3—about half the time, 4—often, 5—always

I seek out and force myself onto climbs that will teach me new skills or shore up techniques at which I lack proficiency, even if it means I may fall and look bad in front of other climbers.
1—seldom or never, 2—occasionally, 3—about half the time, 4—often, 5—always

I direct my practice sessions—and perform specific drills—that will expand the breadth and depth of my skills.
1—seldom or never, 2—occasionally, 3—about half the time, 4—often, 5—always

I work boulder problems, sequences, or entire routes beyond the point of crude success with the goal of developing precise, economical movement skills and superior technique.
1—seldom or never, 2—occasionally, 3—about half the time, 4—often, 5—always

Analysis and Advice

Add up your scores for each question and record the total here: _____.
See chapter 3 for specific instruction and practice drills.

Physical Training

I thoughtfully design workouts to train up my weaknesses and ultimately to provide the greatest payoff for the time I have available to invest in training.
1—seldom or never, 2—occasionally, 3—about half the time, 4—often, 5—always

I plan my training far in advance to prepare for a specific climb, road trip, or expedition; or as a way to keep things progressive and avoid overtraining.
1—seldom or never, 2—occasionally, 3—about half the time, 4—often, 5—always

I train and stretch my antagonist muscles (the muscles opposing the prime movers in climbing) to maintain muscle balance, reduce injury risk, and optimize strength and endurance in my climbing muscles.
1—seldom or never, 2—occasionally, 3—about half the time, 4—often, 5—always

When strength training, I engage in some kind of reactive training or hypergravity training to condition my nervous system to function more efficiently during severe climbing movements (see chapter 4 for clarification of these techniques).
1—seldom or never, 2—occasionally, 3—about half the time, 4—often, 5—always

At some point during the course of a multiweek training cycle, I engage in some form of stamina training that will test the limits of my physical capacity to endure exercise or climbing activity.
1—seldom or never, 2—occasionally, 3—about half the time, 4—often, 5—always

Analysis and Advice

Add up your scores for each question and record the total here: _____.
See chapter 4 for coverage of physical-training strategies.

Self-Awareness

Throughout the day, in both climbing and everyday life, I am aware of my decision-making processes, the direction and quality of my thoughts, and the outside triggers that affect my thoughts.
1—seldom or never, 2—occasionally, 3—about half the time, 4—often, 5—always

At climbing rest positions, and between attempts and routes, I monitor how I feel (physically and emotionally) and assess the quality of my thoughts and actions.
1—seldom or never, 2—occasionally, 3—about half the time, 4—often, 5—always

At some point during a climbing outing (or indoor climbing session), I solicit my partner (or a climbing coach) for an assessment of how well I appear to be climbing and what aspects of my game need improvement. Alternatively, I use videotape to self-evaluate my climbing every season.
1—seldom or never, 2—occasionally, 3—about half the time, 4—often, 5—always

I ponder—or know—my true motives for the things I do, big and small.
1—seldom or never, 2—occasionally, 3—about half the time, 4—often, 5—always

In making major decisions—those that will determine how I invest my time, energy, and resources—I consider and leverage my hierarchy of personal values.
1—seldom or never, 2—occasionally, 3—about half the time, 4—often, 5—always

Add up your scores for each question and record the total here: _____.
Take this self-assessment every year, and read chapter 5 for more information on increasing self-awareness.

Controlling Your State

I get anxious, tight, and hesitant as I climb into a crux sequence, and I have a tough time preventing this.
1—almost always, 2—often, 3—about half the time, 4—seldom, 5—never

My confidence gets shaken, or I get angry and frustrated, when I struggle or fall on a route or encounter unexpected difficulties.
1—almost always, 2—often, 3—about half the time, 4—seldom, 5—never

I can regain a positive mind-set and optimize arousal at rest positions, between attempts on a climb, or during a competition.
1—seldom or never, 2—occasionally, 3—about half the time, 4—often, 5—always

I engage in self-talk to help maintain a positive, productive state throughout the day, whether I'm climbing or not.
1—seldom or never, 2—occasionally, 3—about half the time, 4—often, 5—always

After a bad day of climbing or a poor road trip, I can quickly shake off the disappointment and regain a positive, productive, future-oriented frame of mind. In fact, I can find a way to enjoy almost any day even if I'm not climbing well or things aren't going as planned.
1—seldom or never, 2—occasionally, 3—about half the time, 4—often, 5—always

Analysis and Advice

Add up your scores for each question and record the total here: _____.
See chapter 6 to learn techniques for assessing and controlling your state.

Goal Setting and Overcoming Adversity

I set specific goals for my daily training and each climbing outing, as opposed to making it up on the go.
1—seldom or never, 2—occasionally, 3—about half the time, 4—often, 5—always

At some point each week, I review my long-term climbing and life goals, then mentally work backward to determine what short-term actions I should take to remain on course to those goals.
1—seldom or never, 2—occasionally, 3—about half the time, 4—often, 5—always

I can maintain a positive, productive mind-set in the face of setbacks or unexpected difficulties.
1—seldom or never, 2—occasionally, 3—about half the time, 4—often, 5—always

When faced with a tough situation or unexpected adversity, I get inspired and accept the challenge.
1—seldom or never, 2—occasionally, 3—about half the time, 4—often, 5—always

In the wake of an adverse situation, I spin the negative outcome into something positive by identifying a lesson learned or determining a way that it has made me stronger.
1—seldom or never, 2—occasionally, 3—about half the time, 4—often, 5—always

Analysis and Advice

Add up your scores for each question and record the total here: _____.
See chapters 7 and 8 for instruction on goal setting and strategies for overcoming adversity.

Concentration and Fear Management

I am proactive in managing risk in order to reduce the fear factor, control arousal, and improve my chances for a safe, successful climb.
1—seldom or never, 2—occasionally, 3—about half the time, 4—often, 5—always

I become distracted and lose my concentration due to activity on the ground or because of the hardships or unknowns of the climb.
1—almost always, 2—often, 3—about half the time, 4—seldom, 5—never

I get nervous and afraid heading up on an on-sight, project, or competition route; I ponder the potential for embarrassment and become anxious because of the uncertainty of the outcome.
1—almost always, 2—often, 3—about half the time, 4—seldom, 5—never

When lead climbing a safe route, I push myself to the complete limit and, if I fall, I fall trying.
1—seldom or never, 2—occasionally, 3—about half the time, 4—often, 5—always

I make excuses (to self or others) for why I might fail on a route before I even begin to climb.
1—almost always, 2—often, 3—about half the time, 4—seldom, 5—never

Analysis and Advice

Add up your scores for each question and record the total here: _____.
Read chapters 9 and 10 to learn more about increasing concentration and managing fear.

Mind Programming

I visualize strategy, process, and the ideal outcome in all important tasks I undertake, both climbing and nonclimbing.
1—seldom or never, 2—occasionally, 3—about half the time, 4—often, 5—always

In preparing for a difficult climb, I strive to preprogram the ascent by vividly visualizing myself climbing the route—and imagining the feel of the moves—before I leave the ground.
1—seldom or never, 2—occasionally, 3—about half the time, 4—often, 5—always

I use self-talk and mantras to maintain focus, aid execution, and sustain effort during a hard workout or difficult climb.
1—seldom or never, 2—occasionally, 3—about half the time, 4—often, 5—always

At some point in my weekly training, I try to simulate the moves and muscle action needed for a current project or upcoming climb.
1—seldom or never, 2—occasionally, 3—about half the time, 4—often, 5—always

On rest days, during quiet times, or before going to sleep, I engage in meditation, visualization, or some form of mental exercise to prepare my mind and body for future activities and goals.
1—seldom or never, 2—occasionally, 3—about half the time, 4—often, 5—always

Analysis and Advice

Add up your scores for each question and record the total here: _____.
See chapter 11 to learn numerous mind-programming techniques.

Behavior Modification

I am able to create motivation to train or climb when I'm feeling tired, depressed, and unproductive.
1—seldom or never, 2—occasionally, 3—about half the time, 4—often, 5—always

I can give up things (activities, foods, possessions, or relationships) that I recognize are holding me back from my goals.
1—seldom or never, 2—occasionally, 3—about half the time, 4—often, 5—always

Once I've identified them, I am able to break bad habits of mind and technique that limit my ability and slow progress toward my goals.
1—seldom or never, 2—occasionally, 3—about half the time, 4—often, 5—always

When I find myself procrastinating or dwelling on the apparent benefits of inaction, I can create positive energy and take some action toward a worthy goal, and thus invert the negative tendency and create forward momentum.
1—seldom or never, 2—occasionally, 3—about half the time, 4—often, 5—always

When criticism or other outside factors trigger negative thoughts and feelings, I can quickly let go of the angst and regain a positive, self-confident state.
1—seldom or never, 2—occasionally, 3—about half the time, 4—often, 5—always

Analysis and Advice

Add up your scores for each question and record the total here: _____.
See chapter 11 to learn more about behavior modification.

Executing a Mental-Training Program

When I get up in the morning, I immediately think positive, productive thoughts that will help prepare me for the challenges of the day.
1—seldom or never, 2—occasionally, 3—about half the time, 4—often, 5—always

In the days, hours, and minutes leading up to an important climb, I utilize rituals and routines that past experience has proven to put me in the best frame of mind and physical state for peak performance.
1—seldom or never, 2—occasionally, 3—about half the time, 4—often, 5—always

I study a route extensively to develop strategies for a successful ascent, imagining possible sequences, gear placements, and rest positions as well as developing what-if scenarios to aid risk management.
1—seldom or never, 2—occasionally, 3—about half the time, 4—often, 5—always

If I'm feeling anxious or scared before a climb, I take a mental inventory of past successes and remind myself of my experience and preparation in order to create a more effective mental state for climbing.
1—seldom or never, 2—occasionally, 3—about half the time, 4—often, 5—always

In preparing for and engaging in a climb, I detach from outcome-oriented thoughts and the need to succeed and instead dwell on the process of climbing and the experience of the moment.
1—seldom or never, 2—occasionally, 3—about half the time, 4—often, 5—always

Analysis and Advice

Add up your scores for each question and record the total here: _____.
See chapter 12 to develop a more effective brain-training program.

Table 1.3 Interpreting Your Self-Assessment

Upon completing and scoring all ten parts of the self-assessment, it's beneficial to summarize the results in a table to provide a simple overview of your relative strong and weak areas. Transpose your total score from each section of the self-assessment onto the table below.

Self-Assessment Area	Score	Chapter
Willpower and Self-Concept	_____	1
Motor Learning and Technique Training	_____	3
Physical Training	_____	4
Self-Awareness	_____	5
Controlling Your State	_____	6
Goal Setting and Overcoming Adversity	_____	7 & 8
Concentration and Fear Management	_____	9 & 10
Mind Programming	_____	11
Behavior Modification	_____	11
Executing a Mental-Training Program	_____	12

Your total score in each section is less important than the relative scores of each section to the others. The lowest-scoring sections reveal the aspects of your mental game that are most holding you back—notice that each section has a corresponding chapter with in-depth instruction. It's also beneficial to analyze your answers question by question to identify specific weaknesses (questions scoring a 3 or less), which should become the bull's-eye of your brain-training program.

Scoring this self-assessment may be a somewhat humbling endeavor. Since the mental domain is a common weakest link for many climbers, it's not surprising that the typical climber will score less than 18 points in most sections. Consider that the lower your scores, however, the greater your potential for untold improvement given a commitment to mental training!

Part Two
Brain Training

Brain Physiology and the Functions of the Mind

In his foreword to the book *The Three-Pound Universe,* legendary science writer Isaac Asimov stated that "the human brain is the most complicated organization of matter that we know." While this might seem like a gross exaggeration, neurologists estimate that the three pounds of living tissue between our ears possesses 100 billion neurons, each capable of interacting with up to 100,000 other neurons. The possible number of neuronal connections, then, is an astronomical number more than 10 to the hundredth power (a 10 followed by 100 zeros is known as google). To put this complexity and the potential brain power into perspective, consider that the estimated number of atoms in the known universe is 10 followed by 80 zeros. Thus, Asimov's statement indeed seems accurate—the human brain may really be the most complex object in the universe!

From this perspective, Wolfgang Güllich's provocative statement describing the brain as the most important "muscle" for climbing also seems spot-on. But how does the magnificent human brain direct all physical and mental skill, provide intelligence and memory, and allow us to learn endlessly? Furthermore, how does this fist-size living supercomputer enable us to imagine and execute amazing feats, such as going to the moon or climbing monoliths like El Capitan or Mount Everest?

The brain is a human being's most dynamic organ—it is shaped by the sum of our experiences, both what we do and what we have done.

This chapter will explore, albeit superficially, brain physiology and function and the powers of the brain's cognitive realm (the mind). Along the way you'll be introduced to numerous powerful concepts from the fields of neurophysiology and neuropsychology that directly relate to effective training for climbing. Throughout, I have attempted to avoid unnecessary complexity and excessive use of scientific jargon—consult the glossary for definitions of key terms. Should these fascinating topics of the brain and mind pique your interest, use the references in the back of the book as a starting point of your extended study.

Katie Brown climbing Dew Line *(5.11c) at Lake Louise in Banff National Park, Canada.*
KEITH LADZINSKI

An Overview of the Nervous System and Brain Function

The nervous system consists of the central nervous system (CNS) and the peripheral nervous system (PNS). The brain and spinal cord in turn make up the CNS, with the brain acting as the primary governor of conscious and unconscious bodily function and seat of cognitive function. All other neuronal processes throughout the body make up the PNS, which enables us to sense and react to the stimuli of the world. The main functional unit of the nervous system is the neuron, and it's the synapses that form among brain neurons that empower us to be thinking, acting beings of intelligence and physical skill.

Let's delve a bit deeper into the dynamic processes of the brain so that we can better understand the many aspects of cognitive function and motor learning to be covered in the chapters ahead. I'll begin with a primer on the physiology of brain function, and then delve into the exciting new field of neuroplasticity, including some tips on how you can change your brain and improve in everything you do!

The rather technical, scientific nature of this section may tempt you to skip ahead to the next chapter—I implore you not to! The knowledge you will glean from the upcoming pages will empower you to better apply the brain-training techniques described in chapters 3 and 4. As the saying goes, "Knowledge is power"—or, in this case, "brain power"!

An Introduction to Brain Physiology

Neuroscientists describe the brain as having three parts: the forebrain, midbrain, and hindbrain. Several lobes of the cerebral cortex make up the forebrain, which controls the higher mental functions of thought, reason, and abstraction. The mid- and hindbrain primarily control autonomic functions such as heart rate, respiration, and other unconscious functions that maintain homeostasis. While the mid- and hindbrain are similar to those of animals, the neocortex (of the forebrain) is far more developed in humans, providing greater cognitive ability, including the analytical and anticipatory skills critical to survival.

Perhaps the most widely known aspect of neurophysiology is the apparent localization of certain functions. Nineteenth-century French surgeon Paul Broca was the first to propose localization of brain function after he observed damage in the left frontal lobe of stroke patients who lost their ability to speak. From the late nineteenth century through the mid-twentieth, other surgeons expanded on Broca's idea by isolating other areas that were apparently dedicated to functions such as language, sensory perception, and motor skills. Similarly, it was gradually accepted that the left and right hemispheres of the brain presided over specific functions—a concept known as lateralization. It was posited that the left hemisphere dealt mainly with logic, reasoning, numbers, linearity, and analysis, while the right hemisphere dominated in spatial, creative functions involving imagination, color, shape, pattern, and such.

By the late twentieth century, however, rigid models of localization and lateralization began to lose favor among neuroscientists (although concepts of lateralization and applications to learning are still widely promoted). Research on sensory substitution by Professor Paul Bach-y-Rita and others showed how a given area of the brain could adapt to a loss of a sense. In a blind person, for example, the part of the brain normally used to process vision adapted to perceive objects through tactile perception (as in reading braille) and enhanced sound discrimination.

The advent of functional MRI further dispelled the rigid model of lateralization. MRIs have revealed specific differences in brain activity among individuals exposed to identical sensory stimuli. Another significant finding is that 95 percent of right-handers have their language functions in the left hemisphere, whereas only 19 percent of left-handers have their language function based in the right hemisphere. Furthermore, other abilities such as memory, motor control, and cognition have been shown to be spread equally across the two hemispheres. So the utility of applying the "left brain, right brain" model is limited, and it's a questionable practice to determine preferred modalities for learning based on a person's handedness.

In summary, while the brain's two hemispheres indeed have some specialized functions, these are not absolute or fixed. In general, the left hemisphere excels at temporal conceptualization, including analytical, logical, and causative, while the right hemisphere tends to preside over spatial conceptualization such as visualization of objects in three dimensions and gestalt. Great differences exist among individuals, however. Thus, learning strategies are best based on an analysis of known personal intelligences rather than application of lateralization concepts.

How Neurons and Synapses Run the Show

Neurons, and the connections they make with other neurons, are the source of the brain's vast power and potential. Neurons have three parts: dendrites, the cell body, and the axon. Dendrites are treelike branches that receive inputs from other neurons. The cell body, or soma, contains DNA and sustains the life of the cell. The axon can be thought of as a kind of living wire that carries electrical impulses at very high speeds to dendrites of nearby neurons.

A synapse forms where a dendrite of one neuron connects with an axon of another. When an electrical signal reaches the end of the axon, it releases a chemical neurotransmitter into the synapse that either excites or inhibits the dendrite of the adjacent neuron. When brain neurons excite and "fire" together, there's a strengthening of the connection between them. This is the essence of learning, skill development, and memory, as well as all bad habits of thought and reaction. All external stimuli, as well as your thoughts and your actions, converge in the synaptic space between neurons. And regardless of whether it's self-directed or just happenstance, neurons that fire together will wire together. This cornerstone principle of neuroscience—neurons that fire together wire together—explains how the brain makes new connections that are strengthened with repeated firings.

> **All external stimuli, as well as your thoughts and your actions, converge in the synaptic space between neurons. And regardless of whether it's self-directed or just happenstance, neurons that fire together will wire together.**

Like a thickening cable, practicing a skill over and over (or making a cognitive association to a specific stimuli) will fire and wire neurons and strengthen the connection (and thus the skill or association).

The potential number of novel combinations of neurons that can fire together is almost limitless. The estimated hundred billion brain neurons can interact with just one or many thousands of other neurons, so as stated earlier the possible number of synaptic connections is almost unfathomable. The upshot, then, is that we have unlimited potential to learn, forge new distinctions and associations, and develop skills. In the context of climbing, this means that there is always room to learn and refine skills (both mental and physical), even for the very best climber with decades of experience.

There is always room to learn and refine skills (both mental and physical), even for the very best climber with decades of experience.

A commonly used analogy in explaining brain function is to compare the firing of neurons to the binary code of computers. While there is some similarity in the sort of "on-or-off" connections of brain neurons and microchips, the brain is also mediated by analog processes such as the release of chemical neurotransmitters at synaptic junctions. Furthermore, the brain's most extraordinary power, that of consciousness and deep subjective awareness, is uniquely human and not replicable in the realm of the silicone microchip. Neuroscientists remain unsure of just how these noncorporeal manifestations of the brain arise. It is posited that arcs of neuronal conduction, modulated by electrochemical processes, produce the phenomenon of the mind. Our mental powers, then, arise from a complex neuromatrix—our thoughts, willpower, intentions, and awareness spring to life like spirits in a material world.

Neuroplasticity

The most exciting aspect of the human brain is its ability to change—a process known as neuroplasticity. Interesting, until a quarter-century ago it was widely believed that the brain became relatively fixed and "hardwired" after childhood. Through a series of groundbreaking studies, however, neuroscientists have discovered that the brain possesses a remarkable potential for motor and sensory plasticity. This recent realization shatters the limitations of the old fixed-brain paradigm and empowers all humans to modify and elevate brain function, if they choose to do so. For example, stroke sufferers can regain part or all of their lost functions given the knowledge of learning or training protocols and the motivation to apply them. Similarly, students can accelerate learning and improve memory recall, athletes can learn to move with greater efficiency, and we can all break bad habits, improve patterns of thought, and develop greater willpower by training our brains to change.

Michael Merzenich, called by some the world's leading researcher on brain plasticity, has developed a wide range of brain exercises to improve cognitive functioning, treat mental disorders, and accelerate learning. He targets specific processing areas, called brain maps, which he believes can be modified through training, perhaps changing hundreds of millions or even billions of connections among neurons. Merzenich's work is far reaching as it has been used to accelerate learning of foreign languages and to help deaf people hear (one of his innovations led to the development of the cochlear implant that has helped countless deaf hear again). More generally, Merzenich's experiments have shown that the shape of the brain changes according to what we do in our lives. "The brain," he says, "is a living creature with an appetite," but he emphasizes that the process of positive change requires mental exercise, discipline, and proper nourishment.

Thanks to the work of Merzenich and others, it's now understood that our brains are changing every moment of every day as neurons fire in response to stimuli. Considering the many millions of neurochemical reactions that take place per minute, we can see that the brain is prolific at wiring new synaptic connections.

The ultimate question is whether the new connections that are constantly being established are helping or hurting you. Are the new associations going to increase the quality of your thoughts and actions, or will they hurt your cause? A major factor, of course, is the nature of the stimuli reaching your brain through your five senses.

Ponder for a moment the vast, wide-ranging stimuli that reach you each day—the people, events, and situations, as well as self-directed stimuli such as what you read, watch on TV, or view on the Internet. This massive amount of sensory input and the resultant associations and actions shape your plastic (malleable) brain every day. The bottom line, then, is that who you are today may be more a matter of past sensory inputs and your subsequent actions than any other factor, such as your genetic material (DNA) or where you were born.

The brain is a living creature with an appetite.

It should now be apparent that there is nothing more important than managing sensory input and directing your actions (and reactions) in order to control the shaping of your brain. In his fascinating book *The Brain That Changes Itself,* Norman Doidge emphasizes that "everything your 'immaterial' mind imagines leaves material traces. Each thought alters the physical state of your brain synapses at a microscopic level."

In the context of climbing (and life), developing a positive frame of mind, increasing personal efficacy, and maximizing experience are directly related to how well you guard your brain from negative inputs and self-direct consumption of positive inputs. You must also strive to increase your awareness of the nature and quality of your actions, since each action (or decision not to act) also wires new synapses. Given the prime directive of "training your brain," this book provides you with dozens of distinctions, tips, and training techniques to help you take control of neuroplastic change.

Types of Neuroplastic Change

Studies on rats (the usual subjects) have shown that stimulating the brain with novel inputs in new environments makes it grow in almost every conceivable way.

The Training Implications of Neuroplasticity

- **Neurons that fire together wire together.** Whether you climb with sound technique or sloppily thrash through moves, you are wiring these habits of movement into the brain. Therefore, it's essential to climb each move and route with the best technique possible, always striving to elevate quality of movement.

- **The brain has unlimited capacity to learn.** Therefore, you have unlimited potential to improve climbing technique, forge new distinctions and associations, and develop new skills. There is always room for improvement, even for the best climber in the world!

- **The brain is a living creature with an appetite.** The brain is constantly changing based on what we think, sense, and do. The process of positive change requires mental and physical exercise, disciplined control of sensory input, and proper nutrition and rest.

- **Each thought physically alters brain synapses.** Developing a positive frame of mind, increasing personal efficacy, and maximizing experience are directly related to how well you guard your brain from negative inputs and self-direct consumption of positive inputs.

- **Mental and physical training impart change on the structure of the brain.** Mental training and skill training create new synapses, while strenuous physical training increases vascularization. Since the greatest changes occur in response to exposure to novel, complex situations, it's essential to regularly challenge yourself with new types of climbing and training.

Mental training in rats—achieved by placing rats in a large cage with a changing set of objects for play and exploration—increased brain weight by 5 percent in the cerebral cortex and up to 9 percent in the areas that the training directly targeted. Trained neurons developed 25 percent more branches, thus increasing the number of synaptic connections per neuron. In a somewhat analogous study in humans, postmortem examinations revealed a larger number of branches among neurons, and greater brain thickness and volume, in people who had more education and lived in a more stimulating environment.

Neuroplastic change in the brain isn't limited to just creating more synapses. Studies have revealed that animals raised in complex environments possess a greater volume of capillaries per nerve cell. (More capillaries enable a greater supply of oxygen and nutrients to reach brain cells.) This increase in capillaries proves that the gross structure of the brain was altered as a result of experience.

Perhaps the most fascinating study involved "climber" rats that were challenged to learn complex motor skills (sound familiar?). The study examined four groups of rats, each group being exposed to different conditions. One group was presented with an elevated obstacle course to be traversed. Over the course of one month of practice, these "climber" rats developed the motor skills necessary to easily and regularly send the traverse problem (crank on, bro!). A second group of "exerciser" rats were put on a treadmill to run for one hour per day. A third group of "voluntary exercisers" had free access to an exercise wheel, which they used frequently. The fourth group did no exercise—the researchers called these rats "cage potatoes."

After a month of the exercise protocol detailed above, the researchers examined the brains of the rats to determine how the blood vessel volume and number of synapses might have changed. Both groups of exercising rats showed higher densities of blood vessels than either the climber rats or the cage potatoes. Not surprisingly, however, the climber rats, which developed motor skills via "traverse training," possessed the greatest number of synapses per nerve cell. The conclusion, then, is that different kinds of experience change the brain in different ways. Physical exercise increases vascularization of the brain, whereas learning new mental and motor skills increases synaptic connections.

Applied to human climbers, it would seem that rigorous training of any kind will lead to increased vascularization of the brain—thus providing more oxygen and nutrients to help maintain a clear, sharp mind in severe and stressful situations. Developing new synapses, however, requires skill practice of increasing complexity and exposure to novel situations. It could be argued, then, that the act of frequently pushing yourself on new and challenging rock climbs—which provides both rigorous physical exercise and exposure to complex skill-building situations—will grow the brain with both new capillaries and synapses!

Most recently, scientists have begun to study whether pure mental training can elicit changes in the brain. With the help of the Dalai Lama, neuroscientist Richard Davidson studied a group of Buddhist monks who had spent more than 10,000 hours in meditation. In the experiment the monks' brain activity was monitored while they engaged in compassion meditation—generating a feeling of loving kindness toward all beings that permeates the whole mind so that no other thoughts can surface. The monks' brain activity was compared with a group of novices attempting the same form of meditation. The novices showed only a slight increase in high-frequency (gamma wave) activity, while the monks experienced dramatic increases in gamma waves of the sort that had never before been reported in neuroscience literature! Furthermore, functional MRIs of the monks' brains revealed that the left prefrontal cortex (the seat of positive emotions) lit up with activity, indicating increased blood flow to this region. Based on this and other research, Professor Davidson surmises that mental training can foster a higher level of consciousness and physically change the brain.

In summary, it is now clear that the brain literally grows stronger with training. Research has shown that by regularly engaging in focused, challenging activity—physical or mental—you impart change on the structure of the brain. Any physical or sensory activity, as well as thinking, imagining, and learning, and even cultural

By regularly engaging in focused, challenging activity—physical or mental—you impart change on the structure of the brain.

activities such as learning languages or listening to music, will lead to neuroplastic change. This change can be helpful or hurtful, depending on the nature and quality of the inputs and the new associations that are formed. In the end, the brain is a human being's most dynamic organ—it is shaped by the sum our experiences, both what we do and what we have done.

An Overview of the Mind and Memory

In this section we shift our study from the material brain to the immaterial mind. While neuroscientists can physically examine the brain and many of its functions, the mind is an intangible electrochemical phenomenon of the brain that is less understood and even somewhat controversial among philosophers. Nonetheless, it's generally agreed that the mind is the seat of self-consciousness and the source of cognition, memory, analysis, imagination, and many other mental states.

While the five physical senses of sight, hearing, taste, touch, and smell are our avenue to experience, it's the mind that provides us with the self-awareness to recognize and interpret sensory stimuli. The mind also endows us with the sixth sense of intuition, as well as the mystical feelings of spirituality that many of us experience. The scope of mental function, then, extends beyond the physical to the metaphysical.

Given the mind's broad purview, it is clear that climbers can benefit in many ways by better understanding the functions and powers of the mind. In the coming pages you will learn about important topics such as the nature of awareness, your "three minds," and memory. Then, in part three of *Maximum Climbing*, we'll build on this foundation with dozens of techniques that you can leverage to enhance experience and performance!

Awareness

Awareness is a relative concept that encompasses a continuum from the basic ability to sense and perceive (as in lower forms of animal life) to the uniquely human "higher awareness" of self and one's thoughts. Basic awareness of internal sensation and stimuli of the external world spring forth from the brain stem, whereas higher forms of awareness such as consciousness and deep self-awareness depend more on the neocortex.

As a simple model for better understanding cognitive awareness, you can think of levels of awareness as degrees of wakefulness. When you mentally space out while belaying a slow leader, your awareness of self and surroundings is much less than when you are on the sharp end running it out on severe terrain. In this way, your awareness is largely a function of your need for mental attentiveness—you need to pay acute attention on the sharp end, whereas your attention may slack off somewhat when belaying a lead climber on a safe route. You need a high level of awareness to best process internal and external stimuli, analyze the data and

Everything humans have conceived and achieved is a manifestation of pure thought.

make decisions, and take action in a complex situation, whereas a lower level of awareness will suffice for processing a less complex environment or executing a well-learned motor skill.

The key, then, is to become aware of your need for awareness and, through the power of will, elevate your awareness when needed to perform—mentally or physically—in an important or trying situation. As covered in chapter 1, exercising your willpower to take action or increase awareness is a master skill that will grow stronger with use. You can also enhance awareness via other mental pathways such as meditation and concentration training (both will be covered in part three).

The Infinite Powers of Your Three Minds

The mind is an immaterial function arising from the neurons and synapses of the material brain. As physical beings possessing a three-pound brain, it's (forgive the pun) mind boggling to consider that everything humans have conceived and achieved on planet Earth is a manifestation of pure thought.

The powers of the mind operate on three levels: the conscious, preconscious, and unconscious. The conscious mind comprises our thoughts, perceptions, memory, imagination, intention, and emotion. Despite this broad scope, the conscious mind represents only a small part of our total mental powers. Operating below the consciousness level are the preconscious and unconscious minds, which assist us in all we do and provide the amazing sixth sense of intuition. Let's examine each aspect of the mind and determine its role in climbing.

The Conscious Mind

The conscious mind is the stream of consciousness comprising all our thoughts, memories, imagination, and analysis. It most often manifests as nonvocal self-talk—the incessant stream of ideas, questions, desires, fears, doubts, worries, and other thoughts—but it is also revealed through our words, expressions, and actions in the present moment.

Perhaps the most profound aspect of conscious thought is that it ultimately leads to your behavior as well as the subjective quality of your life. In this way you re-create your life every day according to the thoughts you hold in mind. Buddha summarized this simple yet immensely powerful concept by stating, "What we think, we become."

Perhaps the most profound aspect of conscious thought is that it ultimately leads to your behavior as well as the subjective quality of your life.

Therefore, there is nothing more important than seizing control of your conscious mind and directing it in the most productive way. Far too many people let thoughts of the past consume their conscious mind—and worse yet, they imagine a dismal future based on an extrapolation of the past. The future, of course, is revealed moment by moment, and it is completely open to the influence of willpower! You can change the future, then, only by directing your thoughts and actions in the present moment. So to become a better climber—or better anything—

it's essential to focus your psychic and physical energy on making the most of the moment you are in.

Achieving a positive and proactive modus operandi is easier said than done, however. Not only is there the strong pull of myriad outside influences, but the direction of your conscious mind—your "normal" ways of thinking—may be a deflecting force as well. A key distinction of conscious thought is that it's never neutral. Your thoughts at any moment are either productive or counterproductive—they are either helping or hurting you. A good way to distinguish and become self-aware of these two very different states of mind is to recognize them as a doer mind and an undermining mind. Let's take a look at each state of mind—consider which is your dominant mode.

- **Doer mind.** The doer mind is forward thinking and process-oriented. It imagines a goal and concentrates on learning, training, and discovering the things needed to reach the goal. The doer mind has a positive tone that finds enjoyment in each moment. It analyzes setbacks in search of a silver lining or clue for future success, knowing that progress is under way even when things aren't going as planned in the moment. The doer mind is eternally optimistic—my friend Todd Skinner exemplified the doer mind perhaps better than anyone I've ever met. Young children and adult peak performers (in any endeavor) are the individuals most living with a doer state of mind. You can recognize them as the "busy bees" who don't waste time gossiping or complaining—they are just too darn busy acting, imagining, and experiencing!

- **Undermining mind.** The undermining mind dwells on the failures of the past and extrapolates them into the future. It chronically analyzes and judges, and it's prolific in finding the flaws in self and others. The undermining mind obsesses over bad results and apparent barriers to future progress, and in doing so it magnifies past failures and present challenges. The undermining mind is most recognizable by negative self-talk, unproductive self-criticism, and unwarranted self-doubts. It is also revealed in frequent criticism of others, as a pseudo way to elevate the self.

Sadly, the undermining mind prevails among many teenagers and adults conditioned by the chronically critical minds of some peers, teachers, family, and the media (TV and Internet abound with the drivel of critics—guard your mind!). You can easily spot these "professional critics" because they are consumed either by complaining about their own "bad" situation or by criticizing others.

The Preconscious Mind

Since the conscious mind can only manage one or two tasks at a time, the majority of actions we engage in are turned over to the preconscious and unconscious minds. The preconscious mind (often called subconscious) is masterful at multitasking. For example, in climbing you tend to focus your mind on one critical task at a time (say, reaching up to the next hold or placing a piece of gear), so it's the preconscious mind that directs the many subtle actions needed at the same moment (such as maintaining proper muscle tension throughout your body, finding the optimal location for your center of gravity, and directing your breathing rate, among many other things). Such preconscious

To become a better climber—or better anything—it's essential to focus your psychic and physical energy on making the most of the moment you are in.

function operates just below consciousness, and its constituents can easily shift to the conscious level when needed (in the above example, your conscious mind can instantly switch to the task of maintaining balance or adjusting muscle tension and breathing).

The capacity and effectiveness of the preconscious mind in climbing (or any task) grows with practice and increasing competency. Thus, an elite climber can move quickly and smoothly up a difficult climb thanks to the preconscious mind's prowess at accurately directing many of the necessary motor skills—the conscious mind only needs to address the most critical tasks (spotting the next hold or throwing a lunge). A beginning climber, by contrast, moves more slowly and hesitantly because of her need to consciously think about the many different aspects of moving, staying in balance, locating the holds, and such. Through many hours of practice, she can condition her preconscious to take over an increasing number of tasks, thus increasing her quality and rate of movement.

The process of projecting a hard climb is a perfect example of training the preconscious mind. In the initial stage of working the route bolt-to-bolt, the conscious mind labors in directing a vast range of actions, from locating holds and directing sequence to managing muscle action, balance, and body position. With additional rehearsal, however, an increasing number of these actions can be turned over to the preconscious mind. Eventually, the bulk of the mental workload can be turned over to the preconscious mind, at which point the climb begins to feel doable. Then on redpoint, the conscious mind directs only the most critical tasks, while the preconscious mind oversees the rest of the action. It is really quite amazing how many tasks the preconscious mind directs—body position, balance, rate of movement, muscle tension, and even placement of the hands and feet on certain holds—in the act of redpointing a well-rehearsed route.

The Unconscious Mind

Below the thin layers of the conscious and preconscious lies the omnipotent unconscious mind. While some controversy lingers among psychologists as to the exact nature of the unconscious mind, it is generally agreed to be a massive storehouse of information and experience—both forgotten and repressed—accumulated throughout your life, as well as the source of survival instincts such as the fear of falling or the fear of pain. Neuroscientists have shown that the unconscious mind processes information that is passed over by the conscious mind (a vast amount of subtle sensory input) or too brief in existence to register with the conscious mind. It's also been learned that sensory inputs are registered by the unconscious mind more than one hundred milliseconds ahead of conscious perception. In aggregate, unconscious powers of the mind are what enable us to react quickly and unconsciously in certain situations; more important, they provide us with the sixth sense of intuition.

In climbing, this intuitive sense is invaluable. Intuition directs myriad subtle physical adjustments and actions that are imperceptible to the conscious and preconscious mind. The simple act of walking requires thousands of biomechanical actions to work in concert, so just imagine how big a role the unconscious mind plays in climbing! What is more, the unconscious mind plays a large role in problem solving and intuiting a sequence when on-sighting. Based on the aggregate experience of every climb and move you've made, the unconscious mind will often provide you with intuitive guidance that leads you to find just the right body position—first try—needed to climb through a novel sequence.

Based on the aggregate experience of every climb and move you've made, the unconscious mind will often provide you with intuitive guidance that leads you to find just the right body position—first try—needed to climb through a novel sequence.

Similarly, the unconscious mind is the source of the gut feeling that leads you up the right path or saves you just moments before making a serious, perhaps even fatal, mistake.

Since such intuition is experience-based, a novice will possess little intuitive sense compared with a veteran climber with thousands of climbing days under his belt. It should be no surprise, then, that many accidents are the result of bad judgments by inexperienced climbers. While many climbing judgments are indeed conscious decisions, some of our most important decisions are guided by intuition. For example, it's intuition that provides the insight into whether or not a loose block will hold your weight, if a piece of gear will hold a fall, or whether a slope is at risk of avalanching. All of these critical subjective judgments, though consciously made, are guided by the invaluable sixth sense of intuition.

Another important aspect of the unconscious mind relates to its ability to consume and archive sensory stimuli. Many times a good or bad subjective feeling, which surfaces for no apparent reason, is the result of an association stored in the unconscious mind. Similarly, most of our habits (good or bad) are unconsciously directed as a result of long-term conscious and preconscious conditioning. Even a personal tendency toward action (or procrastination) or being constructive (or critical) is largely guided by the unconscious mind as programmed by past experiences and thoughts.

This is an immensely powerful distinction—your thoughts and experiences program your unconscious mind—and you must learn to masterfully control this process if you are to maximize your experience and performance. While I will delve deeper into this subject in chapter 11, I want to conclude this section on the powers of the mind by stressing the importance of guarding sensory input and controlling your thoughts. Just as you can program your unconscious mind with positive experiences and thoughts (including visualization), the unconscious mind is affected by negative people and negative thinking. The bottom line: The most important thing you can do to improve the quality of your climbing and life experience is to guard your sensory inputs and, as best as possible, self-direct the programming of your unconscious mind by controlling your conscious thoughts.

Your thoughts and experiences program your unconscious mind— and you must learn to masterfully control this process if you are to maximize your experience and performance.

Memory

Memory is the process of information retention in which knowledge and experiences are stored for future recall. Unlike computers, which digitally store bits of data, human memory is extremely complex and the archival of information is influenced by many factors, such as the emotional pleasure or pain of an experience. Memory is often broken down into two classifications: short-term memory (STM) and long-term memory (LTM).

Short-term memory stores information that's currently in use. Most people can hold five to nine items in STM for a few seconds (as in remembering a phone number) simply by concentrating on them for a moment. STM can hold the information more easily if it's chunked into a smaller number of items—for example, chunking down a ten-digit phone number into three or four parts. In climbing, STM is crucial when looking ahead to sort out and remember an upcoming sequence. On a less conscious level, but no less important, the STM stores the shape and location of a hold you are now using for your hand and helps facilitate quick, proper placement of your foot on it as you move up. The above processes are vital for effective on-sight climbing when you have to imagine and remember sequences as you first encounter them. The best climbers with the best STM probably remember sequences in chunks, since they can hold more moves in mind by chunking them into groups of moves.

Long-term memory is the brain's amazing capacity to store information for an extended period of time (even an entire lifetime) by way of new synapses and protein synthesis. These enduring memories are either implicit or explicit in nature. Implicit, or procedural memory, is mostly used to store motor skills for later recall. The skill slowly solidifies in LTM as a result of repeated practice, eventually becoming automatic and largely preconscious.

Although you will learn much more about motor learning in chapter 3, knowledge of the longevity of slowly developed motor skills should underscore the importance of developing good climbing technique as a novice (or for an experienced climber during the initial forays at a more advanced skill). Upon storing bad technique into LTM—for example, sloppy footwork or overgripping handholds—it will be difficult to eradicate the technical flaws. They will tend to resurface when you encounter stressful sequences that limit your conscious control of technique.

Tips for Improving Your Mind, Memory, and Intuition

- **What you think, you become.** Each day you re-create your life according to the thoughts you hold minute by minute. Improving your situation or performance in anything begins with seizing control of your thoughts and becoming positive and productive in the moment.

- **Embrace a doer mind-set.** Instead of dwelling on the failures of the past (the undermining mind-set), allow only forward-thinking and goal-oriented thoughts to fill your mind. Find enjoyment in every moment and search for silver linings and clues for success in apparent setbacks that you encounter.

- **The intuitive sense is experience-based, so seek novel experience.** While novice climbers naturally lack intuitive abilities, logging experience in a wide range of climbing situations will rapidly develop intuitive powers. Err on the side of caution in your formative outings, but gradually expand your journeys into challenging, unknown situations in accordance to the strengthening guidance of your intuitive sixth sense.

- **Your unconscious mind is always learning, so be aware of the people, media, and situations you engage.** Guard your senses from negative people and strive to direct the programming of your unconscious mind by maintaining a positive, goal-oriented frame of mind.

- **You can improve your memory through conscious effort.** Enhance short-term memory by chunking data into more memorable groups or sequences. Fortify long-term memory by adjoining positive emotions and vivid images to the concept or sequence you wish to remember.

Explicit or declarative memory is used for conscious recall of specific facts, numbers, shapes, and such. Explicit memory is quick to store in LTM, but it is also quick to erode if not used or reviewed. Learning a person's name, or a complex sequence on a route for that matter, but forgetting the name or sequence at a later encounter is an example of this. These memories both involve storing data into LTM, data that may be overwritten and forgotten as similar data is stored into LTM (such as meeting new people and learning new sequences). Enduring long-term memories tend to store as concepts and pictures—great spellers and scientists alike utilize pictures and concepts to fortify their memory, and you should, too!

Enduring long-term memories tend to store as concepts and pictures—great spellers and scientists alike utilize pictures and concepts to fortify their memory, and you should, too!

An important discovery of neuropsychologists is that explicit LTM involves the forebrain, and includes the hippocampus, which is the seat of the brain's emotion system. The upshot of this finding is that explicit memories will store more quickly (and remain longer) when they are accompanied by strong emotion. Thus, it's quite likely that you can recall right now almost every detail of your greatest ascent—the emotion of the ascent has helped anchor the storage of the LTM. Similarly, of course, memories charged with negative emotion are also likely to remain in LTM.

The take-home idea here is that you can consciously manage your emotions to influence storage of LTM. For example, you can better anchor a sequence or event in LTM by adjoining it with the true enjoyment of the climb and the challenge. Conversely you may be able to lessen the storage of a bad situation by remaining emotionally neutral and stoic as the event unfolds.

Brain Training to Maximize Skill and Technique

t's a popular coaches' adage that physical practice develops "muscle memory." In reality, the muscles have no memory—it's the central nervous system and representations of skilled movement in the brain's cortex that provide us with "movement memory" in sports and in living. The muscles simply respond to the beck and call of the brain, which is the governor of all motor skill and movement.

Developing climbing skills, then, is primarily a matter of training the brain. It's a fact that every climbing move you make not only originates in the brain, but also changes the brain. Your patterns of movement, good or bad, are constantly wiring the brain with new or refined neural associations. For example, climbing sloppily—with bad footwork, poor posture, and inefficient use of the muscles—will further wire these patterns until they become hard-to-break habits. This underscores the paramount importance of keeping a vigilant watch over your climbing technique and regularly engaging in targeted skill practice to encode high-quality representations of movement. This process of monitoring quality of movement and directing practice to increase the breadth and depth of your skills is the essence of brain training.

You are not what you climb; you are how you climb. For "you," substitute your brain.

Whereas mental training (to be covered in part three) addresses cognitive skills, this chapter on brain training focuses on the processes of acquiring motor skills and practicing to develop a high level of skill and excellent technique. According to the Law of Imperfection (defined in chapter 1), even elite climbers can further refine their technique and climbing efficiency—and for the average climber, a massive windfall of gains can be obtained through brain training!

No matter how good you believe your technique is already, I guarantee that you can improve markedly by applying the material in this chapter. Not only are there always more skills to learn, but with a disciplined effort you can reduce technical flaws, seal off energy leaks, and learn to move with more economy. Your pathway to these gains begins with increasing your knowledge of the processes of motor learning

Rob Pizem stemming up the classic **El Matador** *(5.11a), Devils Tower, Wyoming.*
KEITH LADZINSKI

and skill acquisition. You then need to act with discipline and willpower to apply the material in all your practice climbing, both indoors and out. Resist the lust for constantly projecting hard routes (a flawed but common MO) and remind yourself that the process of refining and expanding skill with practice is never-ending and in fact essential to becoming a better climber. Even Tiger Woods, the most dominant athlete in the world, spends long hours practicing to improve technique and better groove critical skills—so why shouldn't you?

As we depart on our study of motor learning and effective practice, I should point out that this chapter does not provide instruction on specific climbing techniques. Consult chapter 4 of *Training for Climbing* for a review of fundamental techniques, as well as *How to Rock Climb* or *Learning to Climb Indoors* for detailed technical instruction and illustrative photographs.

Motor Learning and Skill Acquisition

In ascending a boulder, cliff, or mountain, you are expressing skilled movement. While climbing may seem to be a relatively simply and intuitive skill, moving with balance and precision in the vertical plane is actually quite complex. The exquisite, flowing movements of an elite climber result from a harmonious aggregate response to the contractions of agonist and antagonist muscles, and a wealth of sensory exteroception and proprioception. This complex process of acting with skill and will, while ingesting a vast array of sensory stimuli, requires many years to master. And despite the unattainable goal of perfection, it's in striving for perfection that you depart on a trajectory toward true mastery.

Despite the unattainable goal of perfection, it's in striving for perfection that you depart on a trajectory toward true mastery.

Following is a short course on motor learning and skilled performance. You will learn many powerful concepts that you can put to work immediately in order to enhance the quality of your time spent practice climbing. Not only is this information important for every serious climber, but I consider it essential knowledge for climbing coaches to understand and maximally leverage in training their students. As much as any other chapter, regularly revisit the pages that follow in order to remain mindful of these training concepts and practice strategies.

Types of Skills and Transference of Skill

Skill is defined as the capability to bring about an end result with maximum certainty and minimum time and energy. Climbing skills possess motor and cognitive components. Developing motor skills is covered in this part of the book, while the cognitive skills are detailed in part three.

Another important distinction is that between discrete and serial skills. A discrete climbing skill is a single movement with a definite beginning and end—a mantel, lunge, high step, down pull, lieback, deadpoint, and the like. String many discrete skills together, however, and you now have a more complex skilled action called a serial skill. Like a gymnast performing a routine, a climber must successfully execute specific moves, but also possess the skill to link all the moves into a complete ascent. This explains why, in preparation for a redpoint ascent, you can't just practice the individual moves—it's equally important to practice connecting the moves, since this is a new skill in and of itself.

Also relevant to the process of learning and application of motor skills is the matter of skill transference, which relates to how practice of a skill in one activity carries over to enhance performance of another, different activity. Research and anecdotal evidence both confirm that transference is either small or completely absent, even between seemingly similar activities. The complexity, coordination, and integration of skilled movement are so specific that they derive very little help from other skilled movements. Therefore, practice at crack climbing will improve crack climbing skill, but not face climbing ability. Furthermore, engaging in any type of "cross-training" activity will also fail to improve climbing skill. Kicking a Hacky Sack, snowboarding, slacklining, or what have you, is a waste of time for the purpose of improving climbing skill (although these activities may develop cognitive attributes, such as focus, that may translate to climbing).

Sources of Sensory Information

Inherent to skilled performance is the need to receive and understand sensory information from the environment and your body. In climbing, the amount of information to process moment by moment is remarkably vast. Most obvious is the data collected through our senses regarding the climb and the surrounding environment. More subtle, but exceedingly important, is the wealth of information provided by our body relating to balance, muscle function, and quality of movement, among other things. Let's examine more closely the two sources of sensory information.

Exteroception

Sensory information from outside the body is called exteroception. Of the five traditional senses, vision is the primary source of exteroception for physical activities such climbing. Not only does vision provide the data needed to discover holds and unlock sequence, but it also offers a wealth of less conscious input on the spatial and temporal aspects of our movements.

Less obvious, but still valuable, is exteroception via touch and hearing. Whether you are aware of it or not, your sense of touch provides essential data on rock texture and quality of contact with the hands and feet. Every moment that you are on a climb, either your conscious or preconscious mind monitors this tactile input, enabling you to make subtle adjustments of grip and foot position. The auditory sense provides other novel environmental data, such as warning of approaching rockfall and confirming that a carabiner gate has closed (hearing that important snap of the gate), among other things.

Proprioception

Proprioception is your internal sense of body position and movement in space (also called kinesthesis). No matter what you do physically, proprioception provides the brain with a high bandwidth of sensory data from the nerves in all of your muscles, tendons, and joints, as well as from the vestibular apparatus of your inner ear (which allows you to sense orientation with regard to gravity). This vast amount of sensory feedback from the limbs and inner ear is processed unconsciously in doing simple tasks such as walking, cranking pull-ups, or dancing up an easy climb that requires little thought. More complex tasks, however, require conscious attention to proprioception—and it's the awareness and diligent use of this information that separates master climbers from the mass of climbers.

Awareness of specific aspects of proprioception, or what I call proprioceptive cues, varies on a continuum from extremely coarse and general on one end to exquisitely subtle and well defined on the other. Beginning climbers initially possess a coarse, limited sense of internal feeling as they climb. For example, they may sense the basic quality of a foot placement, whether they are in balance, and, most obvious, how pumped they are getting! This most basic proprioception is important, but it represents just a tiny fraction of the broad bandwidth of proprioceptive cues that an elite climber can perceive and leverage.

With increasing experience (hundreds of hours of climbing) and a determination to grow your awareness of proprioceptive cues, you will come to recognize a steady stream of valuable movement cues from your body's internal sense organs. When practicing a new skill or working a move on a hard boulder problem or project climb, it is highly instructive to ask yourself, *How does it feel when I do it the right way [most efficiently] compared with when I do it the wrong way?* Making this distinction empowers you to detect flawed execution and make corrective adjustments on the fly. This subtle but immensely important skill is one of a handful of master skills that you must will into being if you want to pursue your ultimate potential in climbing.

Becoming an intermediate or advanced climber, then, will correlate to your deepening sense of proprioception in a wide variety of climbing situations. Each type of rock, cliff angle, type of climbing, body position, and family of moves provides unique proprioceptive feedback that you must learn to interpret in order to move with fluidity and high efficiency. Much of this proprioception (and the resultant physical adjustments) occurs preconsciously when you are climbing submaximal sequences. Crux movements and many novel moves, however, demand full attention to proprioception, thus leaving little remaining cognitive focus for other purposes. Many falls off crux moves that you have rehearsed and seemingly wired—or off easier moves when on-sighting—are the result of poor attention to proprioceptive cues.

The bottom line: The more subtle the level of proprioception that you can perceive, the better you will be able to climb given your current skill level and physical abilities. Serious climbers, therefore, are serious about developing their awareness and use of proprioceptive cues.

Table 3.1 Proprioceptive Cues for Movement Training

Slabs	Vertical	Overhanging	Crack
• Feel relaxed throughout the upper body.	• Feel your center of gravity evenly positioned among all points of contact or centered over a dominant foothold.	• Feel your weight hanging on straight arms with relaxed biceps—except on big moves, feel your biceps contract.	• In finger cracks, feel your fingers twisting and biting in the crack, while your forearms feel somewhat relaxed.
• Feel soft forearms.			
• Feel a natural bend at the hips that shifts your center of gravity over your feet.	• Feel more weight on your feet than on your hands.	• Feel "soft forearms" when you are hanging on good holds; feel taut forearms when pulling a small hold or pocket.	• In hand cracks, feel the muscles in your palm squeezing and contracting, while the forearm muscles feel more relaxed (wiggle fingers to relax your forearm muscles).
• Feel your shoe edging or smearing on the rock.	• Feel the quality of your shoe contact with the rock.		
• If smearing, feel your heels hanging low and calf muscles stretching.	• Feel your fingers' touch on the rock, and relax them to the point just shy of letting go.	• When climbing straight on (facing rock), feel your legs and hips turning out and your feet pulling your center of gravity closer to the rock.	• When jamming thumbs-down, feel your elbow torque downward to secure the jam.
• Feel the majority of your weight on your feet.	• Feel tension in your torso increase and decrease as needed to optimize leverage between your hand- and footholds.		• In fist cracks, feel your hand muscles contract strongly while forearm muscles contract partially.
• Feel weight shifting side-to-side as you stand up over each foot.		• When twist locking, feel tension throughout your torso—feel the tension connect your hand and foot contact points.	
• Feel relaxed and steady belly breathing.	• Feel your leg drive propelling upward movement, while you sense your arms playing a secondary role.	• When twist locking, feel your center of gravity drawing in close to the rock (more over your feet).	• Feel the crack securely squeezing on your toes or foot.
• Feel a sense of calm and lightness throughout your body.	• As much as possible, feel relaxed through your arms and shoulders.		• Feel your weight positioned over your feet.
		• Between hard moves, feel relaxation through your biceps and shoulders.	• Feel your arms relaxing as much as possible.
	• Feel relaxed, steady breathing, except for when you need to hold your breath for a hard move.	• Feel relaxed, steady breathing, except during maximal moves.	• Feel leg drive propelling the upward movement. Feel your arms playing a secondary role.
			• Feel relaxed, steady breathing, and an inner sense of calm.

Above is a generalized list of proprioceptive cues to foster the development of higher sensory awareness. Strive to grow your kinesthetic awareness to the point that you can develop your own list of proprioceptive cues for specific types of climbing moves. It's an immensely beneficial practice to write down the specific proprioceptive cues you discover when learning a new move or working project. The process of regularly thinking about and writing down proprioceptive cues is the most direct pathway to developing excellent technical and movement skills.

Three Stages of Motor Learning

Motor learning is the process by which we acquire physical skills. Regardless of the skill, learning occurs in three identifiable and overlapping stages: the cognitive, motor, and autonomous stages. Let's examine these learning stages and identify the hallmarks of each, the keys to improvement, and the coaching implications.

Cognitive Stage

The cognitive stage of learning involves a lot of thinking (hence the name) about technique and moves, along with repeated trial-and-error attempts to execute novel moves. This first stage of learning is more visual than feel-oriented, so it helps to be shown a move and then verbally guided through execution. Early attempts are clumsy, inefficient, and jerky, expending energy and strength in wasteful ways. This is the normal modus operandi during your first few weeks or months as a climber, as well as when you are more experienced and make the first few attempts at a new type of climbing (crack, slab, pocketed face, et cetera) or on a route that's especially hard for you.

Success by way of thrashing up a climb is really a failure when it comes to learning—it wires bad habits of movement into the brain, thus developing bad technique rather than good technique!

In preparing for a climb, you tend to examine the route from the ground in an effort to figure out the moves and rest positions, and then you attempt the climb via toprope or, perhaps, leading bolt-to-bolt. The results of such early attempts typically are rough and imperfect. With continued practice, however, the quality of performance improves as you learn the feel of the moves via sharpened proprioception and knowledge of the climb.

Given the many and complex types of climbing, it may take weeks or months to advance through the cognitive stage when learning a new climbing skill set (for example, crack climbing). Two keys to effective learning are letting go of judgments relating to poor performance (view errors as clues for improvement), and not rushing or overwhelming yourself by trying many different types of climbing during initial sessions. Most important, strive to develop good technique by repeating moves (and entire routes for that matter) until you can climb them smoothly and efficiently. Remember, success by way of thrashing up a climb is really a failure when it comes to learning—it wires bad habits of movement into the brain, thus developing bad technique rather than good technique!

It's during this first stage of learning that a climbing coach is most valuable. Not only can the coach demonstrate new skills and proper ways of movement, but she can also provide you with verbal cues to guide proper posture, body positioning, tactics, and problem solving. The coach's feedback should be positive and highly specific, yet not overwhelming in volume—the focus should be on correcting major flaws, not tweaking minor technical details. Finally, it's only in this stage of learning that the coach (or others) should provide significant beta, or sequence instruction.

A beginner generally lacks the experience to see some of the necessary holds and to read complex sequences, so providing beta is actually a good way of growing experience and creativity in sequencing.

Motor Stage

The motor, or associative, stage is less a product of self-conscious effort and thought than one of automatic increases in the efficiency and organization of the activity by the nervous system and brain, as a response to continued practice. The brain wires new neural associations as a result of regular practice of a class of skills and multiple attempts at a specific movement. The climber exhibits more fluid, confident, and economical movement. Energy expenditure decreases, and the natural momentum of the body and limbs is used to advantage. This marked increase in economy of movement is the hallmark of the motor stage of learning.

When working a climb, this stage is represented by the attempts at redpoint when the moves and clips are known, and the goals are to develop efficiency and conserve power and endurance for the cruxes. The underlying factors involved in this stage differ from those that lead to early success. Here they involve improving proprioception, the accuracy of limb movement, the speed of detection and correction of minor errors, and the sensitivity of the performance to anxiety, doubt, and so on. These things are obviously less available to conscious awareness or control and are thus acquired only through dedicated practice and the chase of perfection.

In this stage the goal of action becomes more refined and demanding. The moves must be done efficiently with strength to spare, not eked out in desperation. Early, crude success should not be accepted as "good enough" since this will not lead to the best ultimate development of technique and efficiency. Having demanding goals has been shown experimentally to produce both better performance and faster gains. The goal should be to perfect movement and dominate at a certain grade, not just get by at it.

Coaching input during this stage should be far less than during the cognitive stage. The climber must be allowed to self-diagnose errors and make a first attempt at correction. In many cases, the coach may want to save feedback until after the climb—then, in a relaxed setting, talk through specific errors and techniques to practice in the future. Two important keys to rapid learning during the motor stage are broadening the skill set through exposure to new types of moves and climbs, and extensive use of proprioceptive cues to increase awareness and feel of technically correct movement. The climber should be encouraged to talk through (and even write down) what he feels when performing specific moves, although the coach may need to draw out this information by asking, "How does the move feel when you do it correctly versus when you do it poorly?"

Autonomous Stage

The final stage of learning is called the autonomous stage. At this point many climbing moves are automatic and require very little conscious attention, because movement has reached a stable and polished form. You can often do other things while in this state: For instance, you can carry on a conversation while driving a car, or you can decipher and send a moderate route in perfect form on-sight. This apparent ease of execution is one aspect of the flow state or "zone" so often touted by elite athletes. In climbing, it is reached only through dedicated, disciplined, long-term practice.

Veteran climbers with many years or decades of experience exemplify autonomous performance when they fluidly on-sight the majority of nonmaximal climbs they touch. The average climber with just a few years' experience may experience this level of automatic, efficient movement on a well-rehearsed redpoint ascent or when on-sight climbing well below maximum ability. Given the complexity of climbing, it usually takes more than ten years to reach a consistent autonomous stage of mastery. Still, such elite climbers always have room for learning and refining skills, and the very best embrace a lifelong, ever-learning mind-set toward exploring their potential.

As the name implies, climbers in this performance stage need little input from a coach—the fundamentals are well known and the climber is capable of self-correcting errors and self-directing practices and training. Coaching input here should focus on questioning the climber about how he feels, with the goal of enhancing his awareness of lingering (often very subtle) technical and mental constraints on performance, and helping develop an effective long-term training strategy.

Table 3.2 Characteristics of Motor Performance Stages

Cognitive Stage	Motor Stage	Autonomous Stage
Stiff-looking movement	More relaxed movement	Smooth/fluid movement
Hesitant or timid approach	More aggressive and confident	Aggressive and confident
Muscles through moves inefficiently	More efficient movement	Styles through moves efficiently
Needs to work moves repeatedly	Figures out moves quickly	On-sights most moves
Needs much coaching/beta	Needs less input/feedback	Solves moves and recognizes errors by self
Poor proprioceptive feel	Better proprioceptive feel	Excellent proprioceptive feel
Rapid energy burn	More economical use of energy	Highly economical climbing

How We Execute Climbing Skills and Novel Moves

Despite being as intuitive and natural as walking or running, climbing can be a remarkably complex and demanding activity. Consider that the climbing gyms and crags of the world offer a playing field of infinite variation and demand for skilled performance. Compound this with the potential for adrenaline-releasing risk and the perplexing challenge of ascending a gigantic wall, and it becomes apparent that climbing is indeed a most complex sporting activity.

The goal of this section, then, is to provide a primer on the theory of skilled performance that empowers you to learn and develop climbing skills most effectively and rapidly. While the mass of climbers stumble through the maze of trial-and-error learning, your knowledge of how the brain wires motor programs and executes novel moves is a lever that opens the door to techniques for accelerating technical improvement (described in the next section).

Motor Programs

Discrete climbing skills are directed by motor programs wired into long-term memory. These motor programs, which define and shape movement, become more stable, elaborate, and long lasting as you progress through the three stages of motor learning described earlier. With consistent, quality practice, the programs become highly precise and largely unconscious, thus freeing attention for other matters such as finding the next handhold or remembering the sequence. Conversely, climbing skills that you rarely practice (or avoid) will be represented by less detailed, unstable motor programs that may lead to poor execution and require high attentional demands.

A highly skilled climber can often look at a section of rock, see the moves, and know what skills he will need to employ. For example, he might view a short boulder problem and see a lieback move that leads to a backstep move, followed by a 2-foot deadpoint move to a good hold. In ascending the boulder problem, motor programs for "lieback," "backstep," and "deadpoint" yield a sort of movement script directing essential details of movement, like the muscles to be used and in what order, the force and duration of each contraction, and such. Still, the motor programs will not specify every aspect of movement, and so the climber will make many tiny reflexive, preconscious, or conscious proprioceptive adjustments that modify the commands of the movement script.

A less skilled climber may be challenged in many ways by the same boulder problem. First, she may lack the experience and cognitive skills to "see" the necessary moves. Furthermore, she may possess less refined motor programs for the lieback, drop-knee, and lunge skills that are necessary to ascend the sequence. Chances are, she will need numerous attempts to feel out the moves and gather proprioceptive feedback on body position, the muscles to be used, and the force of contraction, among other things. Repeated blocked practice attempts may eventually lead to a successful ascent of the boulder problem.

Performing Novel Skills

The hallmark of an expert climber is the ability to on-sight climb at a high level on a wide variety of terrain and rock types. But how does this climber execute novel moves with a high rate of success? After all, our playing field has infinite variability—so even a well-traveled professional climber will fail to experience every possible move and body position. Understanding how novel movements are generated will empower you to practice more effectively so that you can become a master at on-sight climbing through moves you've never before experienced!

Let's use the boulder problem example above, which concluded with a deadpoint to a good hold exactly 24 inches away. Given the infinite variability of climbing moves and rock surface, it is unlikely that the climber will have previously performed a deadpoint move, from a backstep position, to a hold exactly 24 inches away. However, if the climber has thrown deadpoint moves from several different distances (say, from 15, 21, 28, and 30 inches away) and from different body positions and rock angles, he will likely be able to execute the novel move on-sight. This is because all the different deadpoint moves call the same "deadpoint" motor program into use, and this motor program is scaled to fit the novel situation according to a learned set of rules, called a schema.

A schema is a set of rules, developed and applied unconsciously by the central nervous system, that enables you to adjust a motor program for different environmental conditions (hold location, rock angle, friction properties, and such) by changing parameters of muscle force, body position, and speed of movement. Becoming a proficient on-sight climber, therefore, isn't just a matter of learning all the different classes of skills (jamming, side pulling, down pulling, lunging, flagging, et cetera); it demands that you practice these skills in a wide range of configurations and settings. Such variable practice (more on this in bit) refines the existing schema-rule for each generalized motor program, thus allowing more accurate estimation of the necessary parameters for execution of a skill in a novel situation.

The practical application of schema theory should now be obvious: Upon learning a new climbing skill, say finger jamming, you'll want to practice finger jamming in cracks of different sizes, on different wall angles, and on rock with different frictional properties. Doing so will expand your use of the finger-jamming schema-rule to effectively ascend finger cracks at almost any crag on the planet. The same goes for other climbing skills—strive to expand their use to a variety of rock types and terrain, and you will be on your way to becoming a master of rock!

Conversely, if you climb at only a few cliffs and favor a specific type of climbing, you will develop fewer motor programs and less refined schema-rules for each. These motor programs, no matter how well learned, will work only for similar situations— and they may not apply particularly well at the outer limits of difficulty at these crags. Worse yet, when you travel to new areas, your limited skills and schema-rules will leave you climbing at a much lower grade or flailing on routes of the grade you're accustomed to sending at your home area.

The Importance of Feedback in Developing Expert-Level Skill

In wrapping up our study of motor learning, I must stress the importance of growing your awareness of feedback in all your climbing endeavors. No matter the task, you must consciously compare the ongoing feedback with the desired goal to determine the nature and amount of error. You are then empowered to amend your actions in a way that improves efficacy and moves you closer to your goal.

The desired goal in learning to climb should be to expand your skill set, improve quality of movement, and practice in ways that will accelerate your journey toward becoming an advanced climber steeped in autonomous-level performance. Making the most of both extrinsic and intrinsic feedback will hasten progress up the learning curve. Let's examine these two critical types of feedback.

Extrinsic Feedback

Extrinsic feedback is information provided by some outside source, such a belayer, coach, or videotape, that augments your internal sensory feedback. Extrinsic feedback is an inherent part of cognitive-stage learning, in which a beginner receives extensive verbal instruction to guide learning of new skills and proper movement. As you progress to intermediate-level ability (the motor stage), it's important to accept— and ask for—a lesser amount of extrinsic feedback. Growing your abilities demands that you learn to utilize the high bandwidth of internal feedback (more on this in a bit) in place of extrinsic feedback in self-analyzing and self-correcting movement error. Advanced climbers need very little extrinsic feedback in daily climbing and training activities, although the objective feedback of a coach is valuable in the case of a performance slump or long-term plateau in improvement.

A most common form of extrinsic feedback is beta—highly specific instruction on the proper sequence for a given climb. Beta is extremely helpful in developing hold recognition and sequencing skills during the formative stage of learning. As you progress beyond the cognitive performance stage, however, continued use of beta will handicap the development of problem-solving skills and other advanced cognitive abilities. What's more, long-term reliance on beta will lead to a false sense of ability in that your climbing performance will degrade significantly when beta is not available. The bottom line: Beyond your first few months as a climber, make it a practice to shut off beta from your partner (or others); the exception is those rare cases when beta is essential for safety or speed.

Intrinsic Feedback

Intrinsic feedback is sensory information received via your five senses and proprioception gleaned from your muscles, tendons, joints, and the vestibular apparatus of the inner ear. The most obvious intrinsic feedback is what you visually observe as the gross results of your efforts: falling off a move, seeing that a hold is not what you expected it to be, or discovering that a sequence you visualized won't work. Most climbers, regardless of ability, have good awareness of such basic intrinsic feedback.

It's the more subtle intrinsic feedback of "feel" (proprioception) that beginners— and many nonbeginners as well—lack awareness of. It's understandable, of course, for a novice to lack the subtle senses of touch, body position, and levels of muscular tension, for example, due to the aggregate overwhelm of fearful thoughts, technical struggles, and getting pumped! As your quality of movement improves (the motor stage) and you gain greater control over fear and excessive muscular tension, the more subtle proprioceptive cues begin to reveal themselves. Still, you need to direct your attention inward to fully harvest the proprioceptive cues and come to understand and leverage them completely. Growing your awareness and use of proprioceptive cues is a mental skill that you need to develop through disciplined effort.

As described earlier in this chapter, it's a beneficial practice method to talk through and write down proprioceptive cues that you discover for specific types of moves and crux sequences of project routes—this process will foster uncommon sensory awareness, accelerate motor learning, and put you on the fast track to the higher grades. For many advanced climbers use of proprioceptive cues will become largely preconscious; the exception may be in stressful, effortful moments when movement quality suffers and you need to proactively modulate tension and consciously utilize proprioceptive cues to maintain high-quality movement.

Lessons from the School of Motor Learning

- **Accept that you don't know it all and that you have a vast potential to improve.** Regardless of your level of expertise, know that there's always room for improvement. No climber ever graduates from the school of motor learning!

- **Embrace a beginner's mind-set.** Foster a constant curiosity to discover new moves, distinctions, and proprioceptive cues. Be a voracious learner.

- **Engage in scheduled practice sessions.** Commit a portion of your indoor climbing time to practicing skills, rather than constantly focusing on sending boulder problems and routes. Dedicate occasional outdoor climbing days to practicing weaker skills and gaining exposure to new types of climbing.

- **Withhold judgment of your climbing performance during practice sessions.** Let go of the need to perform—leave your ego at home—and concentrate on learning skills and refining movement, even if means falling and looking bad.

- **Repeat newly learned moves to develop accurate knowledge of proprioceptive cues.** Take mental note of the specific cues and consider writing them down to help lock them into long-term memory.

- **Train and climb with an open mind.** Aspire to glean wisdom from all you do—acute awareness of subtle distinctions of mind and body is a common trait of all master climbers.

- **Accept feedback from a coach (or others) without ego.** Recognize that constructive feedback is essential to elevating your game. Make it your long-term goal, however, to develop the acuity to self-diagnose and self-correct technical flaws as your awareness of intrinsic feedback grows.

Practice Strategies to Accelerate Acquisition of Skill and Good Technique

If you want to accelerate improvement—and develop superior technique—then you must know how to practice most effectively. Acquiring a new skill requires a progression through the three stages of motor learning before you will be able to use the new skill efficiently and intuitively. Depending on the difficulty of the skill, this process may take anywhere from a few hours to a few years. With disciplined practice and an intense belief that you soon will become excellent in the skill, however, the process of learning fundamentally sound climbing technique is hastened and will feel less arduous.

Conversely, impatient and undisciplined individuals who try to shortcut the learning process will develop poor habits of movement and lackluster techniques that will handicap performance for years to come. For example, lunging, thrashing, or foot pedaling through a sequence that could have been finessed by learning a new move, technique, or body position is a classic mistake of climbers obsessed with sending over proper learning. Another example plays out when a competent gym or face climber first attempts to learn crack climbing. The common tendency is not to commit fully to jamming the crack and instead to paw up the face on either side of it. In this case you will rapidly fatigue and likely exclaim that the route felt way harder than its grade (which of course it did, since you weren't using the proper technique).

Ultimately you must convince yourself that no matter how hard a new move feels at first, it will become easier to execute as the result of diligent practice. Make it your modus operandi to practice moves until you can do them in the most efficient, fundamentally correct way (and eschew thrashing!), and you'll soon be viewed as a climber of great technique. To this end, here are nine brain-conditioning practice strategies that will accelerate motor learning and foster superior technique. Use them every time you go climbing and you'll be on the fast track to maximum climbing.

 Engage in Regular Practice Climbing

While it may seem obvious that you must practice regularly in order to improve at climbing, it's a fact that many climbers don't engage in regular practice. A vital distinction to make each time you go climbing is whether the purpose of the outing is to practice or to perform. Performance climbing is all about on-sighting, redpointing, and sending max boulder problems. Practice climbing, on the other hand, is about learning new moves, refining technique and proprioceptive cues, and improving quality of movement with less concern about climbing outcomes. So then, what is the optimal ratio of practice climbing to performance climbing?

If you are a relative beginner (cognitive stage), then climbing for practice is paramount. Invest the majority of your time practice climbing below your maximum level with the intention of refining and smoothing out movements and learning new skill sets. If necessary, hangdog on toprope to practice a specific move repeatedly and discover the most efficient technique for executing the sequence. Most important, avoid getting on routes so over your head that you make little progress. There's little to be gained by flogging yourself in this way, and there's a good chance you will wire poor habits of movement and get unnecessarily frustrated and flummoxed.

More experienced climbers (motor stage) should roughly split their time between climbing for practice and performance. In this stage, begin and end your session with periods of practice climbing; use the middle portion of your climbing time to work and send routes near your limit. Most important for the intermediate climber is to avoid ad-lib climbing with the crowd and instead to always climb (for practice or performance) with a specific purpose or outcome in mind.

Elite climbers (autonomous stage) should spend the majority of their time climbing for performance. Possessing highly refined skill sets, these rare individuals (the top 5 percent of all climbers) should mostly go climbing to work near-maximum boulder problems or routes, on-sight in high volume, and establish new levels of performance on big walls or in the mountains. Still, these experts can benefit from practice as long as it's highly focused and targets a known weakness—climbing extremely easy routes or repeating rudimentary drills that you have well perfected, while perhaps fun, has little training value. Effective practice, then, must train something directly related to a current or upcoming project. For example, you could engage in simulator training of a crux sequence on a current project or crank out many anaerobic endurance laps on a specific kind of climbing (cracks, for example) that you will encounter on an upcoming wall route. Such elite practice climbing is obviously very physical in nature, and thus the line blurs between practicing motor skills and training physical constraints.

Use Trial and Error to Problem-Solve Specific Moves

As an infant you learned to crawl and walk via a trial-and-error process, so why not learn to climb this way as well? In climbing, the trial-and-error method is best applied in solving a crux move and experimental learning of a specific technique or narrow class of moves.

For example, you might use trial and error to practice a new move on a bouldering wall, or you might hang on a toprope and test out different possible solutions to a difficult crux. This process of self-discovering solutions is superior to using beta to circumvent the difficulty. In employing trial and error, however, it's essential that you keep an open and innovative mind-set—trying the same failed movement repeatedly will only lead to frustration, tension, and hampered learning. Make a game out of trying to imagine and test crazy solutions, and you are more likely to stumble onto the best solution.

Beyond solving specific problems or practicing a set move, the trial-and-error method of learning lacks effectiveness. For example, it would likely take you many years to discover the many fundamental techniques of rock climbing via a trial-and-error approach—reading John Long's *How to Rock Climb* or taking climbing lessons is a far more effective approach!

Seek Out and Absorb Quality Instruction

As mentioned above, climbing is a complex activity that is exceedingly difficult to learn by your own devices. Seeking out quality instruction as a beginner is tantamount to being guided through a complex maze with a detailed map of the territory. Even intermediate and advanced climbers can benefit from outside input on climbing and training strategy. A wide range of media are now available on the subject, and you need only look as far as the local climbing gym or crag to learn from a coach or model the moves of more advanced climbers.

Modeling is an immensely powerful technique for opening your mind to new moves and climbing strategies. It's best used in a climbing gym where you can observe the movements, positions, techniques, and tactics of another climber, and then immediately give them a try on your own. Make a mental picture of what you want to attempt and use that vision as a starting point. Experiment, modify, and make the move your own. You can also model what you observe at the crags. In addition to actual moves, take special note of the tactics used by high-end climbers. For example, observe how they work crux sequences, the pace at which they climb, how they find clever rests, and so forth.

Finally, seek out high-quality educational material (books, DVDs, and Web sites) to leverage the experience and expertise of others. By reading this book on brain training, for example, you are tapping into knowledge that took me more than thirty years to learn, discover, and develop—this book, then, represents a massive shortcut in gaining highly specific and powerful knowledge that would take years (or decades) to discover on your own. Of course you must consume all instructional material (and the anecdotes of others) with a critical, discerning mind. Not everything you read or hear is true, or necessarily good advice, given your current ability level.

Use Blocked and Variable Practice in Learning New Skills

Blocked practice—identical repetitions of a specific move—is the most popular method of practicing a hard climbing move because it produces rapid learning of the skill in that specific situation. In striving to learn how to do the twist-lock move, for example, you would repeat the same twist-lock move again and again in order to refine your body position, discern the appropriate application of force with each limb, and discover the most telling proprioceptive cues for optimally performing the move.

Upon development of feel and early success at a new skill, however, a radical change is needed. Further blocked practice will have little value and may even result in a false sense of confidence and poor use of the skill in settings different from that practiced. In our example, suppose you only practiced the one basic twist-lock move you first learned at the gym. Despite your success at that specific twist-lock move, you will struggle and likely fail on twist-lock moves on different wall angles and on the infinite playing field of outdoor climbing. Therefore, upon achieving initial success at a new skill, you must graduate to variable and random practice (covered below) if you want to develop the capacity to execute the new skill proficiently in novel situations. The tried-and-proven way to do this is with variable practice.

Suppose you've just learned the twist-lock move on a vertical indoor wall with large, positive holds. To incorporate variable practice, you would now change the "route conditions" slightly and attempt the same twist-lock move again. After a few reps in this new setting, you'd again modify the route by changing the hold spacing and wall angle to further expand use of the skill. Continue this progression to the point that you can perform the twist-lock move in a variety of random settings. Such variable practice will refine the schema-rule that directs effective execution of the twist-lock motor program over the wide range of conditions (angle, hold size, rock type, frictional properties) that you may encounter in the future.

Employ Fatigued Practice to Complete Skill Mastery

Beyond the initial successful trials of a new move or skill set, practice should be performed with variable conditions and levels of fatigue and never again blocked. This may increase your rate of failure at doing certain moves—but remember, performance isn't your goal, practice is! Besides, this concept actually makes good sense. If you want the ability to stick a deadpoint (or some other hard movement) in the midst of a dicey lead climb while pumped, you'd better log some repetitions of the movement in various states of fatigue during practice.

Here's the best approach. Use the first thirty minutes of your workout (while fresh) to train new skills, before moving on to chalk up some mileage on a variety of routes or testing yourself on a few harder redpoint attempts. As fatigue increases, shift your climbing to known routes and boulder problems that you have fairly wired—the goal is to climb with good technique and control, despite the high level of fatigue. In the context of a two-hour climbing gym workout, this rule emphasizes the benefit of squeezing in a greater volume of climbing practice ascents over doing just a few performance ascents with extensive rest in between. The long rests and performance climbing might make you look better, but the greater volume of climbing, including the fatigue practice, will make you climb better!

A similar training strategy involves downclimbing a route immediately following your ascent. There are many benefits to this practice beyond the obvious one of doubling the pump. If you know you're going to downclimb a route, you become a more observant and focused climber on the way up. What's more, since poor footwork is a leading handicap for many climbers, there's a lot to be gained from controlled downclimbing, which demands intense concentration on footwork.

At first you will find downclimbing to be difficult, awkward, and very pumpy. As your hold recognition improves, however, and as you learn to relax and fluidly reverse the route, you'll find that downclimbing a route sometimes feels easier than upclimbing! This is because your eccentric (lowering) strength is greater than your concentric (pulling) strength, and due to the fact that by leading with your feet while downclimbing you learn to maximally weight them and conserve energy. All of the above make downclimbing an excellent application of fatigue practice climbing.

Employ Restricted Practice Drills
to Improve Weak Skills and Enhance Proprioception

Studies have shown that the best way to improve weak skills is not by favoring compensatory functions (as is the natural tendency) but instead by consciously limiting such compensation and directing targeted practice of the weak skills. Following are four drills that restrict compensatory functions and force learning of several important techniques; see if you can develop a few other "restricted" drills that target specific skills. Beginner- and intermediate-level climbers should use these drills regularly to train up lackluster techniques and thus wire new, more effective neural associations in the brain.

- **Frog-leg drill.** This drill teaches the important technique of pushing with both feet simultaneously, much the way a frog would extend its legs in jumping. Beginning with both hands and feet on the wall, step up with one foot and then the other until you are in a sort of squatting position with your knees out to the side and crouching into the wall. Now press down with both feet in one continuous motion, and then advance one hand and then the other. Use your hands primarily for balance, not pulling—let your legs do most of the work. Repeat this process, and subvocalize the mantra *step, step, push, reach, reach.* Continue up the route striving for smooth movement and a steady rhythm in advancing hands and feet.

- **High-step drill.** On a relatively easy route (one that would surely not require the use of a high step), force yourself to ascend using only high-step foot moves. With hands and feet on the wall, begin by high-stepping with one foot onto a hold near hip level. Now rock over this foot—think about shifting your center of gravity overtop the high foot—and then drive downward with that foot and advance your hands until you reach a straight-leg position. Now high-step with the opposite foot and repeat the process to continue upward movement. The rhythm of execution for this drill is *high-step, shift weight, push, reach, reach.*

- **Tennis-ball drill.** A common technical flaw that kills climbing performance is overuse of the arms and overgripping of handholds. You won't be able to do this if you climb with a tennis ball in the palm of each hand! This is a great drill to develop the vital skill of optimizing your use of feet, improving the position of your center of gravity, and developing enhanced proprioception. Rope up on an easy route with lots of large holds, and then begin climbing (toprope) by using the tennis balls to "grip" the handholds. Clearly, your hands will only be useful for maintaining balance, so relax and allow your legs do all the work. Concentrate on shifting your weight from one foot to the other, while attempting to keep your upper body relaxed and tension-free. If you fall off the climb repeatedly, move to an easier climb with larger holds. Ideally, you should be able to "dance" your way up without falling. Use this drill regularly and you'll develop uncommonly good movement skills and proprioception through your torso and legs. (Toproping a climb blindfolded is excellent drill to develop proprioceptive feel throughout your entire body.)

- **Straight-arm drill.** Use of straight-arm positions is critical for conserving upper-body energy. Thus, the goal of this drill is to climb a route while trying to maintain straight arms at least 90 percent of the time. Strive to use straight-arm positions anytime you aren't moving, such as when resting or scanning the wall above you. Practice maintaining straight arms when stepping up or adjusting your feet. In the case of a foot placement out to the side, you may even be able to leverage off a side-pull hold using a straight arm. Continue upward favoring mainly straight-arm positions, despite that fact that it will feel contrived at times. In forcing this overuse of the straight arms, you will learn to move and rest with high economy.

Engage in Randomized Practice to Enhance Skill Recall

The ability to on-sight a sequence of novel moves on foreign rock is the ultimate goal of your skill practice time. To this end, the best workout approach is a randomized free-for-all of skill types. This highly effective method is widely used in other sports and should not be overlooked by climbers as optimal training for the unknown.

There are two approaches to randomized training of climbing skills. First, on an indoor bouldering wall, attempt to link a sequence of very different moves—contrive an unusual sequence that will call a wide range of skills into use. Make several attempts at sending the complex sequence. Alternatively, team up with a friend for a round of the Stick Game. Take turns pointing (with a broomstick) each other through an unusual sequence of widely varied skills and movements. Don't get too wrapped up in performance outcomes—if you link a random series of moves, then you are a winner in terms of developing superior climbing skill.

Another powerful method of random skill practice is to climb a series of widely differing routes in rapid succession. A commercial gym with many different wall angles, a few cracks, and a roof or two is ideal. Team with a partner and toprope ten to fifteen routes of different character over the course of an hour or so. The first route may be a vertical face, the next a slab, the third a finger crack, the fourth an overhanging pumpfest, the fifth a hand crack, the sixth a roof route, and so on. This rapid recall of a wide range of motor programs and tactical skills is like taking skill-fortifying steroids!

 Practice Climbs to the Point of Near Perfection

Another important rule for effective learning is that you must strive to achieve near perfection of specific climbing techniques, and not be satisfied to just get by at them. This is an immensely powerful concept that's unknown to or ignored by many climbers who simply want to send, even if it's with sloppy technique and a large dosage of thrash.

Let's consider the common approach of calling an ascent "successful"—and moving on to the next climb—at the point you send a route without falling. In doing this redpoint ascent, you probably struggled and fought through the hardest moves, and thus climbed the route with less-than-perfect technique and economy. So while you indeed succeeded in sending the route (good job!), you may have also succeeded in reinforcing the bad habit of climbing with lackluster technique (let's work on that).

This is a vital distinction that you may want to write down and turn into a personal mantra: Becoming an outstanding climber comes only by way of a constant resolve to master techniques and long complex sequences to the point of near perfection.

A good analog of this process is the way an Olympic gymnast practices a routine repeatedly with the goal of achieving true mastery of all its elements. In climbing, this approach might seem superfluous, especially since no one is scoring the quality of your ascent. However, taking the time to practice techniques—and entire climbs, for that matter—to the point of near perfection is one of the best investments you can make in your future ability. Commit to regularly practicing in this way and I guarantee that you will depart on a new trajectory toward climbing excellence.

If you still aren't convinced as to the effectiveness of this practice strategy, let me tell you about the legendary boulderer John Gill, who in 1959 climbed V9 (that's 5.13c/d) when the rest of the climbing world was struggling to climb 5.10! It was Gill's modus operandi to practice many boulder problems to the point of perfection, even after he had successfully ascended a problem. His goal was to perfect movement (not just get by at it) and to achieve a heightened state of kinesthetic awareness (proprioception) and experience. The upshot of his efforts is that in addition to being the strongest climber of his era, John Gill was also likely the mostly technically advanced and proficient.

The take-home idea here: Make it a regular practice to climb a boulder problem or route a few more times after the initial ascent. While you don't have to do this with every climb, it's a powerful practice strategy to employ on routes that possess new types of moves or long, complex sequences that you could surely climb more efficiently with practice. After sending a route your first time, return to practice-climb it a few more times (same or different day), but without the pressure of needing to successfully send the route. Treat this as nothing more than practice—narrow your focus onto improving quality of movement and pay no mind if you happen to fall off in the process. Set the goal to tighten up crux sequences by climbing with more precision, speed, and economy. Make a game out of elevating the quality of your ascent with every practice run, and know that with every lap you are becoming a more technically sound climber.

 ## Embrace a Long-Term Perspective to Learning and Keep Challenging Yourself

Despite the rapid improvement you will experience (or have experienced) in your first few years of climbing, it's a fact that you can continue to learn and improve for many more years to come. Climbing is an extraordinarily complex activity with motor and cognitive skills that take a decade or more to learn. So while you may progress to the verge of elite-level bouldering or sport climbing in just a few years, applying your abilities to wider range of climbing pursuits will take many more years. Becoming a true master of rock requires a sustained love of the sport and a dedication to learning that lasts a lifetime.

The key to sustaining an upward trajectory over the long term is to challenge yourself regularly and avoid settling into one form of climbing for too long. Mastery demands the ability to perceive and distinguish subtle differences in the rock, hold configuration, and techniques and tactics needed, among many other very fine distinctions. Being able to digest a vast amount of information, figure novel sequences and strategies on the fly, and ascend confidently and economically in completely unique situations is a capability born of diverse experience and many hours of laboring in the steep. This rare capacity is ultimately about challenging both brain and body, which is exactly what master climbers like Chris Sharma, Peter Croft, Lynn Hill, and others regularly do.

Tips for Enhancing Skills
and Climbing Technique

- **Engage in regular climbing practice.** Frequently go climbing with the intention of learning new skills and improving quality of movement, with little regard for absolute difficulty. Climb on as many different types of rock, wall angles, and areas as possible to build diverse skills and true climbing expertise.

- **Practice new skills and techniques early in the session while you are physically and mentally fresh.** Strive to discover the novel feeling of each move—take note of the proprioceptive cues of your successful attempts at it.

- **Use blocked practice to accelerate learning of new moves.** During the initial trials of a new move, skill, or sequence, focus practice on repeated attempts until you develop feel and quality, controlled movement. After two or three successful repetitions, cease blocked practice in favor of variable and randomized practice.

- **Employ variable practice to expand command of newly acquired skills over a wide range of conditions.** Vary the route conditions (angle, hold size, rock type, and so forth) greater than you expect they will vary in real-life climbing situations. Note how proprioceptive cues for a given move change as the rock conditions change.

- **Practice known skills, core skills, and recently sent routes in various levels of fatigue to increase mastery and to build long-term retention.** Strive for crisp, economical execution despite your fatigued state.

- **Use random practice to enhance recall of widely varying skill sets.** Climb several very different routes back-to-back in order to mandate recall of many different motor programs.

- **Model the techniques and tactics of advanced climbers.** Modeling is a highly practical way to learn new moves and climbing strategies. Also, seek out high-quality media to obtain sage advice and expert tips that will accelerate learning.

- **Aspire to dominate at a climbing grade.** Focus practice on routes at or just below your maximum difficulty and resist the urge to constantly work routes beyond your ability level. Eschew constantly hanging on the rope as a modus operandi.

- **Resolve to find the best way to do a move or sequence and resist the urge to just thrash up the route and deem that acceptable.** As a practice method, climb a route several times to identify the proprioceptive cues that will guide you to the most effective and efficient movement.

- **Possess a long-term perspective to learning to climb.** No matter how fast you improve or how hard you climb, realize that you can still improve technique and learn new skills—even after ten or twenty years or more!

The bottom line: If you wish to pursue your genetic potential and maximize climbing experience, then it's essential that you avoid repeating familiar patterns of climbing and instead forge a new and exciting path. While climbing the same routes at the same local crags can be great fun, elevating your abilities demands new, challenging experiences and the willingness to experience the frustration and failure common to exploring the unknown. One good way to keep things changing is to vary your climbing preference every season—that is, gym climbing in winter, bouldering in spring, adventure or traditional climbing in summer, and sport climbing in fall (or some variation on this theme). Ultimately, you will need to determine your own path into the mountains and discover what great adventures the future holds.

Brain Training to Maximize Strength and Endurance

The last chapter described how the brain learns and directs motor skills, such as the wide range of complex movements inherent to climbing. In this chapter we'll examine how the brain governs the recruitment of the muscles and modulates exercise intensity to prevent injury and death due to overexertion. As you will soon see, this concept has powerful implications in terms of how to train most effectively in order to condition your brain to allow a higher absolute level of physical performance.

The pain of exertion is something all climbers know well, whether it comes via an effortful push up a boulder problem, lead climb, or 8,000-meter peak. It could be argued that aggressive climbers have a masochist tendency, since pushing physical limits always comes with a dose of pain and sometimes even excruciatingly sustained discomfort. In bouldering, the pain tends to be more acute as arm muscles and pulped tips scream during maximum efforts. Multipitch and wall climbing can produce searing forearms as well, although the pain of full-body fatigue and mental strain are often the primary limiting factors. Alpine climbing is perhaps the most arduous of all climbing endeavors: Aching legs and lungs and a throbbing chest and head impel a slower rate, or termination, of movement. Interestingly, in all the above examples it's the brain that causes a climber pain and subsequently degrades performance, not the arms, legs, and lungs (or other body parts) that seem to be hurting and begging for relief.

Train the brain and your body will follow!

Although the process is not completely understood, the brain monitors bodily functions and modulates physical output to maintain internal conditions within tolerable limits—a state called homeostasis. The brain constantly assesses parameters such as oxygenation of the blood, lactic acid and hydrogen ion concentration, and core temperature, among other things, sending pain signals and "stopping thoughts" as well as mandating a reduction of muscle fiber recruitment in order to protect the body from injury and death. This protective mechanism is extremely conservative, however, and it causes a poorly trained or weak-willed athlete to slow down or cease activity far short of his limit. Legendary bodybuilder and governor Arnold

Joe Kinder sending the stunning Golden Direct (5.14c/d), Cathedral Crag, Utah.
KEITH LADZINSKI

69

Schwarzenegger summarized this concept many years ago with the simple statement that "the mind always fails before the body."

The powerful implication of this overprotective brain mechanism is that you can extend your limits by training the brain to allow continued climbing to a higher level of power output before it sends pain signals and stopping thoughts. Additionally, you can learn to use willpower to extend performance even further, despite the onset of brain-directed stopping thoughts.

One climber who exploited this process and exemplified the stretching of personal boundaries is Reinhold Messner, arguably the greatest alpinist of all time. Shortly after his remarkable solo ascent of Everest without oxygen, exercise physiologists tested Messner to determine his VO2 max (the measure of maximum oxygen uptake and the traditional metric for aerobic capacity). Shockingly, Messner's VO2 max was 48.8 milliliters of oxygen per kilogram of body weight per minute, a value that is only slightly above the average VO2 max of an untrained individual. (For comparison, many elite endurance athletes have a VO2 max exceeding 70; seven-time Tour de France winner Lance Armstrong's VO2 max was measured at a near-record 85.) How then could someone with unremarkable aerobic capacity perform this most extraordinary mountaineering feat?

The best athletes in strenuous, painful endeavors, such as running, rock climbing, and mountaineering, learn to overcome stopping thoughts and willfully press out physiological boundaries.

First, it's quite likely that Messner possesses other physiological traits in his favor, such as high cardiac output, high lactate threshold, and high neural drive. These trainable attributes, along with vast experience at altitude, likely conditioned his brain to delay protective reduction of power output, thus allowing Messner to perform at an exceedingly high level given his modest VO2 max. What's more, when Messner's brain finally began to issue stopping thoughts, you can bet that his iron will empowered him to continue upward, albeit at a slower pace dictated by the brain. The bottom line: The best athletes in strenuous, painful endeavors, such as running, rock climbing, and mountaineering, learn to overcome these pain signals and willfully press out physiological boundaries.

I trust that you agree that this is a fascinating topic and an exciting angle to this brain-training program for climbers. Upcoming I'll cover training methods to enhance stamina, muscular endurance, and strength by means of conditioning the brain to delay its overprotective signals as you push your limits on boulders, on cliffs, or in the mountains.

Theories of Fatigue and Factors Limiting Performance

Before I present the specific training strategies, I want to provide more detail on the mechanisms believed to produce the feelings of fatigue and limit physical performance. Possessing a basic conceptual understanding of sports science will empower you to best apply the training strategies that follow. This topic is still not completely understood by sports scientists, and there are two somewhat different conceptual models on what ultimately limits performance. Let's first examine the widely accepted Cardiovascular/Anaerobic Model, and then delve into the newer Central Governor Model that's now gaining acceptance among researchers and sports scientists.

Cardiovascular/Anaerobic Model

The conventional theory of fatigue and performance limitations during sustained exercise is the Cardiovascular/Anaerobic Model. According to this model, fatigue is an involuntary drop in performance caused by a loss of homeostasis. During strenuous exercise, for example, the muscles' ability to produce adenosine triphosphate (ATP) may reach some low threshold value that limits muscular contraction while rising blood lactate levels may cause muscles to lose pH balance—resulting in pain, cramping, and loss of function. Similarly, long-duration aerobic activity eventually leads to declining blood glucose levels and depletion of glycogen (muscle fuel), which results in a slowdown or end of exercise. Another factor can be reaching maximum oxygen uptake (VO2 max), which may lead to oxygen debt and a subsequent drop-off in performance. In each of these examples, fatigue is a signal from the body that you have reached some personal limit. The body then forces a reduction in exercise intensity to prevent a catastrophic functional breakdown.

In summary, the Cardiovascular/Anaerobic Model states that fatigue signals from the muscles and a coincident decline in performance occur because the body has reached its physical limits. Effective training to enhance performance, then, is simply a matter of exercising in a ways that elevate these functional constraints (increasing VO2 max, glycogen reserves, lactate threshold, and such).

Central Governor Model

While all the fatigue-inducing factors outlined in the previous theory are certainly at play during intense exercise, the idea that fatigue results directly from the muscles is now being challenged. New research suggests that it is actually the brain that initiates stress signals (pain) and triggers stopping thoughts to arise in the conscious mind, based on cues received from the muscles.

The new Central Governor Model (CGM) of fatigue was first proposed by Dr. Timothy Noakes, a marathon runner and a professor of exercise and sports science at the University of Cape Town, and it is now gaining traction with other researches, coaches, and athletes. According to the CGM, fatigue is a sensation sent by the unconscious mind to the conscious mind to prevent loss of homeostasis and complete exhaustion. So what you feel during strenuous exercise—*my arm muscles hurt* or *my legs or lungs ache*—is actually the brain sending a message to slow down so as to avoid serious injury or death. Additionally, the brain involuntarily reduces neural drive in order to reduce power output and protect the body from irreversible damage.

The Central Governor Model remains somewhat controversial among sports scientists, but emerging research is lending support and increasing the number of advocates. As the theory goes, power output during exercise is regulated in the brain by the central governor (believed to function from the frontal lobe, parietal lobe, and visual cortex). Efferent control of the muscles is based upon a black-box calculation that integrates afferent feedback signals from the muscles and heart, as well as sensory feedback of the external environment (weather conditions, terrain, and such), knowledge of ongoing results (competitive place or proximity of the endpoint of performance), and unconscious calibration based on past experience. Integrating all this data, the central governor is constantly assessing how the organs and muscles are faring and what modulations are needed to maintain homeostasis. So it's the brain that interprets increasing blood lactate, elevated body temperature, and decreasing glycogen supply, among other signals, as being stressful to the body, and it's the brain that in turn issues pain sensations and stopping thoughts.

Figure 4.1 The Central Governor Model

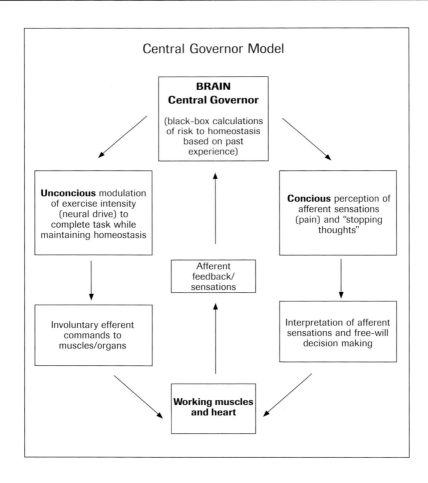

You could argue that there's little difference between the Cardiovascular/ Anaerobic Model and the Central Governor Model, given that both ultimately lead to fatigue based on what's happening in the muscles. However, the CGM's theory that the brain is the sole governor of fatigue is a crucial distinction with powerful implications. And therefore, since fatigue is not an absolute physiological event within the muscle—fatigue is actually a brain calculation and efferent response—it is possible to extend or even elevate performance in the face of the brain's distress signals!

One recent study that supports this theory tested a group of cyclists. Australian researchers measured power output and muscle fiber activation during a rigorous one-hour mock time trial in which the cyclists performed six one-minute maximum sprints interspersed throughout the hour of sustained exercise. The results revealed that power output and muscle activation decreased with each successive sprint (as you would expect). Surprisingly the sixth sprint, performed during the last minute of the time trial, showed a significant increase in power output and muscle fiber recruitment! If the muscles themselves were the end-all in terms of fatigue signals (that is, fatigue is an absolute result of high blood lactate, dwindling ATP, increasing oxygen debt, and such), then the cyclists would have been unable to increase power output in the final stage of the time trial.

With consistent, disciplined effort to employ greater willpower in all you do, the largely untapped power of your mind will grow stronger and more capable of carrying you through extreme situations.

The Central Governor Model, however, can explain this finding in two ways; it may also help you understand instances when you climbed onward through massive fatigue or realized a "second wind" on a big wall or alpine climb. First, knowing the end of the trial was near, the brain reassessed its estimates of energy reserves and afferent signals from the muscles and heart, and it determined that it could allow a higher work output during the final minute of the time trial (without loss of homeostasis and risk of injury or death). Furthermore, the cyclists' knowledge that the final sprint would be followed by cessation of the grueling exercise may have empowered some to overcome, by the conscious power of will, the brain's pain signals and stopping thoughts.

It's interesting to note that two parallel pathways operate within the Central Governor Model: the objective realm of the material world governed by the forces of mechanistic determinism and the subjective realm governed by will (see figure 4.1). As exemplified in the preceding study (and perhaps in your own experience), willpower of the mind can exert a causal influence over strict determinism. While I believe that extreme physical activity is sometimes modulated solely by objective physiological constraints (per the Cardiovascular/Anaerobic Model), it is likely that performance most often falters because we obey or succumb to the brain's overly conservative signals to cease physical activity. The best climbers, then, are not necessarily the strongest physically; instead they likely possess uncommon mental strength and willpower that enables them to hang on longer and continue upward despite the brain's rising chorus of pain sensations.

In conclusion, we can distill two important training implications from the Central Governor Model. First and foremost, you can enhance and extend performance through the power of your free will. With consistent, disciplined effort to employ greater willpower in all you do, this largely untapped power of your mind will grow stronger and more capable of carrying you through extreme situations. Second, engaging in high-intensity or long-duration training (and climbing) to a high level of fatigue will recalibrate the brain to be less conservative in directing work output during extreme physical activity, thus enabling you to perform longer and nearer your body's true absolute limit. To this end, the next two sections will detail several specific training protocols for improving muscular endurance, stamina, and strength.

Brain Training to Increase Muscular Endurance and Stamina

Let's first define muscular endurance and stamina, since some people incorrectly use these terms interchangeably. Stamina is the ability to engage in low- to moderate-intensity activity for an extended period, such as running for an hour or two, or even climbing all day. Stamina is somewhat a function of aerobic capacity (VO2 max), but it's largely influenced by available fuel supply (resident glycogen stores and carbohydrate consumption during exercise) and mental toughness (the will to endure pain and reach your goal).

Muscular endurance is the capability to sustain high-intensity anaerobic activity for a minute or more, or to maintain a high power output through several bouts of intense activity with only brief rest breaks in between. Examples of muscular endurance at work include climbing a long, strenuous sequence without stopping, ascending a steep leg-pumping slope, or enduring multiple bouts of high-intensity exercise. What's more, failure on a near-limit rock climb often seems to come down to a lack of local forearm muscle endurance (although you must always consider whether poor technique or mind control is really to blame), as the hallmark muscle pump and burn seems to mandate an end to your effort. Your peak level of muscular endurance (anaerobic capacity) is a function of your limit (maximum) strength, your muscles' ability to tolerate and remove blood lactate, and your will to sustain strenuous activity despite painful stress signals from the brain.

Per the Central Governor Model described above, the brain limits power output and creates pain sensations and stopping thoughts so that we terminate activity long before we risk catastrophic injury or death. Effective training, then, must not only address specific physiological constraints (aerobic and anaerobic capacity), but also train the brain to better interpret afferent feedback from the blood, muscles, and other organs, thus increasing the brain's threshold for shutting down muscular activation during strenuous exercise. The key is to train in ways that closely simulate the demands of your goal climbs, and in doing so to stretch your limits in anaerobic and aerobic endurance to establish new central governor experience and fatigue set points.

An intriguing question is this: How much of the improvement from such training is a result of physiological adaptations, and how much comes from neuroplastic change (recalibration of the brain's central governor and increase in willpower)? A recent study of cyclists engaging in interval training helps answer this question for us. In the study the cyclists realized statistically significant improvement in as little as six interval-training workouts. This would seem to be too short a period of time for the performance gains to be the result of physiological adaptations such as increased capillary and mitochondrial density. Perhaps more probable, the six challenging interval-training sessions recalibrated the central governor to allow a high power output. Each successive workout gave the brain additional data to better calculate the demands of the activity and create a new higher fatigue threshold before it modulates power output for protective purposes. Finally, the grueling interval-training sessions developed mental toughness that allowed the cyclists to continue longer despite pain signals from the brain. In aggregate, it would seem that the performance gains from such interval training are as much a result of brain modifications as muscular adaptations.

The four following endurance and stamina workout strategies will enhance physiological constraints on performance as well as recalibrate the central governor to a higher fatigue set point and foster willpower to overcome stopping thoughts and stretch your limits. Since this is a brain-training book, I have purposefully kept the exercise descriptions brief. Consult my books *Training for Climbing* and *Conditioning for Climbers* for detailed, illustrated coverage of these exercises and more.

 ### Climbing Intervals

Climbing intervals are the gold standard for training anaerobic endurance, because the exercise routine is tremendously specific to how we have to climb on hard routes. Consider that most long boulder problems or roped routes possess a couple of hard sections (or more) as well as intermittent sections of easier terrain or rest stances. Such stop-and-go climbing likely pushes you in and out of the anaerobic threshold—you get pumped and start breathing harder on a hard section, and then you recover somewhat when you reach easier moves or a rest position. Climbing intervals simulate this exact scenario by alternating one to four minutes of strenuous climbing with an equal or longer period of easy climbing or rest (1:1 to 1:2 work-to-rest ratios). You can perform these intervals on a bouldering wall, or as a series of toprope or lead climbs.

My favorite interval-training protocol, developed many years ago for use on my original small home wall, utilizes a pyramid scheme to challenge both body and brain in a highly effective way. You can use this training strategy on any overhanging home or commercial wall as long as there is enough terrain to move around in order to alternate between difficult and moderate movements. The protocol is simple, yet rather grueling.

Begin by climbing for one minute, during which you climb through some very strenuous sequences, but also move onto easier terrain to prevent failure before one minute has elapsed. Rest for exactly one minute, and then begin a two-minute burn on the wall, again alternating between hard moves and more moderate sections. Feel free to pause on a large hold to shake out for a moment and chalk up. The key is to hang on to the wall for the full two minutes despite the growing muscular pump. (If you aren't getting pumped, then you need to get on a steeper wall, use smaller holds, and execute harder moves.) Now take a rest for two minutes. The third climbing interval is three minutes long. Again, do whatever hard sequences you can manage, but do move on to larger holds if needed to survive the full three minutes. Take a rest for three minutes. Next up you climb for four minutes—this is the crux of the climbing interval. No doubt, your forearms will be screaming and your brain will trigger stopping thoughts in your conscious mind, but fight to hang on for the complete four-minute interval. After resting for four minutes, you will reverse the pyramid with another three-, two-, and one-minute burn, each followed by an equal rest period. In all, this protocol will take you through seven intervals totaling thirty-two minutes of combined climbing and rest time.

It's vital that you stick to the time schedule exactly. If you're training alone, use an egg timer to get your intervals just right. Ideally, recruit a training partner to join you in the session so that one of you is resting while the other is climbing. Use a stopwatch to time the intervals precisely. Perform this interval pyramid up to twice weekly, and you will notice significant improvement in your anaerobic endurance (as well as your willpower to climb on through pain) in as little as six workouts. Less fit climbers may want to initially reduce the pyramid by one step, doing just the one-, two-, and three-minute intervals before reversing down the pyramid with the closing two- and one-minute intervals. This total of five climbing intervals will take just eighteen minutes. Advanced climbers may want to add a five-minute interval, however, making for an even more grueling and beneficial workout comprising nine intervals and taking a total of fifty minutes.

 ### Running Intervals and the Tabata Protocol

Competitive runners view interval training as the gold standard for increasing one's capacity to sustain moderate- to high-intensity running and race-day pace. The physiological and brain adaptations from running intervals can also be a boon for serious rock climbers. While the act of running intervals is hardly specific to climbing, its effects on the cardiovascular and anaerobic energy systems are not far different from a long, multicrux or multipitch route. If you engage in any form of long, strenuous climbing, you can be sure that running intervals will improve your performance, in terms of improved total stamina and anaerobic endurance, accelerated recovery between climbs, and recalibration of the central governor.

The most common interval-training program is to run alternating fast and slow laps on a track. Although you can also run intervals on a road or trail, the ease of setting a goal and gauging distances makes running on a track preferable. For initial training sessions, set out to run 2 miles—that's an aggregate distance of fast and slow laps. As a rough gauge, your fast laps should feel like 80 to 90 percent of your maximum speed and result in your getting significantly winded. Try to hold the fast pace for a complete lap, and then pull back to a jog for the slow lap. Continue alternating fast and slow laps (or half laps) for a total of eight laps. A more advanced interval-training program would involve 3 to 4 total miles of fast–slow interval couplets.

The Tabata Protocol is a highly specific method of interval training that is popular among elite athletes in speed-oriented sports; but serious climbers can benefit from this training strategy too. Developed by Dr. Izumi Tabata at the National Institute of Fitness and Sports in Japan, the Tabata interval is twenty seconds of high-intensity exercise followed by ten seconds of rest (a 2:1 work-to-rest ratio). This interval is repeated eight times to create four minutes of the most punishing training you can imagine.

The Tabata Protocol differs from traditional interval training in three ways. First, the twenty-second work interval is much shorter than traditional intervals. The second difference, then, is that this shorter work interval must be performed with 100 percent exertion. Third, the rest interval is just ten seconds, which is so brief that very little recovery can occur before the next work interval begins. Research has shown this protocol to be uniquely effective in producing gains in both anaerobic and aerobic capacity, although longer rest intervals are superior for training anaerobic recovery (removal of lactic acid and other metabolic by-products). Consequently, climbers can benefit from use of both the Tabata Protocol and the traditional interval-training methods described above.

You can leverage the Tabata Protocol in several ways to enhance your climbing performance. The most obvious is to alternate twenty seconds of sprinting and ten seconds of walking for a total of eight run–walk intervals—likely the most insane four minutes of exercise you'll ever engage in!—to increase your total anaerobic and aerobic capacity (VO2 max). Applied to climbing-specific exercises, you could use the Tabata Protocol to train pull-muscle endurance (Lat Pull-Down Tabata) and forearm endurance (HIT Strip Tabata). In both cases you would exercise (or climb) at maximum intensity for exactly twenty seconds and then rest for exactly ten seconds. Repeat this Tabata interval eight times. Add weight to your body (hypergravity) if needed to make the twenty-second work intervals maximal, in terms of both physical and mental exertion.

 Long-Distance Training

The most popular method for developing stamina is long-duration aerobic training. Applying this method to climbing involves performing a high volume of low- to moderate-intensity exercise lasting several hours or more. Frequent long days of climbing are undoubtedly the best stamina-training tools for rock climbers—training doesn't get any more specific than this! For the average weekend warrior, however, putting in ten to twenty full-length climbing days per month is improbable. Engaging in regular aerobic activity is the best training alternative for triggering the numerous adaptations within the cardiovascular system (such as increased heart stroke volume, VO2 max, and intramuscular capillary density) and creating new central governor set points. In the aggregate these adaptations will increase your stamina, ability to function at altitude, and willpower to endure exhaustive climbing endeavors.

This is a classic train-as-you-climb strategy. If you have the resources nearby, then no training could be more specific than chalking up many long days on the rock. You could do this in the form of climbing as many routes as possible from sunrise to sunset at a cragging area or by racing up a Grade IV or V route in a day. Ideally, the goal would be to engage in two or three all-day climbing workouts per week—do this for a few months and you'll develop amazing climbing stamina! For many climbers, however, it may only be possible to train this way a few days per month. In this case, you will need to engage in some high-volume aerobic training as an adjunct to all-day climbing.

The aerobic-training goal is to engage in four, forty-five- to ninety-minute aerobic workouts per week with a focus on mileage over speed. This could be any combination of running, swimming, cycling, brisk hiking, and trail running. As your conditioning improves, consider increasing the number of workouts to six or eight per week. To do this—and to help make these workouts fit with your other life activities—you will need to double up on some of your workouts. For example, you might go for a long run in the morning, and then go for a bike ride for an hour in the evening, or vice versa. If you engage in such two-a-day workouts, it is best to take at least a six-hour break between the two workouts. This is clearly an advanced aerobic-training program, but it might be just the ticket to up-regulate your central governor in the weeks leading up to a long wall climb or high-altitude expedition.

Brain Training to Increase Muscular Strength and Power

Muscular strength and power are highly distinct functions that involve brief, intense force production. Muscular strength, often called limit strength, is the ability to exert maximum force in a single all-out effort (irrespective of time), as in crimping on a minuscule handhold or pulling hard through a strenuous move. Power is the application of force with velocity—think of it as explosive strength—as in popping a deadpoint, making a fast pull and reach, or throwing a lunge.

Given the brief duration of maximum strength and power at work, the factors that lead to fatigue and limit performance are vastly different from those of muscular endurance and stamina. A primary limitation in maximum strength and power output is the supply of adenosine triphosphate (ATP) and creatine phosphate (CP) stored in the muscles. The supply of these fuels limits maximal force production to less than fifteen seconds (although ATP is continually synthesized within the muscles and it replenishes with just three to five minutes of rest).

While the central governor plays a lesser role in modulating such maximal movements, the brain is a major factor in directing application of strength and power. It's ultimately the brain that dictates recruitment of muscular motor units via neural drive (the amplitude of the impulses impelling motor units to fire) and by cycling motor units within a muscle in order to sustain steady force production as long as possible. As an example of this amazing process, consider the act of holding steady a one-arm lock-off position for a few seconds. During this maximal activity, the brain cycles the firing of motor units to maintain a steady lock-off; it rests some motor units (groups of muscle fibers) while it fires others. Maximum strength and power production are greatly influenced by the quality of coordination and synchronization of this motor unit recruitment.

Two final factors that limit strength and power production are the Golgi tendon organ (GTO) and willpower. The GTO is part of the autonomic nervous system; it protects tendons by limiting the recruitment of motor units below some threshold amount. In a manner quite similar to the central governor, the GTO restricts power output to a level far below the likely point of catastrophic tendon damage. Unlike the central governor, however, GTO function is completely involuntary and essentially instantaneous in reaction since its neural pathway only travels from the sensory receptors in the tendon to the spinal cord and back, and not the longer round-trip to the brain and back. Still, the sensitivity of the GTO can be influenced through training. Specifically, reactive training methods (more on this in a bit) will somewhat disinhibit the GTO to allow a higher level of maximum strength and power output.

A recurring theme in this chapter is the idea that you can leverage willpower to extend physical performance to new levels. In executing maximal efforts of strength and power, your ability to summon immense willpower is the ultimate wild card. Whether it's by way of a quiet, intense focus or an ecstatic "psych-up," learning to maximize volition may be the factor that ultimately leads to a personal-best outcome.

A recurring theme in this chapter is the idea that you can leverage willpower to extend physical performance to new levels.

To close out this chapter, I'll introduce you to three training strategies for elevating your maximum strength and power. While not appropriate for out-of-shape, injured, or novice climbers, these techniques should be a regular part of every serious climber's training program.

 Hypergravity Training

The fact that the training load while climbing is always body weight or less represents one of the greatest limitations in developing strength. Therefore, the concept of hypergravity training (adding extra weight to your body while performing certain controlled climbing movements) is revolutionary in terms of opening the door to a higher level of performance.

The importance of training at progressively higher intensity and with heavier loads cannot be overstated. When you carefully expose your fingers (and other upper-body pull muscles) to a load and intensity not previously experienced at normal body weight, the neuromuscular system will respond to offer a high level of maximum strength. The dramatic gains in strength that result from hypergravity training are due to both neurology enhancements (such as motor unit synchronization and neural drive) and hypertrophy (muscle cell growth).

The four best applications of hypergravity are weighted pull-ups, weighted fingerboard hangs, weighted bouldering, and Hypergravity Isolation Training (HIT). If you feel that your level of finger, lock-off, or pulling strength is the same as last year, then I guarantee that you can break this plateau by incorporating some of these exercises into your weekly training routine. See *Training for Climbing* or *Conditioning for Climbers* for more in-depth coverage of hypergravity training as well as how to best integrate this technique into your workout program.

 Reactive Training

The National Academy of Sports Medicine defines reactive training as a quick, powerful exercise that involves a forceful eccentric contraction followed immediately by an explosive concentric contraction. This advanced training technique (often referred to as plyometric training) holds great potential for advanced climbers looking to increase their contact strength and power. It's also rife with risk for those who misuse reactive training exercises such as campus training, lunging exercises, and other explosive movements.

When used properly, however, reactive training will actually strengthen tendons and ligaments—and, of course, the muscles too—and thus increase your resistance to injury when out climbing a physically stressful move or sequence. Consequently, I advocate a limited amount of reactive training for intermediate climbers, with an increase in volume and intensity of reactive training as you enter the elite category. One qualifying rule that no climber should overlook is that reactive training will be more harmful than beneficial if performed while injured. In particular, any finger, elbow, or shoulder problems must be rested and rehabilitated before you engage in reactive training of any type.

First used by Russian athletes in the 1960s, reactive training was originally applied to climbing by the late Wolfgang Güllich with the advent of campus training. Given that reactive training involves fast, dynamic movements, the resistance used (training load) must be significantly less than in the maximum strength-training exercises describe earlier. For many climbers, the resistance will need to be less than body weight in order to allow for the rapid movement and directional change that's essential for effective reactive training. The resultant adaptations of such speed training are primarily neural (disinhibition of the Golgi tendon organ and increased motor unit synchronization and neural drive), so reactive training alone will produce little in the way of hypertrophy. Still, the numerous neural adaptations of properly executed reactive training will result in highly practical—and often surprisingly noticeable!—gains in lunging ability and contact strength.

In *Training for Climbing* and *Conditioning for Climbers*, I detail several reactive training exercises of varying difficulty and injury risk. The safest, and therefore the most appropriate for nonelite climbers, are reactive exercises performed at less than body weight and with some measure of control. For example, One-Arm Lunging and Campus Touches are two reactive exercises that most healthy intermediate climbers can incorporate into their training with little risk. By contrast, reactive exercises that involve full body weight and double-handed, drop-and-catch movements are extremely stressful and appropriate only in small doses for injury-free elite climbers.

Complex Training

Complex training is a cutting-edge training method used by elite athletes in many power-oriented Olympic events. Applied to climbing, the complex training protocol described below is one of the most advanced strength-training concepts available. Since introducing complex training to climbers in the first edition of *Training for Climbing* in 2002, I have heard from countless climbers around the world who have leveraged this technique to increase their grip strength and upper-body power. You can, too, as long as you are a relatively advanced climber (solid at 5.11 or V5) with no recent history of finger, elbow, or shoulder injuries.

Complex training involves coupling a high-resistance, maximum-strength exercise with a power-oriented, high-speed exercise. Research has shown that performing these two very different exercises back-to-back—and in the order of strength first, power second—produces gains in strength and power beyond that achieved by performing either exercise alone.

Incorporating complex training into your program can be done several different ways; the key is, again, the back-to-back coupling of a maximum-strength exercise and power exercise. To get started, you might climb a very fingery near-maximal boulder problem and then immediately do a set of One-Arm Lunges with each hand. Taking things up a notch, you could send a hard boulder problem with a ten-pound weight belt around your waist and then immediately ladder hand-over-hand up a campus board (without the weight belt on). To up the ante further, you could alternate doing a set of Hypergravity Isolation Training (with ten to forty pounds around your waist), and then immediately do a set of double dynos on the campus board (at body weight).

Table 4.2 *Maximum Strength and Power Training Exercises*

Maximum Strength Exercises	Power Exercises
• Hypergravity bouldering	• One-Arm Lunging
• Hypergravity Pull-Ups	• Campus Laddering
• Hypergravity Fingerboard Hangs	• Campus Lock-Offs
• Heavy Finger Rolls	• Feet-Off Bouldering
• HIT Strip Training	• Campus Double Dynos

The table above lists several highly effective exercises for developing maximum strength and power. You can create a complex training couplet by executing two of these exercises, one from each column, back-to-back with no rest in between. See Training for Climbing *for details on performing each exercise.*

This latter strategy of combining HIT and a reactive training exercise such as campus training should be a staple technique of elite climbers, and it may represent the single best training protocol for pursuing absolute genetic potential for finger strength and upper-body power. Begin by doing just three coupled sets, and over the course of a few months increase to a maximum of six to eight coupled sets. Rest for five minutes between coupled sets.

Obviously, complex training is an advanced technique that produces both high passive and dynamic stresses—it should only be utilized by well-conditioned climbers with no recent history of injury. Furthermore, its use should be limited to once every three or four days, and it should be cycled on and off about every two weeks. Finally, complete recovery from a complex workout could take as long as three to five days. Any other strenuous training or climbing during the supercompensation period would slow recovery and may limit the benefits of complex training.

Part Three

Mental Training

CHAPTER FIVE

Increasing Self-Awareness

Any study of the mental aspects of climbing performance must begin with increasing self-awareness. Self-awareness is the ability to monitor your internal climate, comprising your thoughts, physical sensations, and emotions, as well as the quality of your actions in the material outside world. Becoming a better climber, then, demands that you foster a higher level of awareness in each of these areas, so that you can regulate your internal states in the quest for maximum climbing.

Although self-awareness is a human endowment, we all differ and it is less well developed in many individuals. Consider people who take the same dysfunctional actions over and over, despite the clear evidence that these actions are getting them nowhere. For example, the climber who repeatedly falls off a crux without recognizing there's an easier sequence, or the person who climbs day after day to the point of injury. Another classic example is the climber who strength trains intensively in the quest to climb harder, when poor footwork and lack of mental control are the real barriers to achieving the next grade. The common theme in these examples is that lack of self-awareness will perpetuate ineffective and perhaps even harmful behaviors, and thus maintain a very unproductive status quo.

To become better than we are, we must first become aware of what we are.

Conversely, examine the most effective people you know—athletes, businesspeople, students, or parents—and you will discover that they are individuals of remarkably high self-awareness. They are quick to recognize and correct a flawed approach, unproductive emotions, or limiting ways of thinking. These masters of self-awareness and self-regulation (more on this in the next chapter) will become peak performers in most any endeavor they put their minds to.

In climbing, the pinnacle of self-awareness is an acute on-demand monitoring of your internal climate and outward efficacy. In ascending a difficult or dangerous route, for example, the goal is to monitor your arousal and muscular tension, the quality of your movements, the direction of your thoughts, and the perceived effectiveness of your risk management strategies. Given this high level of self-awareness, you are empowered to make tiny course corrections on the fly that will maximize your chances of completing the climb and, at the very least, lead you to making a proud effort and living to try another day.

Alex Honnold on his astounding free solo of the 1,200-foot **Moonlight Buttress (V, 5.12d), Zion National Park, Utah.** CELIN SERBO

It's instructive to think of levels of self-awareness as a continuum from extremely coarse to superfine, much like varying grits of sandpaper. Having only a basic level of self-awareness is akin to sanding with extremely coarse 60-grit sandpaper—it will only enable you to smooth out gross imperfections and yield a poor final product. Possessing acute self-awareness, however, is like sanding with 600-grit sandpaper. It allows you to identify the smallest imperfections and produce a polished, top-shelf final product.

Applied to climbing, novices will naturally possess coarse self-awareness that enables them only to recognize and correct gross errors (mental, technical, or physical). Elite climbers, having spent many years fostering a superfine level of self-awareness, are empowered to detect and correct the smallest of errors in their movement, training, and strategy, among other things.

Your quest to improve self-awareness must similarly involve a multipronged approach that shines the light of higher self-awareness on the following areas:

- **Thoughts.** More than any other thing, you are defined by and produce in accordance with your thoughts. Becoming fully aware of the nature and quality of your thoughts is obviously an essential first step to improving your performance in anything.

- **Body and emotions.** Your body is the vehicle for creating and achieving, and your emotions are the fuel that propels the experience. Self-awareness of your physical and emotional state is therefore tantamount to captaining your journey.

- **Strengths and weaknesses.** You cannot correct a problem that you are not aware of—for example, poor footwork or poor self-awareness! Recognizing and training up weak areas is fundamental to elevating your game.

- **Actions leading to results.** Sensory acuity is your awareness of feedback and results, and it's a vital skill for maximizing efficacy. The ultimate goal is to quickly and accurately discern the productivity of your actions, the effectiveness of strategies employed, and the trajectory of emerging results. Acute awareness of such feedback facilitates rapid course correction and increases the probability of success.

- **Values and self-image.** Values ultimately guide the choices you make, while self-image is your core concept from which beliefs, personality, and the confidence to achieve emanates. Understanding what drives you and nurturing a positive, empowering self-image are central to maximizing experience and achievement.

Before we examine each of these areas more closely, I want to stress the importance of remaining nonjudgmental and self-accepting throughout your journey to higher self-awareness. Becoming self-aware of the myriad small things that you need to improve upon can get you down if you let it. Thus, it's essential that you reframe all the flaws and weaknesses you identify as really being clues for success! Instead of ignoring or covering up your mistakes and weaknesses, you must embrace them with an enthusiasm and future-oriented vision that transcends your current situation and acknowledges your great potential to improve.

Self-Awareness of Thoughts

Self-awareness of thoughts is the act of "thinking about what you are thinking about." Psychologists call this inward-directed thought process *metacognition,* and it is the most basic and important mental skill you can develop. Metacognitive ability is essential for identifying goals, developing strategy, monitoring learning and progress, and determining whether your current thoughts are helping or hurting you.

In becoming conscious of your thoughts, you can seize control of the analysis, planning, and decision-making processes that ultimately determine the direction and vigor of your actions. Individuals with poor self-awareness of thoughts tend to be reactive in their decision making or follow a path of least resistance that requires little original thought, initiative, or effort. Following the crowd or acting in the same well-known ways of the past is the easiest path, but it won't get you to that special place you want to be.

Self-aware individuals, however, understand the power of their thoughts, and they are quick to identify flawed ways of thinking. They hold in mind a clear vision of their mission, develop novel plans of action, and follow through with optimism and the power of will. Furthermore, they recognize decision making as a watershed event of great importance. They nurture and milk the process and resist the common tendency toward flippant, reactive decision making. They consciously slow down their thought processes in order to factor past experience into decisions, assess risk, and ponder possible unintended consequences.

Self-aware individuals understand the power of their thoughts, and they are quick to identify and modify flawed ways of thinking.

In climbing, metacognition involves thinking about what you are thinking when climbing instead of thinking singularly about the climb. No doubt, many climbers expend most of their psychic energy thinking about the climb: *Where's the next hold? How's my gear? Where's the next rest? Am I going to fall?* and so forth. While all of these outward-directed thoughts are sometimes necessary, effective climbing also requires inward-directed thoughts (metacognition). Only by directing your thoughts inward can you determine the quality of your climbing technique with questions such as: *How's my footwork feel? Does my center of gravity feel properly positioned? Am I overgripping and feeling tense?* Similarly, you can monitor the quality of your thoughts by asking yourself, *How's my focus? Are my thoughts positive and process-oriented? Am I adequately managing my fearful thoughts?*

Clearly, fostering greater metacognitive abilities is essential to elevating your climbing performance and maximizing experience. You can best develop this capability by striving to increase metacognition in all you do, climbing or nonclimbing, throughout the day. Think of metacognition as a highly generalized ability. Regularly ask yourself questions such as: *What am I thinking? Why am I thinking this? Are these thoughts helping or hurting me? How can I think more effectively? What physical sensations (proprioception) do I notice? How well do I comprehend the material I'm reading? Do I agree with what I'm reading, hearing, or seeing?*

Practicing Metacognition

Stop reading this book for a moment and answer the following questions. Dig deep to obtain answers that are beyond the superficial and that accurately reveal your current situation.

- How well do you comprehend what you are reading? Have you needed to re-read passages to fully understand the message? How can you apply the lessons to your climbing?

- What physical sensations do you feel right now? What muscles feel tense? Can you feel the weight of your body pressing down on the seat of the chair? Do you feel in balance and relaxed, or are you bracing yourself or tensing muscles to maintain your current position?

- What is the direction of your thoughts and emotions? Do you feel positive or negative? How strong or vague are these emotions? Are your thoughts more future-oriented, in the present, or focused on the past?

- Review the past twenty-four hours in your mind and determine the quality of your actions and decision making. Was your decision making mostly reactive and quick, or did you sometimes pause to formulate a more measured decision? What were your strong points of the day (things you did well)? What weaknesses (both major and subtle) can you identify in actions taken? Did you march to your own drummer or did you tend to follow the crowd and get absorbed into group activities? Overall, how do you feel about yourself based on the sum of the day's events?

- Now direct your thoughts toward the future. How well do you know your personal goals for the next day, month, or year? Ponder your current strategy for reaching these goals—is the strategy working or does it need modified to produce the results you desire?

Self-Awareness of Body and Emotions

Emotions are the fuel that supercharges your life with energy. That energy may be positive and productive or negative and destructive. Consequently, becoming aware of your emotional state, as well as emotional triggers, is crucial for optimizing your effectiveness (at anything) and maximizing life experience.

Ask yourself the following questions to increase self-awareness of your emotions. *What is my predominant baseline emotional state? Do I naturally tend toward being optimistic and happy or pessimistic and depressed? Do outside events regularly trigger a change in my emotional state? When I reach a happy or sad state, do I tend to linger there a long time or do I quickly return to my normal baseline?*

Closely tied to how you feel emotionally is your physical state and the sensations that arise. As you will learn in the next chapter, your body exerts a powerful influence over your emotional and mental state. The opposite is also true—your emotions and thoughts can affect your physical state. Consequently, increasing self-

Identifying Emotional States and Common Triggers

Think back over the past week or two and try to identify your most common emotional state as well as the less frequent, yet more dramatic emotional states that you've experienced. Consider both climbing and nonclimbing examples. Write down in the appropriate slots below the people, situations, tasks, or events that elicited a strongly negative, mildly negative, mildly positive, and strongly positive emotional response. Also record approximately how long you remained in the resultant emotional state. The goal of this exercise is twofold: To identify your most common emotional state (your baseline) and to identify common triggers that change your state. Strive to be deeply introspective and write down your answers in as great a detail as possible. Work on a separate sheet of paper if you need more space than is provided below.

Strongly Negative	Mildly Negative	Mildly Positive	Strongly Positive

awareness of your body and its rich language of sensations is an essential precursor to becoming fully proactive and to productive acuity.

Improving physical self-awareness begins with discerning varying degrees of tension (or relaxation) in major muscle groups. Scan your body right now: Which muscles feel tight and tense? Next, consider what other physical sensations your can detect. (It may help to close your eyes for a moment and focus your concentration into a narrow beam that slowly scans the body to detect sensations.) Do you feel in balance or are you bracing? Can you discern the different levels of muscle tension throughout your body? Possessing a subtle sense of kinesthetic feel is a master skill you should aspire to develop, since such proprioception helps guide efficient movements and provides invaluable feedback from the muscles and joints. See page 50 for more instruction on developing proprioception.

Ultimately, we all experience varying emotional and physical states, and in a relative sense there must be some down moments in order to define and appreciate the emotional and physical highs. Our goals, then, are to become more self-aware of our present state and to identify triggers that cause a change in how we feel emotionally and what we sense physically. The more aware we are of the cause-and-effect process, the more we are empowered to effect, or even completely control, that process.

Self-Awareness of Strengths and Weaknesses

It's human nature to focus on traits and engage in activities at which we excel. Consequently, it's a common practice to avoid our weaknesses and to hope that our strengths will carry us through whatever situations or challenges lie before us.

While the preceding approach is quite common, the result of this modus operandi is mediocrity. To excel at any activity, you must be proactive in identifying and training up weaker skill sets and performance handicaps. Achieving excellence, then, is not just a matter of exploiting your strengths to the fullest, but also ruthlessly pursuing improvements in the things that constrain your performance.

Achieving excellence is not just a matter of exploiting your strengths to the fullest, but also demands that you ruthlessly pursue improvement in the things that constrain your performance.

The fifty-question self-assessment in chapter 1 has already sharpened your self-awareness of brain-directed cognitive skills and function. The goal now similarly is to identify your strong and weak areas with regard to technical and physical abilities (see "Score Your Technical and Physical Abilities"). Leverage the results from this evaluation to develop a most effective training program; that is, one that centers on improving your weaknesses, rather than focusing on your strong points. See chapter 12 for guidance in creating a comprehensive training program.

Score Your Technical and Physical Abilities

Evaluate yourself in each area and check the column that best represents your current ability. A most effective training program will then target your lower-scoring abilities.

Technical Abilities	Excellent	Good	Fair	Poor
Precise, quiet foot placements that carry your weight	___	___	___	___
Handholds are gripped lightly; arms play a secondary role	___	___	___	___
Economy of movement (rhythm, pace, poise)	___	___	___	___
Use of rest positions	___	___	___	___
Use of nonpositive handholds (side pulls, underclings, slopers)	___	___	___	___
Use of flagging to aid stability and prevent barndooring	___	___	___	___
Hand–foot matching and manteling	___	___	___	___
Twist lock, backstep, and efficient movement on overhanging terrain	___	___	___	___
Use of creative footwork (heel and toe hooks, and knee locks)	___	___	___	___
Dynamic moves (deadpoints and lunges)	___	___	___	___
Jam crack climbing	___	___	___	___

Physical Abilities	Excellent	Good	Fair	Poor
Lock-off and pull-up strength	___	___	___	___
Contact strength (finger strength on small holds)	___	___	___	___
Muscular endurance of forearm and arm muscles	___	___	___	___
Core conditioning	___	___	___	___
Antagonistic muscle conditioning (muscle balance)	___	___	___	___
Flexibility	___	___	___	___
Stamina (aerobic conditioning)	___	___	___	___
Recovery ability (between climbs and days of climbing)	___	___	___	___

Self-Awareness of Actions and Results

In *Training for Climbing* I presented the Cycle of Improvement, a three-step process cycle that involves setting goals, taking actions, and making course corrections (see figure 5.1). The third step, making course corrections, obviously demands acute self-awareness in order to discern the quality of the actions taken and to determine the course corrections needed to improve the results. Without such self-awareness the cycle breaks down. With acute self-awareness, however, the Cycle of Improvement in fact becomes an upward Spiral of Improvement!

Obtaining a high level of performance in any endeavor—and ultimately reaching your goal—depends on your ability to recognize and leverage ongoing process feedback and results. Process feedback involves subtle proprioceptive and exteroceptive cues that constantly change moment by moment. As a climbing example, you might shift your center of gravity toward a high foot placement and become aware of a growing loss of balance and increasing difficulty in gripping a slopping hold. Based on this proprioceptive feedback, you twist your body and position your inside hip closer to the wall; the result is improved stability, balance, and grip on the rock.

Process feedback, as in the example above, arises in a broad stream from all of your muscles and joints throughout every move of every climb. Yet for many climbers, self-awareness of these vital data is quite low, as only the screaming proprioceptive messages (for example, *I feel my foot slipping* or *I'm about to fall!*) register

Figure 5.1 *The Cycle of Improvement*

in their conscious mind. Elite climbers, however, possess acute awareness of process feedback and they can tap into proprioceptive sensations in an instant to optimize a foot placement, body position, or movement. Gaining such a high level of self-awareness of process feedback comes only by way of a long-term, conscious effort to tap into the subtle physical sensations that constantly spring forth as you climb. Be patient and take the time to develop this critical ability!

On the macro scale, you must also strive to recognize the gross results feedback that provides clues on the effectiveness of your actions and chosen strategy. On the surface such results feedback seems to be simply an outcome of an action taken—for example, falling off a given move or failing on a route. Awareness of these results takes little effort—the message is obvious, right? Well, not really; there's always a deeper message to be found if you possess the self-awareness to look for it.

Making the most of results feedback demands that you search back for the cause of the poor outcome. For example, you might ask yourself: *Is my limiting constraint mental, technical, or physical in nature?* As always, you can sharpen self-awareness by asking a series of probing questions: *Was I climbing too slowly? Is there a better sequence to be found? Is fear preventing me from fully committing to the moves?* Obviously there are countless other questions you could ask, so keep an open mind and play the role of a performance detective who's trying to uncover clues for success. You may recognize the role of metacognition in this process.

Another strategy to improve self-awareness of results is to view yourself climbing or training from an observer's perspective, as if watching yourself on TV. In your mind's eye, examine the strategies you have employed, the ways you've been training, and your overall behavior at the crags and elsewhere. From this dissociated perspective you can be more critical in your assessment, usually without the undesirable side effect of getting yourself down. Can you identify a flawed strategy? Are the same actions being taken over and over without any course corrections? Are training practices ineffective, perhaps failing to address known weaknesses? Do you see emotions getting out of hand and adversely affecting performance?

Ego and arrogance diminish self-awareness—in fact they tend to be mutually exclusive.

This latter idea of emotions getting out of hand and clouding self-awareness is critical. Too much emotion of any kind—even overconfidence—not only overwhelms subtle proprioceptive feedback but can also cause you to miss the more blatant results feedback that provides the clues to correct your course and eventually reach your goals. Ego and arrogance similarly diminish self-awareness—in fact they tend to be mutually exclusive. It should be no surprise, then, that the very best climbers most often exhibit a humble, quiet demeanor that enables them to remain curious, introspective, and highly self-aware.

Perhaps the most fundamental factor in determining your mental health and personal effectiveness is the nature of your self-image. Self-image develops gradually based on your personal experiences, but also largely in response to the evaluations of your family and peers. For example, internalizing judgments relating to your attractiveness, intelligence, physical fitness, and likability, among other things, influences your self-image. Consequently, the accumulation of negative evaluations and criticism—valid or not—can lead to a poor self-image.

Since your self-image influences all you think and do, it is essential that you become aware of it and, if necessary, strive to correct a poor self-image that's resulted from past experience and criticisms. Many people unknowingly harbor a poor self-image that adversely affects their mental outlook, emotions, and efficacy in challenging situations (such as climbing). Worse yet, someone who has possessed a poor self-image for many years may not even recognize it for what it is—they may feel that they have a decent self-image, even though an observer can easily notice a problem.

To become aware of your current self-image, you simply need to complete this sentence: I am [insert adjective]. Do this in as many ways as possible and with the first term that comes to mind: for example, *I am strong, I am shy, I am nice, I am a worrier,* or whatever. Also, consider the nature of self-talk that you blurt out or subvocalize in stressful or challenging situations—is it encouraging or self-critical? The aggregate of your common self-talk and the answers to the question I am ____? will provide a clear picture of your self-image.

Upon gaining awareness of your self-image, you have to next consider the possibility that it is not an accurate representation of your true self. Many people perpetuate a poor self-image when they focus more on bad results and criticism, and overlook or play down their goodness and successes—and such a skewed view limits self-efficacy. If this sounds at all familiar, you can use the following exercise to recalibrate your self-image. Chapter 11 provides additional techniques for improving self-image, modifying behavior, and enhancing performance in all you do. You will see how all three can work in concert.

Recalibrating Your Self-Image

Step outside yourself and, from an observer's point of view, list all your positive traits, personal successes, and contributions, aid, or comfort that you've provided to individuals or organizations. Take an inventory of all things good and true, and successes big and small, being sure to shine the best light on your intentions and actions. I submit that the self-image you hold of yourself should be a reflection of the things you list, and not the sum of occasional mistakes and the criticisms of self and others. Use the list as a daily reminder of your goodness and personal power.

Self-Awareness of Values

Lastly, you need to become self-aware of your true values so that you can invest your time and energy in the most meaningful activities and endeavors. You will feel most happy and fulfilled when you are engaging in endeavors that you view as valuable, whereas you will tend toward unhappiness or indifference when you plod along through low-value activities. Interestingly, many people aren't aware of their hierarchy of personal values and therefore spend many hours involved in lower-value activities that bring them very little pleasure, personal growth, or happiness.

You will feel most happy and fulfilled when you are engaging in endeavors that you view as valuable, whereas you will tend toward unhappiness or indifference when you plod along through low-value activities.

In the exercise on the next page you will rank fifteen common activities that should make up just about all the things you do. By ranking these activities from "most important to me" (number 1 on your list) to "least important to me" (number 15 on your list) you will gain a clear sense of your hierarchy of values—which, by the way, will change as you grow older or as circumstances in your life change. For this reason, it's beneficial to perform this exercise every year or two, just to be certain that you are crystal clear about what you truly value.

Knowledge of your true values is fundamental to personal effectiveness, because you will feel optimistic and energized to act in proportion to the amount of time you are engaged in high-value activities. In completing the "Creating a Hierarchy of Personal Values" exercise, you will hopefully discover that you spend most of your waking hours engaged in high-value activities (the top five items), perhaps a few hours per week in middle-value activities (the middle five of your ranking), and little or no time in the low-value bottom five activities. Should you discover that you spend a lot of time on one or two of the low-value activities, however, you will have identified something that's limiting your productivity and potential for success and happiness. Remember, just as engaging in high-value activities brings a beneficial momentum to your life, partaking in low-value activities becomes a ball-and-chain that limits personal growth and achievement.

Identify what activities you value most, and invest as much of your time and energy in these endeavors as possible. The result will be a day—and life—well spent!

The bottom line: Identify what activities you value most, and invest as much of your time and energy in these endeavors as possible. The result will be a day—and life—well spent!

Creating a Hierarchy of Personal Values

Rank the fifteen activities according to degree of importance, or value, regardless of how much time you actually spend doing them. Number 1 will signify highest value, 15 lowest value. Record the number rank in the blank space provided. Dig down to the core of your very being and analyze how you really feel about the different activities. Should you have trouble determining what two items will be listed as, say, 1 or 2 (10 or 11, or whatever), do a side-by-side comparison and ask yourself: *If I could only do one of these activities, which would it be?* Rank this activity as the higher of the two. When you complete your ranking, create a top-ten list of personal values by writing down your hierarchy of values onto an index card or piece of paper. Hang or place the list somewhere that you will see it daily, so that you can leverage your hierarchy of values in decision making and day planning.

_____ Career-related activities (time at work, working at home, or starting a business)

_____ Creative activities (painting, writing, playing a musical instrument)

_____ Educational activities (time at school, studying, self-directed learning such as reading this book)

_____ Exercise and health activities (working out, planning training, cooking healthy meals)

_____ Family activities (playing with kids, family time)

_____ Financial activities (financial planning and investing)

_____ "Giving-back" activities (nonprofit and charity work, volunteer and stewardship activities)

_____ Home responsibilities (cleaning, doing laundry, cooking, lawn and home care)

_____ Intimate time ("date nights" and time alone with spouse or significant other)

_____ Passive entertainment (watching TV, watching sports, playing video games, surfing the Net)

_____ Recreational and adventure activities (climbing, hiking, hunting, playing sports)

_____ Relaxing, "comfort" activities (shopping, napping, "just doing nothing")

_____ Social activities (time with friends, partying, going to bars/happy hours)

_____ Soothing, "calm-down" activities (snacking, smoking, drinking alcohol)

_____ Spiritual activities (praying, meditating, going to church)

Tips for Increasing Self-Awareness

- **Grow your metacognitive ability (self-awareness of thoughts).** Strive regularly to think about what you are thinking about, then assess whether the thoughts are helping or hurting you. Ask inwardly directed questions to assess your current state. Cultivate process-oriented and positive ways of thinking.

- **Slow down your thought process in critical moments.** Eschew reactive decision making, and instead strive to factor in the choices before you, past experience, alternative approaches, and the likely consequences of a particular decision.

- **Strive to read the physical feelings of your muscles and joints.** What's the message? Which muscles harbor tension? What external factors might have triggered the physical tension you are feeling? Grow awareness of proprioceptive clues in order to improve quality of movement on the rock.

- **Foster higher awareness of your emotional state.** Assess the nature of your emotions and the level of arousal, and then determine whether they are ideal for the task at hand. Identify, and then avoid, triggers of negative emotions.

- **Develop sharpened awareness of your weaknesses.** Take the self-assessment in chapter 1 (and use the skills checklist on page 91) to identify weaknesses. Do this once per year, since your weaknesses are a moving target. If available, elicit the input of a climbing coach. Constantly ask yourself, *What's my limiting constraint?*

- **Search for clues in performance feedback.** Analyze the stream of ongoing results feedback from the climb. What's the message? Do you need to climb faster, slower, or use a different approach?

- **Focus on the process of climbing, not the outcome or your "greatness."** Arrogance and self-awareness are mutually exclusive. Stay in the moment, stay humble, and learn from the climb and experience.

- **Cultivate a deep sense of your personal values—know who you are and what you want.** Establish a ranking or hierarchy of values each year, since you can only optimize decision making and invest your time most wisely by knowing your true values.

CHAPTER SIX

Controlling Your State

Your *state* is how you feel at any moment—the sum of your thoughts, emotions, and physical sensations and energy. Learning to regulate your state is essential for optimizing your performance and maximizing your experience. In this chapter you'll learn numerous powerful state-changing strategies.

When describing their state, people often use general classifications such as being in a "good mood" or "bad mood." It's important to recognize, however, that there is a much broader range of unique states, and each represents a distinctly different foundation from which to perform. A few examples include being psyched, excited, confident, centered, relaxed, mellow, indifferent, sleepy, uneasy, nervous, exhausted, angry, and depressed. Each of these states is made up of a unique level of mental, emotional, and physical vigor, and the aggregate effect plays a very influential role in performance. How well you will climb—or learn, problem solve, and strategize, for that matter—depends on how well you can create and maintain the optimal state for performing the task.

In the stressful situations common to climbing, however, controlling your state can be difficult; in fact, simply maintaining awareness of your changing state can be a challenge. Consider that rising fears and growing sensations of physical fatigue and pain can rapidly consume your conscious mind, thus precluding self-awareness of other more subtle, yet vitally important factors. Climbing efficiency will subsequently decline as you unknowingly begin to overgrip the rock, become increasingly tense, tentative, and mechanical, and lose your volition to push onward. It should be obvious, then, that controlling your emotions, thoughts, and physical arousal goes hand in hand with maintaining self-awareness. Figure 6.1 illustrates the dynamic process loop of self-awareness and self-regulation that you must come to consciously govern if you are to ever realize your potential.

Fortunately, the many powerful self-regulation strategies described in this chapter will equip you to change your state on demand. In a nutshell, changing your state is as simple as changing your current thoughts and physical demeanor. Knowing this, you never again have to be a slave to a bad state. Just change it! One

We must master our state before we can become a master of rock.

Matt Wilder on the first ascent of the R-rated trad line **Viceroy (5.14a/b), Boulder Canyon, Colorado.** ANDY MANN

Figure 6.1 *The Self-Awareness and Self-Regulation Process Loop*

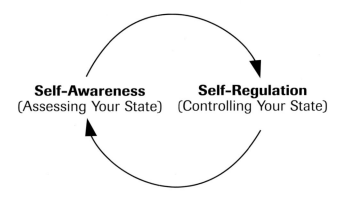

Self-Awareness
(Assessing Your State)

Self-Regulation
(Controlling Your State)

Figure 6.2 *Mind–Body–Emotion Interaction*

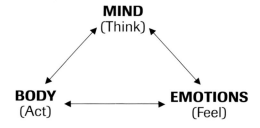

MIND
(Think)

BODY
(Act)

EMOTIONS
(Feel)

Figure 6.3 *Centered Versus Out-of-Center States*

"Centered" state with mind/body/emotion in balance

Overactive mind pulling you out of center

Runaway emotions pulling you out of center

Physical tension or arousal pulling you out of center

important caveat, however. A small percentage of the population experiences clinical depression and other psychological disorders. These present special challenges, and may require the assistance of professional therapy and medication.

Now let's delve deeper into the mind–body–emotion relationship. Figure 6.2 depicts how your thoughts, emotions, and physical feelings are interdependent and dynamically affect one another. Evolving states can run either mind-to-body or body-to-mind, and your emotions amplify and change as a result of the specific mind–body processes at play. Your ultimate goal is to self-direct this dynamic mind–body–emotion relationship, instead of letting outside influences (people and events) run the show.

An example of the mind-to-body process running the show is the way dwelling on a bad event or on your fears will make you anxious and perhaps even depressed. Quite simply, harboring mental stress will yield physical stress.

Conversely, the body-to-mind process at work is evident in how vigorous physical activity can make you feel vibrant, confident, and perhaps even euphoric. Thus, by activating your body you are mentally transported to a different, enlightened dimension.

Peak performers take ownership of their states and are proactive in self-regulating.

The take-home message here is that you always have the choice to change your state. Whether you don't like how you are feeling at the moment or if you feel that a different state would be better for performing a certain task, you can take charge and change the state almost instantly. The master skill is becoming aware of your ever-changing state (see the previous chapter) and then actively managing it using the tools you'll learn on the following pages. The bottom line: Peak performers take ownership of their states and are proactive in self-regulating, whereas less empowered people allow outside stimuli to affect their state, and they may be quick to blame others for how they feel.

Ultimately, your goal is to maintain a balance of your mental, emotional, and physical attributes in order to create a centered state from which you can perform optimally. Allow any one of these attributes to dominate and overpower the others, and it will push you out of center (see figure 6.3). For example, by thinking too much you can suffer from the paralysis of analysis; when your emotions run wild you can scare or doubt yourself off a route; or when you get physically tense and mechanical you lose the ability to climb efficiently. But in being centered, your mind, body, and emotions are all in an optimal zone that yields balanced feedback to one another—you'll know when this happens because your movement will flow almost automatically and unconsciously, in what some people refer to as *the zone*.

In a sport as physically and mentally stimulating as climbing, it can be extraordinarily difficult to get centered. Even when you start up a climb feeling like you're in a good groove, it only takes one botched move, a poor protection placement, or an unanticipated difficulty to throw you out of center as physical tension, mental stress, or runaway emotions take over. It is therefore imperative that you monitor your state and immediately counter any shift out of center.

In the following sections you will learn specific strategies for modulating your state and remaining as close to center as possible. First, I'll detail several body-to-mind techniques, in which you modulate physical tension and arousal to help foster ideal mental and emotional states. Next, we'll examine a few mind-to-body strategies that leverage the power of your thoughts to change your physical and emotional states. The chapter then concludes with two techniques for recalibrating your emotional state to its natural positive set point.

Controlling Your Physical State

In this section you want to take on the perspective of your body as a climbing machine. How well does it perform when you step on the gas to zoom up a difficult climb? Does it function optimally with crisp precision and high economy, or does it sputter along with jerky, tense movements and poor fuel economy?

Excessive physical tension is a villain that robs us of economical movement and hinders performance in any physical activity. And given the high-stress world we live in, tension can manifest itself as we engage in simple tasks and even while at rest. For example, I have discovered that I often clench my jaw when concentrating on a task, and I sometimes tense or move my leg muscles when driving or working on the computer. This unnecessary tension can then spread—from my jaw to my neck and shoulders in the first example, and to my hips and lower back in the second example. Fortunately, now that I'm aware of this common cascade of muscular tension I can be proactive in controlling or preventing it.

You, too, should strive to gain awareness of how tension develops and affects you. Begin by scanning for pockets of tension at different times throughout the day. You want to pay special attention to how physical tension evolves when you step onto the rock—where does tension first develop, and what tense body parts seem to hinder efficient movement as growing mental and emotional stress add to the mix? With this knowledge, you can take an active role in slowing or preventing the rise of performance-killing tension.

Your level of arousal, or excitability, is another factor you want to monitor and control. Assess your arousal on a scale from 1 to 10, with a completely calm and physically relaxed state (ideal when reading or going to sleep) being a 1 and the highly excited and maximally energized fight-or-flight state being a 10 (ideal when running for your life!).

A crucial distinction is that there is no optimal level of arousal for climbing, since different types of routes are best engaged at different levels of arousal. For example, a complex, technical face climb, with its delicate and precise movements, is best performed in a state of low arousal (perhaps a 2 or 3 on the scale from 1 to 10). Conversely, a short, steep, dynamic boulder problem, with its brute power moves, can only be sent with very high arousal (say, an 8 or 9 on the scale). The typical rock climb will fall somewhere between these extremes (perhaps a 4 or 5 on the scale), since you need enough arousal to climb with vigor and focus, yet you don't want to feel so excited that you botch sequences or overgrip holds (see figure 6.4). Some climbs are interesting because they deal up a mix of delicacy and power.

Figure 6.4 *Ideal Arousal for Different Climbs*

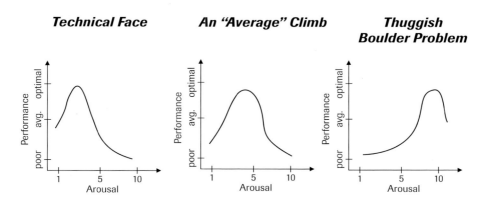

In self-regulating arousal before a climb, it's better to err on the side of setting arousal too low rather than too high. Given the inherent stress of a climb, your arousal will almost always increase as you progress up a route—in the worst case, a full-fledged fight-or-flight response will kick in a shot of adrenaline as you encounter an unexpected or life-threatening situation. While this fight-or-flight response might be beneficial in rare situations, such as running from approaching rockfall or an avalanche, it will kill economy and lead to poor technical performance on most climbs. As a practice, then, it's best to set a relatively low arousal at the beginning of most climbs and then strive to maintain moderate arousal (using the techniques below) as you proceed up the route. The exception is a short, thuggish boulder problem, which would be best attempted in a fully amped state.

Let's examine three powerful techniques for lowering and controlling arousal. Begin using these strategies to optimize your physical state in all you do, both climbing and nonclimbing, and you will increase the quality of your actions and discover a higher level of self-mastery.

Foster Deeper Breathing

Breathing has a profound effect on your physical state. If you don't believe me, try this: Hold your breath for thirty seconds, take one breath, and then hold your breath again for thirty seconds. Chances are your body has shifted to a higher overall level of tension, particularly through your torso and neck. The same thing happens in climbing—as breathing becomes irregular, or even stops during hard moves, your level of physical tension increases.

Interestingly, many people breathe in a way that can give rapid rise to tension in adverse situations. The common method of breathing is a shallow, relatively rapid turnover of air that primarily involves the upper chest. A better breathing technique for controlling tension is to draw slow, deeper breaths that begin from the belly and then progress to fill the midchest and finally the upper chest. This way of breathing maximizes use of your lungs, thus increasing oxygenation of the blood and lowering muscular tension. So by directing slow, deep breaths while climbing and at rest, you promote clearer thinking, faster recovery, and reduced tension throughout your body.

After habitually engaging in shallow chest breathing for many years, at a rate of about 20,000 breaths per day, it can be extraordinarily difficult to change your ways. But the process of change begins with learning conscious breath control in stressful situations, whether it's a traffic jam on the highway, a tough situation at work, or a crux sequence on a route. When you sense rising stress, focus attention onto your breathing and direct slow, deep belly breaths (see "Deep Breathing Technique" below) for a minute or two.

The next step to improving your breathing style is to frequently check in on your breathing in order to consciously regulate slower, deeper breath-play. Do this regularly—at least once per hour throughout the day—and you will gradually condition a new way of more effective breathing that will positively impact your state and, thus, your potential to perform.

When climbing, begin the practice of slow, deep breathing for a few minutes just before you begin to climb—make this part of your preclimb ritual. Then as you climb, make breathing checks as often as possible in order to quell rising physical tension. Use every rest position, or clipping position when sport climbing, to briefly return your focus to directing steady, deep belly breathing. You will climb far better using this strategy compared with just climbing and letting your breathing direct itself, as most climbers do.

 ### *Deep Breathing Technique*

Here's an excellent breathing sequence, promoted by renowned Penn State sports psychologist Dorothy Harris, to use throughout the day and when climbing. Utilize this breathing technique for a few minutes each hour, no matter what you are doing, and you will eventually develop more effective—and unconscious—breathing in all you do.

Imagine that your lungs have a lower, middle, and upper compartment. Begin inhaling through your nose with the goal of filling the lower compartment first. Push your diaphragm downward, and feel your lower abdomen expand outward.

Continue steady inhalation to fill the second, midchest compartment by expanding your rib cage until filled.

Complete the breath by filling the top compartment—feel your upper chest and shoulders rise upward.

Now slowly exhale through your mouth striving to completely empty your lungs.

When practicing this exercise it should take about fifteen seconds for each breath cycle. Take five or six seconds for the inhalation phase (through the nose), hold your breath for a second or two, and then take about eight seconds to slowly release the breath (through pursed lips). When climbing, however, the inhalation and exhalation phases should each take between two to five seconds, with no pause in between.

Direct Muscle Relaxation

Elegant efficiency and perfect economy are the ultimate goals in climbing movement, and muscular tension and overarousal are the enemies of this quest. While true perfection is unattainable, every climber can improve the quality of movement and therefore climb more efficiently. Trust me: No matter how hard you climb now, you can climb harder if you improve your technique and economy.

No matter how hard you climb now, you can climb harder if you improve your technique and economy.

The chief problem among climbers is tension in the antagonist muscles that oppose the prime movers (the pulling muscles). Undue tension in these antagonists causes the agonist (pulling) muscles to work harder than need be, thus increasing the rate of fatigue and compromising smooth movement. Tense climbers are easy to spot—they look mechanical, stiff, and hesitant, and they always pump out quickly. The best climbers possess little unnecessary tension and flow across the rock with an apparent lack of effort.

You, too, can foster this highly efficient and fluid style by controlling tension, rather than allowing muscular tension to control you. As in seizing control of your breathing (per above), reducing muscle tension requires a disciplined effort both on and off the rock. Daily stretching of all the major muscle groups is a good place to start. Engage in five to ten minutes of general stretching twice per day, ideally in the midmorning (when your muscles are warmed up from a few hours of moving around) and again in the evening, when you can best make gains in flexibility.

A modest amount of stretching is also beneficial when you are out climbing. Performing some warm-up activities to prepare the joints and muscles for climbing is always a good idea, as is some mild stretching of the muscles primary to climbing (only stretch after engaging in some warm-up activities or a couple of easy ascents). Most important, and often overlooked, is stretching the antagonist muscles as part of the warm-up process before you attempt a near-maximum climb. By stretching the finger extensor muscles, the triceps, and other push muscles of the torso, you reduce inherent tension in the antagonists and reduce the overcharge in energy expenditure that they can levy on the crucial pull muscles. The result is more relaxed, fluid, and efficient movement!

Self-directing relaxation is also highly effective for reducing tension. Like stretching, you can engage a few minutes of progressive relaxation (see "Progressive Relaxation Sequence" below) anytime during the day to lower your level of muscular tension and arousal. You can execute this sequence, working from your feet up to your head, to reclaim a relaxed state and return to center. Use this sequence anytime you are feeling tense, whether it's before an exam at school, an important meeting at work, or a climb. Progressive relaxation is also useful to enter an optimal state for performing visualization (more on this in chapter 11) or falling asleep quickly.

Also detailed below is the ANSWER Sequence, perhaps the very best relaxation and centering technique for use immediately before climbing and during brief rest breaks en route.

Progressive Relaxation Sequence

Perform this sequence anytime you want to reduce muscular tension, lower arousal, or enter a calm state for reading, learning, or falling asleep. Initially, the sequence may take ten to fifteen minutes to progress through. With practice, however, you'll be able to move quickly through the sequence and reach a highly relaxed state in less than five minutes. Sitting or lying comfortably, in a quiet location, will expedite and enhance the relaxation process.

1. Close your eyes and take five deep belly breaths. Inhale slowly through your nose to a slow, silent count to five, and then gradually exhale through your mouth to a slow, silent eight-count.

2. Keeping your eyes closed and maintaining slow, relaxed breathing, tense the muscles in your right lower leg for five seconds. Feel the tension in your right foot and calf muscles, then let go and relax the muscles completely. Compare the difference in sensation between the tense and relaxed states. Repeat this process with the left lower leg. With both of your lower legs now relaxed think, *My feet and lower legs feel warm and light.* You should now feel your lower legs enter a deep state of relaxation.

3. Next, perform the same sequence in the muscles of the upper leg (one leg at a time). Tense the muscles in your upper leg for five seconds, then relax them. After doing this with both legs, finish up by thinking, *My upper legs feel warm and light.* Feel all tension dissolve as your upper legs drop into deep relaxation.

4. Repeat this process in your hands and lower arms. Begin by tensing the muscles below your right elbow by making a tight fist for five seconds, then relax these muscles completely. Repeat this with the left hand and forearm, and conclude with the thought, *My hands and forearms feel warm and light.*

5. Repeat this procedure on the muscles in the upper arm.

6. Next, shift the focus to the many muscles of the torso (including the chest, abdominal, back, and shoulder areas). Repeat the process exactly.

7. Conclude with the muscles of the face and neck.

8. You should now be in a deep state of relaxation (possibly, you will have fallen asleep by now). Mentally scan yourself from head to toe for any isolated pockets of remaining tension—if you discover any, visualize the tension escaping the muscle like air from a balloon.

Upon completing this sequence, you can open your eyes and commence with an activity (or climb) with a renewed sense of calm and focus. Or you can leverage this relaxed state by performing some mind programming—visualize the process of reaching some of your goals or mentally rehearse a project climb.

The ANSWER Sequence

Perform the ANSWER Sequence before and during each climb and in everyday situations where you need to control tension, anxiety, and focus. Initially, this six-step procedure will take a few minutes to perform. With practice, you'll be able to go through the sequence in about ten seconds—perfect for use at marginal rest positions where getting centered could make the difference between success and failure.

A—Awareness of rising tension, anxiety, or negative thoughts.

Acute awareness of unfavorable mental and physical changes is fundamental to optimal performance. It takes a conscious effort to turn your thoughts away from the outer world toward your inner world. Peak performers habitually make these tension checks every few minutes, so they can nix any negative changes before they snowball out of control. Make this your goal.

N—Normalize breathing.

In climbing, your breathing should be deep, relaxed, and regular. Unfortunately, many climbers breathe unevenly during hard sequences, thus creating tension and degrading performance. Your goal is to foster deep, even breathing throughout the climb. The exception is "holding your breath" (Valsalva Maneuver) to create core tension during a hard move.

S—Scan for specific areas of muscular tension.

In this step you perform a tension check. Scan all your muscles in a quick sweep to locate pockets of tightness. Commonly tight areas are the forearms (are you overgripping?), shoulders, upper back, chest, abdominals, and calves. The best way to relax a specific muscle is to consciously contract that muscle for a few seconds, then relax it and visualize the tension draining from it like air from a balloon (the differential relaxation technique).

W—Wave of relaxation.

Upon completing the tension check above, take a single deep breath and feel a wave of relaxation wash from your head to your toes.

E—Erase thoughts of past events (and possible future outcomes) and focus on the present.

This step involves freeing your mind from the ball-and-chain of undesirable past events. There is no benefit to pondering the last failed attempt or the heinous sequence you just barely fought through. Let go of the past and do not ponder the future—thoughts of the past and future are enemies of excellence in the present. Refocus on and engage the present moment.

R—Reset posture and flash a smile.

It's amazing how much positive energy you can generate simply by resetting your posture and flashing a smile. This final step of the ANSWER Sequence will leave you in a peak performance state and ready to climb into the zone. Trust your skills, have fun, and let the outcome take care of itself.

Alter Your Physiology

While the two previous strategies addressed the common need to lower arousal and muscular tension, there will sometimes be situations in which you need to increase arousal or sustain an energetic state. For example, if you are feeling physically sluggish or lethargic before a workout or climb, it would be highly beneficial to assume a more aroused, energetic state. Otherwise there's a good chance you will blow off the workout or perform poorly on the climb.

Another common problem is low energy levels or a feeling of lethargy during the afternoon hours. Such midday lulls in arousal are often diet-related, and they are easily corrected by consuming the right types of energy foods. Let's examine two techniques for elevating low energy levels.

 ### Change Your Physical Demeanor

Perhaps the simplest way of changing your state is to either change your current posture or do something to elevate your heart rate. For example, simply sitting up straight or standing up with good posture will instantly elevate your mood and sense of well-being. Similarly, if you are feeling depressed, poorly focused, or low in energy, you can dramatically change your state for the better by doing jumping jacks for a few minutes, going for a short run, or doing anything physical that elevates your heart rate.

In the context of climbing, you might do a few jumping jacks or jump up and down a few times to get psyched up for a powerful boulder problem. Or if you'd like to elevate your mood without increasing arousal, as might be ideal before a serious lead climb, you would simply roll your shoulders back, lift your chin up, and crack a big smile. While these techniques might seem unbelievably simple, I guarantee that by using them you will obtain a better state for optimal climbing performance. Of course, only you can determine the optimal arousal level for a given climb—this is something you will learn to intuit with increasing climbing experience.

 ### Use Nutrition to Stabilize and Sustain Energy and Arousal

The foods you choose to eat help determine your overall energy level, physical stamina, mental alertness, and to some degree your mood. The powerful state-altering effects of food are exemplified by the sadly common practice of people eating "comfort foods" as a way to change their negative state. Similarly, there's the practice of consuming alcoholic beverages or taking drugs in an attempt to escape a stressful or depressed state.

More resourceful and empowered people, however, know how to change their state by changing their thoughts or physical demeanor; they also know what foods to eat to support clear thinking, a positive mood, and sustained energy. The focus of this section is the latter idea of leveraging nutrition to foster a more consistently effective state, both on and off the rock. Since this is just a primer on the subject, I encourage you to read the chapter on performance nutrition in *Training for Climbing*.

Central to your physical and mental energy level is your blood sugar. Steady blood sugar levels support steady energy and concentration, whereas blood sugar spikes (and the relative troughs) lead to a roller-coaster ride of energy highs and lows, and often emotional volatility as well. The goal, then, is to consume a healthy snack or meal every few hours throughout the day in order to encourage steady blood sugar. Unfortunately, not all foods are the same in terms of the effect they have on blood sugar levels, and it takes a little bit of effort to select foods that will support steady blood sugar.

Fortunately, there's the glycemic index (GI) to help you select the right carbohydrate sources (see table 6.1). Foods with a high GI cause a rapid increase in blood sugar and often a subsequent insulin release with the telltale energy and emotional trough that soon follows. Low- to mid-GI foods produce more subtle changes in blood sugar and hence promote stable energy level, mood, and concentration. Consequently, it is best to consume mainly low- to mid-GI foods during rest days, in the hours leading up to exercise, and during stop-and-go activities such as bouldering and cragging. Only during sustained, intense exercise and the first two hours following exercise do you want to consume high-GI foods, since the resultant rise in blood sugar will help sustain strenuous activity and best initiate recovery immediately following exercise.

I will stress the importance of proper nutrition with the interesting fact that pound for pound the brain uses up to ten times as much glucose and oxygen as

Table 6.1 Glycemic Index of Common Foods

High-GI Foods (GI > 65)		Low- to Moderate-GI Food (GI < 65)	
Most sports drinks	70–85	Granola bars	61
Most cookies and donuts	66–80	Oatmeal (non-instant)	61
Most candy	65–80	Whole-grain foods	~60
Potatoes	83	Pasta and pizza	30–60
Rice and rice cakes	82	Banana	55
White bread	78	Gorp	~50
Graham crackers	74	Beans	48
Potato and corn chips	73	Most fruits	~40
Bagel	72	Balance Bar	30
Clif Bars	70+	Milk and yogurt	~30
Soft drinks (nondiet)	68	Most veggies	~20
PowerBar	65	Peanuts	14

Tips for Controlling Your Physical State

- **Assess and, if necessary, adjust your physical arousal level every hour throughout the day or whenever an event requires a new level of arousal.** Err on the side of setting arousal too low for technical climbing; set arousal higher for powerful moves and boulder problems.

- **Take control of your breathing.** Learn to use the method in this chapter. Direct slow, deep belly breathing to lower your arousal, release muscular tension, increase oxygenation of the blood, and calm your nerves. Check your breathing at all rest positions, and engage in a few minutes of deep breathing before every climb.

- **Use stretching and self-directed relaxation to reduce muscular tension.** Use the Progressive Relaxation Sequence to lower tension and arousal before you climb, prior to visualization training, and when falling asleep.

- **Alter your physiology to change how you feel.** Stand with better posture and crack a big smile to instantly charge your state with positive feelings. Elevate your heart rate with jumping jacks or a brief jog to increase arousal before a powerful climb.

- **Use nutrition to stabilize and sustain energy levels.** Consume low- to moderate-glycemic-index foods before and during climbs to avoid energy troughs. Eat higher-GI foods only during sustained, strenuous exercise, at the end of the climbing day, and immediately following workouts to jump-start recovery.

muscle. Consequently, when oxygen and glucose supply dwindle, so does brain function—this helps explain why concentration and mental sharpness drop off toward the end of a long workout or day of climbing, as well as when climbing at an elevation higher than you are used to. Hopefully this knowledge will compel you to snack more frequently on lower-GI foods—and to breathe deeply!—throughout long days of climbing.

Controlling Your Mental State

Make no mistake about it: The thoughts you generate and dwell upon are powerful. You can literally think yourself to success or failure.

If you think fearful thoughts, you will trigger anxious feelings and physical tension that will degrade performance. Conversely, positive, process-oriented thoughts help foster a centered state from which you can perform optimally. The premise of this section, then, is that controlling your state and performing your best demands that you seize control of your thoughts and consciously direct them in productive ways.

Becoming a productive thinker is extremely difficult for some people. Years of habitual negative thinking and self-criticism can lead some individuals to believe that they were simply "born this way" and can't change it. While it's a fact that genetics do provide a framework for your development, they do not determine the outcome. You do! The nurturing effect of what you think and do throughout the hours and days of your life has a far greater effect on what you will become than does nature (genetics). So if you have an affinity for thinking that *I can't change my ways, it's just how I am,* I'm calling bull on that right now.

The thoughts you generate and dwell on are powerful. You can literally think yourself to success or failure.

In this section you will learn how to take control of your internal dialogue, which ultimately solidifies into the bricks and mortar of what you become and achieve. This topic of thought control is obviously central to all the chapters within part three of *Maximum Climbing*. (I suggest you fold down the corner of this page so that you can easy return to these thought-control strategies for frequent review.) So consider this to be the beginning of an exciting journey that will elevate the quality your thinking and forever change your trajectory in climbing (and beyond)!

Take Command of Your Self-Talk and Mental Imagery

Our brains are filled with an almost incessant verbal chatter and slide show of mental images. In all we do, whether it's a simple task at home or a complex climbing sequence, we talk to ourselves and conjure mental images relating to the task at hand. Our brains are prolific in generating this ongoing multimedia show, so much so that it's sometimes difficult to turn it off, even when going to sleep at night. The goal, then, is to tune in to, direct, and, when needed, turn off this internal dialogue and imagery.

Your self-talk and mental imagery can be both tremendously useful and exceptionally self-destructive. For example, you might talk to yourself (usually subvocalized) to aid in problem solving and self-analysis, to remind yourself of the fundamentals of proper movement, and to encourage yourself when you are struggling to hang on to a difficult move or finish an exhausting workout. A few examples of helpful self-talk and self-instruction are: *Relax and stay cool; I can do this; Focus on the feet; Keep breathing; Hang on, there's a rest just ahead.* Similarly you might create mental images as a way of testing possible solutions to a crux sequence, visualizing the best route of ascent and developing risk management strategies, and seeing the goal completed in your mind's eye in order to invigorate your efforts. These are just a few of the unlimited ways of using self-directed internal dialogue and imagery to enhance your performance.

Now let's examine a few unproductive, and sometimes even self-destructive, uses of self-talk and mental imagery. You might engage in self-talk that lists all the reasons that you might fail on the climb, dwells on things outside your control, and spew invectives (perhaps even out loud) that destroy your confidence and create negative energy. Have you ever thought to yourself: *I don't think I can do this; Weather conditions are not ideal for this climb; I'm afraid I'll fall and embarrass myself?* Worse yet, you may also invoke fearful images of falling, visualize past failures, and envision your weaknesses, real or imagined. No doubt these are just a few of the ways people sabotage their performances, in climbing and life.

In an activity as tenuous as climbing, entertaining such negative imagery or self-talk is tantamount to strapping a heavy weight to your back. Have you ever felt the weight of your worries and fears hinder your upward movement on a climb? I have. Fortunately, you can seize control of your internal dialogue and make it your strongest ally. By directing encouraging self-talk and by creating mental images that aid your efforts, you spread metaphorical mental wings that lighten your load and boost performance.

Changing habitually or even occasionally harmful self-talk requires that you vigilantly monitor your internal dialogue and immediately redirect any unproductive statements or images. With a sustained daily effort you will gradually create new ways of thinking (thanks to the generation of new synapses and neuro-associations) that are more positive, productive, and automatic. Best of all, elevating your mental state in this way will not only make you a better climber, but also make you feel more emotionally stable as well as positively affect all the people around you. I call this the Skinner Effect, named in honor of the way Todd Skinner could effortlessly impart a positive, energetic state onto everyone in his presence.

Following are two exercises that will help you move toward higher-quality internal dialogue. The first exercise ("Observing Your Thoughts") is simply about gaining awareness of the tone and nature of your self-talk and mental imagery. The second exercise ("Changing Your Self-Talk and Mental Imagery") gives numerous examples of how you can redirect your self-talk and imagery to create a more empowering state.

 ### *Observing Your Thoughts*

Sit down in a relaxed position, close your eyes, and take a few slow, deep belly breaths. Let your current thoughts and concerns escape with each exhalation. Refocus your concentration onto your breathing, and feel the air slowly filling and exiting your lungs. After a minute or two, you should be in a physically and mentally relaxed state.

Next, let your focus of the breathing process dissolve into nothingness, and simply let your awareness wander. Observe your thoughts as they come and go, letting them pass without stopping to dwell on any given thought. Passively monitor your thoughts in this way for five to ten minutes.

Now retake control of your thought processes and review your journey of the past few minutes. What subjects or activities did the thoughts relate to? What was the tone of the thoughts—were they positive or negative in nature? Were your thoughts more future-oriented or focused on the past? Did your mental images depict past memories or goals of the future? Did the images invoke any positive or negative emotions? It may help to write down everything that you remember thinking, imagining, or emotionally feeling.

If you perform this exercise at different times of the day and in different situations, you will notice some similarities in your train of thoughts as well as some differences. It also can be instructive to do this exercise during a rest break between climbs or redpoint attempts. Your goal is to identify the theme of any recurrent negative images or thoughts of self-criticism or failure. Once identified, you must make it a top priority to break the habit of such negative thinking and end the indulgence of reliving past failures or feeling sorry for yourself.

Change Your Self-Talk and Mental Imagery

Once you have learned to recognize unproductive thoughts and images, you must learn to either let them pass with disbelief or convert them into something more productive or encouraging. It's crucial to understand that thought content is not tangible or real unless you believe and act upon it. Therefore you can choose to let any given thought pass you by, viewing it as nothing more than fiction! This can be hard to do with stronger thoughts and vivid images, however. So if you can't simply dismiss a thought as fiction, then you must be proactive in changing the self-talk or mental image into something more productive. (One word of caution: When engaged in risk management planning, never dismiss as "fiction" thoughts of possible dangers, unless they can be ruled out as near impossibilities in the given situation.)

Table 6.2 contains numerous examples of how to modify negative self-talk and mental imagery into something more positive and productive. You will need to identify your own novel ways of harmful thinking and then proactively and creatively invert these thoughts, metaphors, and images into something more beneficial.

Quiet Your Mind with Meditation and Stay in the Present

One of the most pleasurable and addictive aspects of climbing is how it can sometimes quiet your mind and narrow your concentration to the present moment and the move at hand. Nothing else matters when you enter this rare state of single-pointed focus. The rest of the world seems to disappear and all distractions and concerns evaporate from your conscious mind as you engage in what legendary boulderer John Gill called a climber's moving meditation.

This highly distinct state of pure focus and engagement is often difficult to come by in other aspects of life (although it is experienced by others who similarly engage their mind and/or body in a challenging endeavor). Vastly more common in our everyday lives is multitasking, dealing with distractions, and staying connected with people and events around us. These situations, and almost everything else that makes up our day, overwhelm our senses and lead to racing thoughts and rising physical tension. It is no surprise, then, that many people try to quiet their minds with drugs and alcohol or try to divert attention to another reality by watching TV for hours at a time.

In this chapter, however, you are learning how to change your state *naturally.* In the quest to quiet an overactive mind, there are two simple yet powerful strategies that I will present. The first is to quiet your mind once or twice per day

Table 6.2 *Examples of Self-Talk Modification*

Unproductive Thought or Image	Change to . . .	More Productive Thought or Image
This climb looks hard (or impossible).	⟶	This climb looks challenging.
I can see myself falling all over this climb.	⟶	I can see myself making a great effort.
This climb is spanking me; I'll never figure this out.	⟶	With each fall, I'm gaining more data about the climb, and I'll soon figure it out.
I'm feeling scared of this climb.	⟶	I have done other climbs similar to this, and I feel I can give it a strong effort.
I might be too short for this climb.	⟶	My slight physique and light weight are advantages on this climb.
It feels too hot to climb my best.	⟶	My muscles feel warm and energized.
I feel butterflies in my stomach, and I fear that my nervousness will do me in.	⟶	I feel energized and ready to climb, but I will down-regulate my arousal a bit.
This climb looks steep and pumpy.	⟶	I climb steep, pumpy routes in the gym all the time. I have a good chance of sending.
Many people are watching me, and I'm afraid to embarrass myself by falling.	⟶	I climb for myself, not others. I will focus on the process of climbing and enjoy every minute of it!
Despite having adequate rest since the last workout, I'm feeling too lethargic to work out tonight, and I'd rather just watch TV at home.	⟶	I'll go to the gym for a shorter-than-usual workout tonight, knowing that physical activity will make me feel better.

with meditation (see "Using Meditation to Quiet Your Mind"). Meditation has been practiced by Buddhists for millennia as a pathway to peace of mind and enlightenment, and you, too, can use this mental exercise to quiet your mind and regain control in the midst of a hectic world.

Using Meditation to Quiet Your Mind

Meditation is the art of silencing the mind. By meditating once or twice per day for fifteen to twenty minutes each time, you will reduce mental clutter, improve your concentration, lower stress and anxiety, and enhance your performance in the important things in your life. Getting the most out of the practice of meditation requires a commitment to do it daily. Take the attitude that you can't afford *not* to do this each day—schedule a time to meditate, just as you schedule a time to exercise and eat. Here's one way to do it.

Go to a quiet location with no potential for distractions. Shut off your cell phone and any other electronic device that might interfere with your meditation.

Sit up straight in a chair, lie on the floor, or assume some other comfortable position.

Take several slow, deep belly breaths as described in the breathing exercise on page 104. This will begin to relax your body and quiet the mind.

Foster single-pointed focus by concentrating on your breathing—narrow your world to the feeling of air passing in and out of your lungs. Alternatively, you can focus on a small object, such as a candle flame, a cross, or a flower, or you can repeat a mantra such as "calm."

The final step is to advance to a state of no thought at all. You cannot achieve this ultimate state by trying, however; instead you have to let it arise on its own. The best way to do this is to let your single-pointed focus (on breathing, a candle, or whatever) dissolve into nothingness. Perhaps you will experience a few seconds of no thought before something pops into your mind. Instead of resisting this burgeoning thought, simply observe it developing and then let it pass. Return your concentration to your breathing (or other) and upon reaching a single-pointed focus, again let the focus dissolve into nothingness. Achieving no thought is extraordinarily difficult, but with practice you will eventually come to know these moments of highest awareness and spiritual connection with the universe.

Stay in the Moment

The second strategy for reducing cognitive chaos is to narrow your thoughts to the present moment, and pay little attention to the past and future. The past can't be changed, so why dwell on it other than briefly to relive the good feelings or lessons of a past event? Unfortunately, many people waste precious time brooding over past failures or hurtful situations, thus poisoning the present moment with unproductive thoughts and emotions.

Excessive thinking about the future similarly diverts attention from the present moment, and it fosters the tendency toward being a dreamer or worrier rather than

Figure 6.5 *The Now Clock*

Engage this moment—the time to act is now!
(Make a copy of the Now Clock and hang it somewhere you'll see it daily.)

a doer. Future-oriented thinking is only beneficial when it involves targeted goal setting or the formulation of a specific game plan for the attainment of a goal. Other ponderings of what you wish for in the future, without a specific goal and plan for making it a reality, are nothing more than daydreaming, a sort of mental narcotic that provides an escape from the reality of the present.

The bottom line: Strive to mentally stay in the here and now for all but a few minutes per hour. When you discover that you have slipped into past- or future-oriented thinking, immediately ask yourself: *Is there a practical purpose for the thoughts or am I mentally just killing time?* Constantly remind yourself to stay in the present, since all things accomplished evolve from taking intelligent actions one moment after another. When you find yourself losing the momentum of action or dwelling on the past or the future, take a look at the Now Clock (figure 6.5) as your reminder of where to focus your thoughts for peak performance and maximum experience.

 Simplify Your Life—Get Back to Basics!

Do you ever feel like you are in a state of mental gridlock? There's too much to do, too little time to do it, and your head is spinning from it all. Your schedule is overbooked, your phone and e-mail constantly summon you, and there's too little time for the important things in your life. Does any of this sound familiar? If so, it's time to simplify your life and get back to basics. Here's how.

- **Enact a value-based process of scheduling your time.** Consult the list of personal values you developed on page 96, and stop wasting time doing anything on the bottom third of the list. Most important, commit most of your waking hours to the top five items on your list—this will instantly increase your effectiveness and simplify your days.

- **Narrow your circle of friends and associates.** Downsize your social time and group activities to only the events that involve your family and closest friends. Scattering your time and energy among a vast social network might make you feel liked, but how many of your myriad casual friends will be behind you when the chips are down? You are not defined by the number of friends you have, but by the quality of the relationships you have with the people closest to you.

- **Drop the facade.** People waste so much time these days trying to create some bogus image of themselves that will impress the world. Meanwhile, as they are consumed by their charade of being cool, wearing the bitchin' threads, and spewing self-inflating jive, real life is passing them by. Refuse to play this superficial game, and invest your mental and physical energy (and financial resources as well) into the things that really matter. Again, I implore you to see the top five items on your values list, and to invest the precious minutes of your life wisely.

Tips for Controlling Your Mental State

Regularly direct your focus inward and observe the nature and quality of your thoughts. Pause frequently throughout the day, and before starting up a climb, to observe and modify your thinking; use the following strategies to optimize your mental state.

- **Seize control of your inner dialogue.** Direct positive, productive self-talk and create mental imagery that will enhance your confidence and help preprogram your ascent.

- **Supplant negative self-talk and imagery with positive statements and images.** Replace negative thoughts and images with memories of past successes and visions of your goals completed.

- **Use meditation to quiet your mind.** Reduce cognitive chaos and racing thoughts by taking a meditation break. Meditate once or twice per day to foster a calmer mental state in all you do.

- **Narrow your thoughts to the present moment.** Anytime you need to perform, whether it's on or off the rock, focus on the task at hand and eliminate all thoughts of the past and future. Detach yourself from thoughts of possible outcomes—let the outcome evolve organically.

- **Simplify your life and then feel the power!** Multitasking, being constantly wired to electronics, and excessive socializing are enemies of a quiet, focused, agile mind. Simplify your life by nixing low-value activities, narrowing your circle of friends, and cutting ties to people and things that contribute to mental overwhelm.

- **Cut your ties to activities and things that no longer have a meaning, purpose, or value in your life.** As you age and mature, you need to let go of activities, relationships, and attachments that no longer contribute to your central mission and purpose. It's human nature to hang on to the ways of the past, even after you've moved on to new goals and values. There may be many small things that you've carried over from the past or perhaps just one big thing; either way, by letting go of these remnants you free up emotional energy and clear mental space. Can you think of anything that would be advantageous to cut your ties with? For example, knowing everything that you know, is there a relationship or possession that you'd be better off without? If so, liberate yourself, and discover the feeling of life made simpler. Of course you need to act responsibly—there may be people or commitments that you are morally obliged to remain engaged with even though it may not align to your long-term mission.

Controlling Your Emotions

It's fitting to conclude this chapter with a section on controlling your emotions. After all, your emotions provide the energy, or fire, to your states, whether they are productive, unproductive, negative, or positive. You need emotional energy if you are going to maximize performance—you can't accomplish much living in the state of indifference!

As depicted in figure 6.2, your emotions evolve dynamically as a result of your prevailing thoughts and physical demeanor. Controlling emotions, then, comes down to a matter of changing your thoughts and physiology. The preceding sections have armed you with numerous techniques for doing just this. Review, practice, and master these techniques and you will become a master of your emotions.

Below I will introduce you to two more strategies for creating positive emotions. You will learn to create anchors to positive states that you've previously experienced, and to take a mental inventory in order to recalibrate your appreciation of your many blessings.

Anchor Yourself to Positive States

We've all heard a song or smelled a distinct scent that instantly connected us to some past event, good or bad. In many cases the song or smell triggers a remarkably clear visual and emotional flashback to the past experience. This is an example of the power of anchors—that is, when an impactful or novel event has become married or anchored to a distinct mental, physical, and/or emotional state.

While anchors often are created through a pairing of events that are outside your control, you can learn to consciously create anchors for use at some point in the future. The benefit of this strategy is that you can create an anchor to an event or situation during which you were highly effective and in a peak emotional state. Then, at some point in the future, you can trigger the anchor to transfer this positive emotional resource for use in the present moment. Refer to the "Creating Anchors to Positive Emotional States" exercise to learn how to add this powerful state-changing tool to your arsenal.

Similarly potent are anchors to negative states. If you've ever seen or heard something that instantly made you feel anxious or gloomy, chances are that the image or song triggered an anchor to some past negative event. Each of us has unique anchors to past events that make us feel sad, weak, or angry. The key is to identify the specific anchor (a person, place, or thing) and avoid that trigger so you will never relive these unwanted emotions. Alternatively, you can try to break the negative anchor by intentionally triggering a powerful positive anchor (as you will have developed using the Creating Anchors exercise) just as you expose yourself to the negative anchor. Doing this repeatedly—triggering the positive anchor nearly coincident to seeing/hearing the negative anchor—will create a new neuro-association.

 ### Creating Anchors to Positive Emotional States

Recall a particular situation or event when you experienced a strong positive emotional state. You can pick a climbing or nonclimbing event, although a climbing context is ideal if you want the anchor to transfer most powerfully to future climbing situations. Now put yourself back into that experience, taking the time to re-create it as vividly and with as much detail as possible in your mind's eye. *See* what you saw then, *hear* what you heard then, and *feel* the positive emotions of that past moment. Replay the experience in your mind as a mental movie and feel your emotions build to a peak.

Now repeat this exact process but this time, just as the state is about to peak, make a unique gesture with your arm (such as a fist pump), say a word or phrase (for example, *Yes!* or *I feel great!*) that evokes feeling, and visualize a vivid summary snapshot of the event. Dwell on the positive state for a moment, and then release it. Shift your thoughts to something completely different and move your body in a new way.

You have just created an anchor that associates the specific gesture, word, and image with the strong positive emotion of a past experience. Actually, with repetition the anchor becomes a neuro-association (represented by the formation of new synapses) that will grow stronger through repetition. It's essential, then, that you go through the complete anchoring procedure many times over the next week in order to strengthen the anchor.

The anchor you have created is a powerful state-changing tool that you can use anytime to generate a positive emotional state. All you need to do is to fire the anchor—make the gesture, say the word, see the picture—and your brain will re-create the positive emotional state from the past. Within five to ten seconds, you will begin to feel the positive emotions; if needed, fire the trigger again to increase the effect. Use your positive anchor anytime you want to boost your emotional state, whether it's before a big climb or in the wake of some experience that has left you feeling emotionally flat or down. Fire the anchor, feel the positive emotions, and shift into action!

Assume a Grateful Attitude

If you are reading this book, it's a fair assumption that you are in good physical health, live in a modernized country, and have the luxury of engaging in a recreational activity such as climbing. Without a shadow of a doubt, you are therefore better off than the majority of the people on this planet. Given this simple reality check, you (and I) have no good reason to feel depressed or possess chronically sad emotions.

If you are regularly in a bad mood or have a tendency to fall into an emotional funk, I propose that you are thinking yourself into this state by dwelling on (or imagining) a specific bad event or situation. One hallmark of the mind is that it magnifies whatever you focus on—so if you dwell on a bad situation, no matter how finite, it will grow in apparent size and severity. Conversely, if you direct your focus on all the good things in your life (see "Taking a Mental Inventory"), you will magnify good feelings. In fact, if you make it a habit to count your blessings each day, you will completely transform your emotional landscape and become a happier, more productive person.

 ### Taking a Mental Inventory

Engage in this simple thought exercise anytime you notice that you've slipped into a negative emotional state. Better yet, you can proactively create a tendency for inherent positiveness by taking this quick mental inventory upon waking every morning and at night before bed. Here's what to do.

Mentally review all the people, situations, and experiences that you are fortunate to have in your favor. Resist the tendency to simply list material possessions; consider the priceless blessings of family and friendships, wonderful life experiences, your health, and freedom. Also strive to identify the many smaller assets that you might not recognize or appreciate on a daily basis. No doubt you can come up with a significant list that's at least ten or twenty items in length. Given this data, I trust that you will agree that feeling sorry for yourself is unwarranted. Make it a daily habit to acknowledge all your assets, and you will foster consistently positive emotions.

If you'd like to take this exercise another step, spend a few minutes each night writing down everything of value that you learned or experienced that day. Recording this information into a notebook or journal not only updates your inventory of assets, but also helps store the new distinctions, valuable facts and techniques, and memories of the day in your long-term memory.

Tips for Controlling Your Emotions

- **Foster positive emotions that will fuel habitual action.** Strive for acute awareness of your emotional state, and create positive emotional states that favor a bias for action.

- **Create and leverage anchors to positive states.** Use the exercise on page 119 to create anchors that you can recall on demand to create a positive state, anytime and anywhere.

- **Avoid or break negative anchors.** Identify people and situations that trigger negative emotions; alternatively, break the negative anchor by intentionally triggering a powerful positive anchor just as you experience the negative anchor.

- **Direct grateful ways of thinking.** Focus on your blessings, rather than your apparent limitations or shortcomings. Focus on your achievements, good health, and future goals, instead of dwelling on failures and criticisms. Learn to think yourself into a positive emotional state!

- **Take a mental inventory each day.** Spend a few minutes each night reliving your recent achievements, novel experiences, lessons learned, and inspiration gained. Record this information in a notebook or journal in order to enhance learning, as well as to document the precious days of your life.

CHAPTER SEVEN

Goal Setting

E very great invention, amazing ascent, and extraordinary achievement begins as pure thought energy in the human brain, with the mental act of setting a goal. Then, through focused human action, this nonmaterial goal is transmuted into a material object or physical accomplishment. This amazing process of turning creative thought into action and outcome is a human endowment, and hence we are by our very nature goal-seeking and goal-achieving beings.

Nineteenth-century author and naturalist Henry David Thoreau wrote that "If one advances confidently in the direction of his dreams, and endeavors to lead the life which he has imagined, he will meet with success unexpected in common hours." This quote intimates the seemingly miraculous power of goal setting and how, by investing the days of our life pursuing the goals we hold in mind, success will be revealed in its own due time. Furthermore, I believe the success to which Thoreau alludes is not simply worldly success and recognition, but perhaps more so the internal reward of living a life of meaning and experiencing happiness and contentment in the process.

You will accomplish in proportion to your ability to set compelling goals and overcome adversity.

In setting and pursuing great goals, however, you will surely experience some adversity along the way. Pursuing goals and encountering adversity go hand in hand—in fact, they are the opposite sides of the same coin, so you cannot reach great goals without facing some adversity. Sadly, our society has grown to celebrate instant gratification over hard work and perseverance, such that possessing the character to face and overcome adversity is increasingly rare. The moment that adversity hits is, thus, defining—the mediocre masses will cower and quickly backpedal, whereas peak performers persevere by developing new strategies and marshaling their forces to transcend the adversity.

Ultimately, you will discover that the adversities you encounter in climbing (and elsewhere) are transformational. With every hard climb attempted—success or failure—you return to the ground a different person than before. Not only does adversity force you to grow technically, but it strengthens the mind, body, and spirit. It should be no surprise, then, that the great climbers who went on to break barriers

Steph Davis on the first female free ascent of the thirty-five pitch **Salathe Wall (VI, 5.13b), on El Capitan, Yosemite, California.** JIMMY CHIN

or in some way revolutionize the sport—Reinhold Messner, Mark Twight, John Bachar, Todd Skinner, Lynn Hill, and Tommy Caldwell, to name a few—did so by setting grandiose goals and overcoming adversity in their pursuits.

You, too, can break personal barriers and achieve great things by becoming an effective goal setter and goal pursuer. You must also learn to persist in times of adversity knowing that you will be rewarded greatly, both in terms of increased mental and physical fortitude, as well as in taking another step toward the realization of your dreams. On the pages that follow, you will learn powerful techniques for setting goals; then in the next chapter you'll discover several indispensable strategies for overcoming adversity on the way to your dreams. Let's begin this exciting journey with an in-depth study of effective goal setting.

Overview of Goal Setting

I will begin this section with a precept that I believe to be absolutely true: You accomplish in proportion to your ability to set compelling goals. The validity of this principle is evident by the magical force that develops upon setting a goal with emotion and resolve. For that reason, the simple act of setting a compelling goal represents a giant step toward achieving it, and it creates a magnetic attraction that makes it feel like "what you want, wants you."

Sadly, many people live out a myopic life directed by the need for instant gratification. They set only short-term goals that will meet their immediate needs, and they ultimately follow a path of least resistance that translates into little personal growth and mediocrity in most endeavors. Their days lead to weeks lead to years squandered on low-value activities such as watching TV, socializing, surfing the Internet. Ironically, people suffering from this affliction often complain about their lack of progress (in climbing, career, or elsewhere) and how genetics or "the system" is against them. We, of course, know better—what we become is mostly a result of our thoughts and our willpower to do, endure, and achieve.

By stepping onto the goal-setting train, you immediately embark on an exciting journey and new life trajectory. The ride begins with learning how to shape your goals according to your personal values. You will then learn about the differences between outcome, performance, and process goals, and how each type of goal yields a unique motivation to act. Next you will learn the four time frames and six steps to effective goal setting, and you will be taken through several powerful goal-setting exercises that will help define the route toward your goals. The section concludes by stressing the importance of commitment and discipline in accelerating progress, boosting achievement, and increasing the chances that you will someday reach your mega goals.

How Goals Provide Direction and Increase Motivation

One of the amazing things about setting a compelling goal is the way it creates an emotional vector in your life. The vector is defined by both the magnitude of the emotion it elicits and the direction it moves you. Big goals possess great emotional magnitude that will propel you through setbacks and adversity, whereas smaller goals yield much less emotional energy that will last but a short time and perhaps collapse in the face of adversity. It is therefore fundamental that you set your big (mega) goals before setting smaller goals, in order to create the greatest emotional leverage to act in both the short and long term.

Before setting a mega goal that will define your actions in the months and years to come, you must first calibrate your compass to True North by gaining awareness of your values. Developing a hierarchy of personal values, as you have done on page 96, empowers you to set mega goals that match your top-tier values. I can't emphasize enough the importance of aligning your goals with your top values—you will only feel truly happy and maximize your life experience by investing your time and energy into goals that point toward your top-tier values.

In addition to providing direction, goals also create the emotional energy that we call motivation. Don't confuse motivation with physical arousal—loud music and caffeine can produce physical arousal, but they don't motivate. Motivation is based on a reason for acting in a certain way. For example, you are motivated to train in the

With every hard climb attempted—success or failure—you return to the ground a different person than before. Not only does adversity force you to grow technically, but it strengthens the mind, body, and spirit.

gym because you want to increase strength and endurance; you are reading this book because you want to learn how to train your brain for better performance; and you go climbing outside because you want to escape the confines of the flatlands and experience the novel pleasure and exhilaration of moving over stone.

There are actually myriad reasons why we do the things we do. Motivation can come from many places, and some sources generate a more powerful emotional vector than others. Let's examine two general types of motivation: extrinsic and intrinsic.

- **Extrinsic motivation** is based on the desire for external rewards, such as gaining the approval of others, earning money, winning prizes, or obtaining reinforcement for a certain behavior. Coercion and quid pro quo also yield extrinsic motivation, as do many image- and ego-building ventures. Extrinsic motivation, then, plays to the flow of determinism, in which external forces exert control over your life. Although we are all extrinsically motivated to some extent, extrinsic motivation tends to be most controlling among people with a poor self-image or low self-confidence, as well as with professionals who feel they have an image to maintain at all costs, and individuals who lack more compelling internal goals to focus on.

- **Intrinsic motivation** is based on an inner desire to do something for the pleasure or benefit it brings to self. Intrinsic motivation emanates from the personal desire to gain knowledge and pursue mastery in something, experience the pleasure of accomplishment, feel the kinesthetic sensations of athletic performance, taste the true wonder of the world, and experience inner happiness and fulfillment.

Intrinsic motivation is most prevalent among confident, curious, adventurous, and nonconforming individuals, who almost always possess a strong bias for engaging their mind and body in unique ways and without obvious external incentives. The indomitable intrinsic motivation of peak performers relates to the pursuit of clear, compelling mega goals that are perfectly aligned with what they value most.

Since climbing is a recreational activity and not a competitive sport for most, motivation to recreate in the steep begins, and for many stays, intrinsic. We all get into climbing because of the novel challenges and pleasures it provides us, and as a beginning climber the goal is simple: to climb! Our incentive to go climbing is equally basic: to learn moves and develop skills, to stretch our mental and physical abilities, and to taste fear and the attendant exhilaration, but still return to the ground healthy and alive. These intrinsic motivations are pure and long lasting, and they will keep you climbing for many years to come as long as you continually expose yourself to new climbing situations and locations.

With increasing expertise and a growing peer status of being a "good climber," however, motivation can gradually become more extrinsically oriented. For example, the feeling that you need to succeed on a route when others are watching is a form of external motivation, as is the desire to outperform another climber or to win in a climbing competition. An extreme example of extrinsic motivation is the professional climber who feels that he must ascend some radical route to satisfy his sponsors or, worse yet, engages in a dangerous form of climbing in order to be featured in some magazine or DVD. While some extrinsic motivation comes with the territory of being a sponsored or professional climber, it's vitally important to remain connected to—and primarily directed by—your intrinsic motivation. To become completely controlled by extrinsic motivation is to lose your soul, prostitute your passion, and perhaps lose your life, since some of the most dangerous acts and poor decisions in climbing are compelled by external pressure to take a risk, despite a strong intuitive sense not to.

The bottom line: Strive to remain intrinsically motivated, and you will experience great joy and accomplishment, and dodge the pitfalls, pressure, and angst that come with extrinsic motivation. Go to the mountains to recreate because there's no place you'd rather be, climb simply because you love to climb, risk because it's in your soul to do so, and bask in the glory of your efforts (successful or not), and you will be a happy climber for life.

Three Types of Goals

There are three types of goals that you should consider setting in your pursuit of maximum climbing. Let's examine the benefits of process, performance, and outcome goals.

- **Process goals** relate to improvements you'd like to make in your climbing technique, tactics, and mental skills. Setting specific process goals, such as to improve your footwork, increase your economy of movement, and grow your awareness of proprioceptive cues, will put you on the fast track to becoming a better climber. No matter your absolute climbing ability, you can always set process goals in your quest of mastery. While novice climbers will likely have a clear sense of the gross technical errors they need to address, elite climbers need to foster acute self-awareness to uncover the subtle defects that constrain their performance. Either way, by reviewing your process goals at the beginning of each training or practice session, you become empowered to take the actions necessary to elevate your game.

- **Performance goals** are powerful motivators because they provide crisp, objective benchmarks to pursue. Creating a ticklist of climbs to do is the most popular form of performance goal setting. Also common is the goal of a specific climbing grade to achieve; for example to climb 5.10a, boulder V8, redpoint 5.13, and the like. Similarly, you can set training goals that will boost motivation to achieve the physiological changes you desire. For instance, you might set a goal to do twenty pull-ups or to lose five pounds. Training goals are most effective if they are concrete and measurable, as opposed to a less specific goal such as to get stronger. The beauty of performance goals is that you can set a series of progressive benchmarks to achieve that will serve as waypoints on your way to a major long-term (mega) goal. Over many weeks and months, you will experience tangible progress and an ongoing sense of success that will help sustain long-term motivation and discipline.

> **Go to the mountains because there's no place you'd rather be, climb simply because you love to climb, risk because it's in your soul to do so, and you will be a happy climber for life.**

- **Outcome goals** focus on competitive results, awards, and gaining acknowledgment for achievement. Examples of outcome goals include placing in a competition, winning the World Cup, gaining sponsorship, or getting featured in a magazine. While outcome goals can be very motivating, achievement usually depends on the performance or judgments of others. So whereas process and performance goals are flexible and completely within your control, reaching outcome goals is often beyond your control.

In conclusion, setting process and performance goals is fundamental to creating motivation and guiding your path toward long-term goals. Setting outcome goals is less important unless you plan to pursue competition or professional climbing.

Regardless of the type of goals you set, it's critical that you only ponder your goals to help motivate and guide your training, and never during moments of action. Any thought of your goals as you are climbing or competing will divert your focus from the process of climbing and, most likely, incite anxiety and performance-killing pressure. This is one of the most important distinctions in this entire chapter: Goal-focused thinking is a powerful ally in motivating your training for climbing, yet such goal-focused thoughts are your enemies during the act of climbing.

Four Time Frames for Goal Setting

In the upcoming goal-setting exercises, you will learn to set goals in four time frames. Let's take a look at each.

- **Mega goals** are extremely long-term goals that align with top-tier activities in your hierarchy of values. View mega goals as a dream achievement or ultimate outcome to work toward over the next five to fifteen years. The mega goal should be extremely specific and have an approximate date of completion, even though you have scant idea of how to achieve it. Only establish a mega goal in the few activities you most value—having too many mega goals or having conflicting mega goals is tantamount to ensuring that none will ever be accomplished. An example of conflicting mega goals is wanting to become a professional climber or, say, climb the seven summits, while at the same time setting the mega goal to earn a PhD or start a family. Clearly the time and commitment needed to achieve the above climbing goals conflicts with that needed to reach a lofty educational or family mega goal.

  My favorite example of setting a mega goal (and one of my all-time favorite quotes) is when, in 1962, President John F. Kennedy stated in a speech, "We choose to go to the Moon in this decade and do the other things, not because they are easy, but because they are hard, and because that goal will serve to organize and measure the best of our energies and skills." The idea of putting a man on the moon, when we had only one year earlier first put a man in space, may be the most audacious goal of all time. NASA had little idea of how they would send a man to the moon and bring him back to Earth safely, yet given this mega goal and total commitment, it was achieved in less than seven years. The take-home message here: Don't limit your mega goals to things that you can plan a precise course for today—a true mega goal is something you can imagine, but not yet know how to achieve.

- **Long-term or annual goals** are major benchmarks to achieve on the path to your mega goals. For example, you might set a long-term goal to achieve a specific grade of climbing by year's end or to ascend a certain major climb or mountain next year. Either way, it's important that the goal represents a significant step toward the attainment of your mega goal.

  It is possible, however, that you may sometimes set a long-term or annual goal not as a means to an end, but as the end itself. There may be times in your life, particularly in transition periods when starting a new job, beginning school, or entering a new relationship, that you don't have a clear mega goal to work toward. Still, you can sustain a sense of growth and progress in climbing by setting a compelling annual goal to pursue.

- **Medium-term or monthly goals** are specific training targets or to-do climbs that represent a distinct step toward your longer-term annual goals. Your medium-term goals may include what you hope to achieve on a particular climbing trip, such as completing a major climb, sending a project, or breaking into a new grade. Such medium-term goals provide a target to which you can align your day-to-day training; they also enhance emotional energy to take the actions and make the sacrifices necessary to remain en route toward your long-term and mega goals.

- **Short-term goals** aren't much more than a specific to-do list for the day and week ahead. The scope of your short-term goals can be very broad, including training goals, climbing plans, your intentions with regard to nutrition and recovery, and how other major life events and commitments will fit into the day and week before you. Setting of short-term goals—essentially weekly planning—is best done in a training notebook, calendar, or smartphone.

The ability to set and follow a detailed short-term plan of action is a hallmark of all peak performers. As they say, however, "Life can get in the way," as outside forces, myriad distractions, and unexpected urgencies vie for your attention and energy. Thus, it's very easy to get deflected and lose your efficacy in the moment—and as a result your medium-term, long-term, and mega goals can collapse like a house of cards. Perhaps the number one reason people fail to reach their long-term or mega goals is the failure to set short-term goals or the inability to exercise self-discipline in following through with the plan. Peak performers, on the other hand, can block out most distractions, with the mental armor of their intentions, and forge ahead with utmost effectiveness day after day. Strive to develop this master skill and your effectiveness will soar.

> **The number one reason people fail to reach their long-term or mega goals is the failure to set short-term goals or the inability to exercise self-discipline in following through with the plan.**

Strategies for Effective Goal Setting

Effective goal setting is a process comprising specific steps—it is not simply a statement of vague *I wish to* or *I hope to* statements. Research has shown that setting moderate to difficult goals will enhance performance and motivation more than setting easy goals or none at all. Studies have also revealed that it's most effective to set both short- and long-term goals, obtain feedback on progress along the way, and have a source of accountability or a means to objectively verify whether a goal has been meet.

Detailed below is a six-step goal-setting process that incorporates the findings of many research studies. Following these steps is especially important in establishing your long-term and mega goals; however going through the entire six-step process is often unnecessary in setting the more immediate short- and medium-term goals.

1. **Write down your goals.** A goal not written down is but a dream, so it's imperative that you record your goals in a dairy or training notebook. If you don't already, begin keeping a training notebook or climbing journal in which you can record your goals, workout plan, and climbing accomplishments. This documentation is both a great motivator and a keepsake record of your life's many adventures in the steep.

2. **Define your goals specifically and with as much detail as possible.** Make sure that the goals align with your top-tier values from the hierarchy created on page 96.

3. **Make your goals lofty and challenging, but keep them within the realm of being realistic.** For example, wanting to climb *The Nose* of El Capitan in a day, boulder V12, or summit an 8,000-meter peak are all realistic mega goals; however, it would not be realistic for a novice climber to set one of these goals for attainment in the next year or two. The best strategy is to set the mega goal, and then to set a series of incremental annual goals that build toward the mega goal.

4. **Set a specific deadline for medium- and long-term goals, but keep the deadline for your mega goals more general (for example, in ten years).** Goals such as achieving ten consecutive pull-ups by year's end or bouldering a V8 by your birthday will light a fire for action—a fire that burns stronger as the deadline nears. Keep setting incremental goals that advance you toward the mega goal.

5. **Enlist a partner to join you on the journey (toward your mega goal) or recruit a friend or coach to maintain accountability.** Either strategy will add energy to your pursuit of the long-term and mega goals, and make it easy to make the necessary sacrifices in the short term.

Set Mega Goals

Okay, it's time to have some fun, and perhaps change the trajectory of your climbing and life in the process! Let's set a few mega goals—these are the dream goals that align with the top-tier activities in your hierarchy of values. Setting a few compelling mega goals will create a strong emotional vector that will thrust you into action both today and in the long term. Setting the mega goals helps you see beyond the complexities and urgencies of the present. Emancipate yourself from the chaos, cultural influence, and peer overwhelm, and begin a new path to experiencing your own unique and wondrous journey.

Unbridle your imagination and set a mega goal for each of the top two to four activities in the hierarchy of values you established on page 96. These should be major goals that will require at least three to ten years, perhaps longer, to be accomplished. Note that you may not have a specific mega goal for one or more of your top-tier values—you may simply have the general goal of continuing to enjoy growing and achieving in this important life aspect.

Top-Tier Values (from page 96)	Your Mega Goal (if any)
_____	_____
_____	_____
_____	_____
_____	_____

6. **Write down at least one thing that you will sacrifice in order to reach this goal.** This last step is vital and, interestingly, it's a step missing from most traditional goal-setting exercises. Considering what activities, possessions, or stale relationships you are willing to give up in your quest of a major goal is a revealing exercise that might shed new light on what things you truly value. This practice will also open your eyes to the reality that achievement doesn't just come by way of doing more of something or trying harder; it also requires that you eliminate and detach from things that might hold you back. Eighteenth-century British author James Allen aptly summarizes this sixth step by saying, "He who would accomplish little must sacrifice little; he who would achieve much must sacrifice much; he who would attain highly must sacrifice greatly."

Gap Analysis and Developing Strategy

Now that you've set a couple of mega goals, you need to perform a cursory gap analysis of the skills and experience you need to acquire to bridge the gap or, more likely, chasm that lies between you and the goal. Clearly, you won't be able to identify all the things that you will need to do in the coming years in order to reach the goal, but you can make a "guesstimate" of the major steps along the way. Your strategy for achieving the mega goal certainly will need to be modified along the way, but this initial brainstorming strategy session is an exciting and essential starting point to the process.

Since achieving your mega goal is likely several years (or more) away, it's helpful to set a series of annual goals that will advance you progressively closer to your terminal goal. Try to set annual goals that are exciting and compelling as stand-alone long-term goals—this way you will create anticipation for achieving a significant goal in the upcoming year, in addition to enhancing the lure of your more distant mega goal.

As an example, consider the mega goal of wanting to someday climb *The Nose* of El Capitan in a single day (this extremely difficult adventure, often called Nose in a Day or NIAD, has become a popular goal among some traditional climbers). Supposing you are an accomplished crag climber with several years of lead climbing experience, what would your gap analysis reveal as the major skills and steps necessary to make the NIAD a reality?

Given that *The Nose* route on El Cap is a 3,000-foot, thirty-four-pitch route that normally takes three or four days to ascend, you'd need to become extremely proficient at speed climbing to complete the climb in less than twenty-four hours. Not only would you need to become a competent 5.10 crack climber, but you'd also need to be able to ascend many relatively easy aid climbing pitches in short order. Furthermore, you must find a climbing partner with similar capabilities, and then you'd need to practice speed climbing as a team to develop the rope management and climbing tactics needed to race through a large amount of climbing with little downtime. Finally, you'd need to develop a tremendous reserve of physical endurance, by way of consistent training and a regular schedule of climbing twelve-hour-plus days.

Figure 7.1 Nose-in-a-Day Goal Gradient

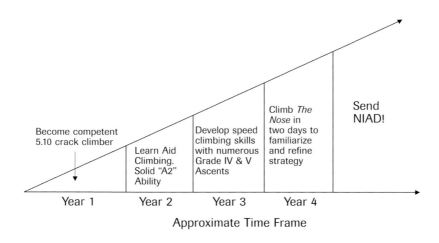

Become competent
5.10 crack climber

Learn Aid
Climbing.
Solid "A2"
Ability

Develop speed
climbing skills
with numerous
Grade IV & V
Ascents

Climb *The Nose* in
two days to
familiarize
and refine
strategy

Send
NIAD!

Year 1   Year 2   Year 3   Year 4

Approximate Time Frame

Once you have identified the most obvious steps for reaching the mega goal (in this case, NIAD), you would arrange the steps in a logical order and create an approximate time line for completion of each step. In this way you are creating a series of seasonal or annual goals that form a stair-step goal gradient toward becoming a climber capable of the difficult NIAD task. Figure 7.1 reveals a progression of long-term goals that might transform a committed climber to being NIAD-capable in somewhere between three to seven years. (If you, by chance, have an interest in pursuing the NIAD as a mega goal, you should read the FalconGuide *Speed Climbing* by NIAD specialist Hans Florine.)

Now you need to create a similar goal gradient that rises toward your climbing mega goal. Since you have likely set mega goals in a couple of different activities (in the exercise above), it's best to have a separate brainstorming session for each. Begin each session with a blank sheet of paper and write down all the major steps in the process of pursuing your mega goal that you can imagine at this time. Consider both the skills that you will need to develop as well as the major benchmark, or annual, goals that you must reach along the way toward your multiyear goal. Arrange each step in a logical order and create an approximate time line for reaching each benchmark goal. Ultimately, you will have created a dated ticklist of steps for reaching each mega goal in your top-value activities. One thing you will need to ponder, however, is how your different mega goals might conflict with one another—you have a finite amount of time and energy available, so you may need to subordinate one mega goal in order to reach another.

Once you have performed a gap analysis and defined an approximate sequence of steps toward your mega goal, you need to establish specific long-term goals (one for each mega goal) to achieve in the upcoming year. Now develop a specific strategy for achieving each of these goals in the upcoming year. It will be advantageous to plot out a month-to-month game plan on a calendar—try to set a specific goal and benchmark achievement for each month. From this prospective schedule you can develop a targeted daily and weekly plan for meeting your monthly goals.

Developing a Short-Term Strategy for Maximum Efficacy

This is where the rubber meets the road—or perhaps more aptly where the shoe rubber meets the rock! The quality of your actions hour-to-hour and day-by-day is the single biggest factor in determining whether or not you will attain your annual goals and mega goals. Each day you make countless, seemingly minor decisions on what to do and how to think at any given moment. A few examples of these minor decisions include: *What should I think about upon waking in the morning? What should*

Tips for Effective Short-Term Planning and Decision Making

- **Spend half an hour each week planning in detail your strategy for the week ahead.** Begin by firmly scheduling all tasks relating to your top-value activities (training, climbing, school studies, career and family activities, and the like), so that you never subordinate an important task to a low-value activity.

- **Set specific process and performance goals for each climbing session.** Set process goals such as to improve footwork, refine movement, or practice visualization skills, and a performance goal or two involving a specific climb to send or a grade to achieve.

- **Take charge of the "moment of decision" by being proactive, rather than reactive, in your decision making.** In making each decision, ask yourself: *Will taking this action, or doing this activity, in some way advance me toward my goals?*

- **Constantly evaluate the effectiveness of your short-term actions.** Are you following through with your weekly plan? Are you achieving your medium-term benchmarks or have you veered off course? Is there a conflicting activity preventing you from taking the necessary actions? Do you need to modify your approach or even develop a new strategy?

- **Become a compulsive time manager—make the most of your waking hours.** Try to take meaningful goal-oriented actions every day, and avoid the excessive "social loafing" of the masses.

I eat for breakfast, lunch, and dinner? What should I do after work or school? Should I work out and climb today and, if so, what should I train? Should I turn on the TV or surf the Net when I get home in the evening or should I spend time planning or working toward one of my goals? What time should I go to bed, and should I engage in some mental training before falling asleep?

Really, every day of your life consists of constant decision making, and thus it's the aggregate of the decisions you make that ultimately makes you! Maximizing daily efficacy, and moving measurably toward your goals, therefore demands a high awareness of decision-making moments and the willpower to slow down the process of choice. By consciously pondering each decision—versus making an quick reactive decision, the way many people do—you are empowered to make the best choice based on your values and goals. Apply this decision-making strategy consistently, and I guarantee you'll improve more and advance farther (in all endeavors) in one year than most people do in three to five years. The proof is visible in the peak performers of the world who, by making the most of each day, do great things in sport, business, social work, and other worthy endeavors.

Every day of your life consists of constant decision making, and thus it's the aggregate of the decisions you make that ultimately makes you!

Short-term effectiveness also demands that you have a solid strategy for action, so weekly planning is an essential part of the process. Dedicate half an hour each Sunday evening (or some other fixed time each week) to plan out the week ahead on a calendar or electronic schedule of some kind. First, fill in must-do obligations such as your time at work or school, family commitments, and such. Next, consider your list of high-value activities and the related mega goals—block in as much quality time as possible for focused action in these areas, including your climbing and training time. After doing this, there's a good chance that your schedule for the week will be nearly filled; use any remaining time to engage in medium-value areas.

Given a well-thought-out, detailed weekly schedule, you are now in the position to act with uncommonly high effectiveness. Still, it takes commitment and discipline to resist distractions and stopping thoughts, and to follow through with the plan. Taking small steps—and an occasional giant leap—toward your goals comes when effective goal setting meets disciplined action. And to this end, you'll learn in the next section how to leverage the unseen power of self-discipline in maximizing your progress and performance.

Self-Discipline and Commitment: The Great Equalizers

It takes great discipline to boulder V12, climb 5.14, summit a daunting mountain peak, and do other great things. In fact, regardless of the grade you aspire to climb, it will take great discipline to reach your mega goals and maximize experience. So what exactly is self-discipline and how can you develop greater self-discipline?

Self-discipline is the ability to steadily act with conscious control, in directing or changing behavior, divesting from things of lesser value, and delaying gratification, in the pursuit of a higher purpose or goal. In climbing, it takes self-discipline to train optimally (not overtraining or undertraining), to consume a healthy diet, and to maintain a calm, controlled demeanor while in the midst of a stressful climb. Perhaps most central to self-discipline is abstaining from things (foods, activities, and other extravagant pleasures) that will diminish personal effectiveness and squander time and energy. In all of the above examples, exercising self-discipline requires the assertion of willpower.

Think of self-discipline as a lever that multiplies your current technical and physical capabilities—and in developing greater self-discipline, you lengthen the lever!

As detailed in chapter 1, willpower is a human endowment that can be highly developed through regular use. So by willing yourself to assert a little more self-discipline each day—by saying no to things that conflict with your goals, and by taking the necessary actions to advance toward those goals—you will not only grow greater self-discipline, but also increase forward momentum, develop more self-confidence, and feel the unique pleasure of total commitment to a goal.

One of the beauties of self-discipline is that it's a powerful compensatory tool. Think of it as a lever that multiplies your current technical and physical capabilities—and in developing greater self-discipline, you lengthen the lever! Fascinating research at the University of Pennsylvania has shown that self-discipline is a better predictor of academic success than IQ. And while they did not study athletic pursuits, I feel that self-discipline is a similarly strong predictor of athletic success. Thus, although ideal genetics don't guarantee that you will achieve climbing greatness, lack of self-discipline does guarantee mediocrity. The bottom line: Developing uncommon self-discipline can make up for what you are lacking in resources, experience, or genetic talent. Self-discipline, then, is the great equalizer!

Possessing Healthy Commitment

I will wrap up this extended study of goal setting and goal pursuit with a discussion of what I feel is a healthy level of commitment to goal attainment. Given the enthusiastic and highly focused approach described on the preceding pages, you might be thinking that *Eric's kind of intense* or *Eric's instruction is a little over the top.* Yes, I've heard this before, but I take it as a compliment—better to be too focused, too analytical, and too disciplined than to be scatterbrained and lazy. But I digress.

Let me now state clearly that there is such a thing as being overcommitted and going overboard in the pursuit of your goals. While self-discipline, perseverance, and commitment are all necessary to achieve uncommon success and maximum experience, it is healthy and in fact beneficial to occasionally take some time off and break from the ways of strict self-discipline. Taking one day off per week, one weekend off per month, and even a few weeks off per year is essential to refresh your mind, rest your body, and prevent burnout. This is a practice utilized by many of the best climbers, past and present—Wolfgang Güllich, Todd Skinner, Ed Viesturs, Chris Sharma, and many others, take (took) time away from climbing after a long season or upon achieving a major goal. You should, too.

In chapter 12 I'll provide some specific guidelines for taking rest days as well as more extended breaks from climbing. But for now I will define three markedly different levels of commitment, including what I feel is a healthy level of commitment.

- **Low commitment** is exemplified by the dreamer who takes little meaningful action toward a goal, follows a path of low resistance, and rarely challenges himself. In climbing, low commitment is seen in the person who, despite setting goals, trains haphazardly, climbs infrequently, rarely pushes himself to the point of falling, and fails to persevere in times of adversity.

- **Healthy commitment** is evident in the passionate person who has a mega goal, a plan of action for achieving it, and a record of taking daily steps toward the goal while maintaining a sense of balance in her life. A climber with a healthy level of commitment trains and climbs optimally (rather than obsessively), exercises self-discipline in determining use of time and in avoiding distractions (people, places, and situations), sacrifices things that will conflict with her goals, and balances her climbing life with other high-value nonclimbing life activities. Healthy commitment, then, is about having a serious dedication to climbing, but not an obsessive devotion that dismisses all other things in life as unimportant.

- **Unhealthy commitment** is marked by obsessive thought and pursuit of an activity or goal at the expense of all other things, including one's physical and mental well-being. Unhealthy commitment to climbing is exemplified by the person who climbs and trains every day or to the point of chronic injury. It is also evident in those who destroy important relationships or sabotage other important life areas in the name of reaching their goals. While climbers with unhealthy commitment may experience significant success for a period of time, they will ultimately end up injured, depressed, and burned out, and hence they are unlikely to reach their mega goals.

Tips for Effective Goal Setting and Maximum Achievement

- **Set a few multiyear mega goals according to the compass of your value hierarchy.** Write down your mega goals and hang them up somewhere that you'll see often. Create a strong belief in the feasibility of reaching your goals even though you cannot yet determine all the steps for reaching them.

- **Perform a gap analysis and develop an approximate long-term strategy of pursuit.** Set an incremental series of annual or seasonal goals that yield a goal gradient that creates forward momentum. Strive for acute awareness of results, and be proactive in making course corrections and developing new strategies, if needed.

- **Engage in detailed weekly and monthly planning with the goal of high efficacy.** Schedule high-value activities first to avoid being pulled off course by lower-value activities or social loafing. Err on the side of being a compulsive planner and having an indomitable bias for action, rather than succumbing to distractions and acting in an inefficient ad-lib manner.

- **Develop the self-discipline to sacrifice greatly in the name of reaching your goals.** Decide what activities, possessions, or sour relationships you can give up in order to free more mental, emotional, and physical energy. Remind yourself that achieving greatly demands that you sacrifice greatly. Conversely, if you want everything, you will get mediocrity.

- **Foster healthy commitment.** Plan intensively, act decisively, and sustain a narrow goal focus during most of your waking hours. However, do allow yourself some leisure downtime and occasional breaks from pursuing your training and climbing goals. Use these days off or annual breaks from climbing to renew your motivation, smell some nonclimbing roses, and maintain some semblance of balance in your life.

CHAPTER EIGHT

Overcoming Adversity

There are only three real sports: bull-fighting, car racing, and mountain climbing. All the others are mere games," wrote great author Ernest Hemingway. I tend to agree with his sentiment, especially given the uniquely dire consequences one may face by engaging in these activities. Although rock climbing is a more controlled cousin of mountain climbing, the potential for experiencing adversity and the specter of paying the ultimate price are ever-present.

Interestingly, it's the acute challenges and problems to be solved, the potential of facing adversity, and the exhilaration of risk taking that draw us to recreate in the vertical extreme. Many of us come to observe that the challenges of the steep can tell us more about ourselves than any other aspect of our lives—like seeing our breath on a cold day, severe adversity can reveal the normally unseen shape of our character. Some of us also discover that in the most extreme moments, when it seems we

You are defined more by how you react to adversity than you are by the ultimate outcome, be it a success or failure.

are but an onion-skin thickness away from eternity, we plumb the depths of our souls and gain a strong sense of the spiritual dimension. All of these experiences verify that climbing is not a mere game—it's a profound sporting pursuit that, perhaps more than any other life activity, can reveal the stuff of which we are really made.

The annals of rock climbing and mountaineering possess so many classic examples of individuals overcoming great hardship and adversity, it's hard to pick a single event that best exemplifies the conquering of adversity. Since this book is dedicated to Todd Skinner, though, it's fitting that I tell you about Todd's 1995 epic ascent on the east face of Trango Tower, in the Karakorum Himalaya.

First, let me give you a bit of background on Todd and his quest to free climb the 3,000-foot east face of Trango Tower, a technical rock route that tops out at 20,469 feet. In the prior decade Todd leveraged his hard free climbing skills to do breakthrough free ascents of the *Salathe Wall* on El Capitan and the *Direct Northwest Face* on Half Dome. Despite the magnitude of these achievements, climbing 5.12 and 5.13 moves on a Yosemite wall might seem easy compared with climbing similar terrain above 18,000 feet on Trango Tower. Still, Todd conceived and believed in the

John Avrette on **King Cat (5.11d), Indian Creek, Utah.** KEITH LADZINSKI

viability of a Trango Tower free climb, and he wasn't discouraged by the cynicism of some veteran Himalayan climbers who learned of his plans.

By Todd's somewhat naïve estimation, the climb could be completed with a commitment to live and climb above 18,000 feet for between ten to fourteen days. As now chronicled in Todd's must-read book, *Beyond the Summit,* he and his team members (Mike Lilygren, Bobby Model, and Jeff Bechtel) ultimately spent sixty adversity-filled days on Trango Tower! Twenty-three days were lost to storms, including a nine-day blizzard that killed seven climbers on K2, just 20 miles away. Moreover, a base camp attendee drowned in a lake, and the team's tents were blown away by an air blast from an avalanche. And then there were the constant technical challenges that the climbers faced up on the wall, as the team had to solve thirty-four pitches of difficult free climbing, clinging with bare fingers in the rarefied air on a Himalayan big wall. In the end, Todd and his partners found success on the far side of their many adversities, establishing the world's first 5.13a, Grade VII climb.

While your climbing goals are likely less audacious than Todd's were, you will surely face plenty of adversity along the way, including some things you can't even imagine today. Obviously, then, it would be advantageous to learn a variety of strategies for coping with adversity. And while failure is sometimes unavoidable, becoming a competent problem solver and adversity conqueror will yield many great successes and help make your mega goals a reality. To this end, the upcoming pages will equip you with numerous techniques for overcoming adversity and becoming a better problem solver.

Strategies for Coping with Adversity

Before I detail specific strategies for overcoming adversity, I first want to illustrate how there is a utility to the adversity that you experience. For one, persevering in the face of adversity develops a hardness factor—perhaps the origin of the "hardman" label affixed to many of climbing's greatest figures, such as Warren Harding, Royal Robbins, Jim Bridwell, and Henry Barber. Furthermore, times of adversity are sterling opportunities for learning and growth—if you persevere, these novel experiences will forge greater mental toughness, stretch the imagination, and in fact boost motivation and commitment. So while the common man tends to avoid situations that might bring adversity, the hardman seeks grand experiences knowing that there is a strong possibility of encountering adversity and that he can likely overcome and benefit from the challenges before him.

Great climbers of today, individuals like Tommy Caldwell and Chris Sharma, are always looking for new ways to stretch their limits and maximally exert themselves—Caldwell does it high up on granite big walls, while Sharma does it on relentlessly steep limestone cliffs and over the deep water of the Mediterranean. Both Caldwell and Sharma have, thus, benefited from the way the brain recalibrates itself when exposed to new challenges and the adversity that's often attendant. Due to their willingness to progressively challenge themselves and consistently overcome adversity, both climbers have in the past decade transformed from accomplished local climbers into world-famous masters of rock with no peer.

Caldwell, in particular, has encountered almost unimaginable adversity as described in the book *Over the Edge* by Greg Child. While on a big-wall climbing trip in the remote mountains of Kyrgyzstan in 2000, Caldwell and his partners (Beth Rodden, John Dickey, and Jason Smith) were captured by al-Qaeda-linked terrorists. Held hostage for six trying days that included witnessing numerous gun battles with the Kyrgyz army and the horrifying execution of a Kyrgyz soldier held captive with them, the climbers escaped by pushing their terrorist guard off a cliff and finding their way back to a Kyrgyz army base. Great adversity struck again just one year later when Caldwell accidentally cut off his left index finger, above the middle joint, with a table saw.

Such adversity would have had even the most rabid climber pondering retirement, yet Caldwell now recognizes these events as being catalysts for his subsequent gains in ability and soon-to-be cutting-edge ascents. Caldwell states in the book *Vertical World*, "I felt that since we lived through it [capture by terrorists], we needed to make every day count. After Kyrgyzstan, and after cutting off my finger, I was always supermotivated, pushing really hard because I felt like I needed to live life to its fullest. I now think I'm climbing better and stronger because of it." And indeed he did climb better—just eight months after cutting off his finger, Caldwell established the sport climb *Flex Luthor*, considered by some to be North America's first 5.15a. In the years that followed, Caldwell directed his energies onto Yosemite's El Capitan, climbing an almost unfathomable twelve free routes up the 3,000-foot monolith.

The hardman seeks grand experiences knowing that there is a strong possibility of encountering adversity and that he can likely overcome and benefit from the challenges before him.

As exemplified in the above examples, adversity is not necessarily a bad thing; it can in fact make you stronger and more capable, if you strive to persevere rather than retreat. Certainly there will be grim situations when you had better retreat and then resolve to learn what you can from the bad experience. More often than not, however, the adversity you face will be surmountable, and it will be frequently less formidable than you first surmise. As a general coping strategy, for use at the onset of an adverse situation, remind yourself that experiencing difficulties is but a natural part of the route-finding and toughening-up process that will eventually lead to the realization of your goals.

Ultimately you are defined not by adversity and your occasional failures, but instead by the way in which you respond to adversity and failure. Following are five powerful strategies for responding to adversity and overcoming moments of apparent failure.

Exercise Your Mental Agility—Be a Spin Doctor!

The first key strategy is to exercise flexibility of perspective. To overcome a setback, you must get outside the mind-set that brought you to this point. Detach yourself from the situation and visualize it from a perspective outside yourself—look down on top of the problem, or project out into the future and look back at the problem. This new view might reveal that the problem isn't as big or serious as you thought; at the least, you may discover a way past the adversity from the less up-close and more emotionally detached perspective. Avoid having a reactive response to the problem and instead make a game out of trying to transcend the setback via mental agility. Be creative and have fun, and soon you will discover the clues to overcoming the adverse situation.

Here is a powerful technique for quickly regaining a positive, resourceful state anytime you experience a setback or begin to slip into the negative end of the emotional scale. I call it "becoming your own personal spin doctor." I'm sure you've seen spin doctors at work on TV—typically political campaign managers and Hollywood publicists—trying to shine a better light on, or in some way make positive, the verbal or behavioral slip-ups of their clients. In a somewhat similar fashion, you can take the adversity you face and spin it into something positive. By finding a way of turning a negative into a positive, you can often sustain forward momentum on a task, maintain a positive mind-set, and not waste valuable energy fretting about something that can't be changed.

You can use the spin doctor strategy to cope with almost any misfortune, big or small. For example, suppose you arrive at the base of the route you had planned to work on, only to find another climber starting up the route. Rather than getting anxious and succumbing to negative emotions, you can spin the situation a number of positive ways. First, you can remind yourself that you always climb better after a few warm-up routes, so why not go and send a few preparatory climbs and then come back in an hour or two? Another positive spin job is that you might benefit by watching the other climber work the route—perhaps you can even help each other by alternating attempts on the route, thus using a team approach to unlocking the best sequences.

Let's consider another example. Suppose you've got a late start on an alpine climb and then a few hours later you are forced to retreat due to deteriorating weather conditions. Instead of berating yourself about the late start, you could consider how much more dire the situation would be if you were caught on the upper part of the climb in the approaching storm, which would indeed be the case if you had gotten that early start you had planned. Given this spin, you can return to camp with a more positive attitude, and prepare to launch an earlier start the next day.

As an East Coast climber, I realized many years ago that I would have to learn to deal with bad weather in a productive way. In my youth I would frequently go on climbing trips despite bad weather forecasts; when rain then found me on a climb, I would positively spin the situation by telling myself that this adversity was essential preparation for some future climbing situation I would face. Again and again I was able to convince myself that whatever adversity I faced in climbing, no matter how unpleasant, would increase my hardness factor and make me a more capable climber down the road. This approach also helped me remain positive and productive in the moment.

A very memorable example of this, from back in my formative days, was being snowed off New Hampshire's Cannon Cliff one April weekend in 1981. After shaking off the initial disappointment, my partner, Jeff Batzer, and I decided to drive south looking for better weather—and a positive finish to our weekend—at the Shawangunks. The next day I surprised myself in sending, despite cold conditions, a very difficult route named *Foops* (5.11c), thus becoming one of the youngest climbers to succeed on this famous roof climb. So in less than twenty-four hours I managed to turn a disappointing retreat from a big wall into an exciting success on one of the 'Gunks' most celebrated routes!

No doubt, you will face untold adversity in your future; but always know that you can spin most adversities into something positive if you unbridle your imagination and find the way. Strive to become a world-class spin doctor who creates positive emotions and finds strategic advantages in even the most untoward situation—this is always more advantageous than dwelling on your misfortune and making yourself feel worse. Make a game out of spinning your adversities into potential successes and, as legendary alpinist Mark Twight instructs, "Relish the challenge of overcoming difficulties that would crush ordinary men and women!"

One final thought: It's important to recognize that being an effective personal spin doctor is mostly an internal way of thinking and using positive self-talk, and not a method of creating excuses to feed yourself or other people. Embracing the reality of your challenging circumstances—and not making excuses or blindly ignoring the seriousness of your predicament—is vital in order to effectively overcome, and perhaps even survive, a bad situation. The process of spinning a negative event into having some silver lining is simply a technique for preserving a positive emotional state as you encounter and deal with adversity. While not a risk management or self-rescue strategy, maintaining a positive mental state in trying times can make all the difference in the world.

 ## Use Optimism as a Tool

For many people optimism is simply a way of wrestling with their emotions or hiding from the problems of the present moment. For peak performers, however, optimism isn't just a way of thinking—it's a tool, or mental lever, for coping with and overcoming adversity.

In using optimism as a tool, you must first acknowledge the brutal facts of your present situation. Assess all aspects of your current position; this may take just a minute or two in a relatively minor crag climbing predicament, or it could take many hours to sort out a chaotic situation on a mountaineering expedition. Either way, collecting as much data as possible is an essential first step. Next, determine the severity of the situation: Must you begin a retreat or initiate a rescue, or can you regroup and find a way to climb on?

Leveraging optimism then comes into play as you, with the brutal facts held in mind, try to find an argument for or way to proceed onward with the climb. Can you push one pitch higher to test the waters? Can you return to camp and start anew tomorrow? Or, knowing that you've endured so much already, can you endure another day; and if so perhaps you can endure another day after that and another day after that, and eventually reach the top of the wall or mountain? It's this exact process that helped Todd Skinner and his partners prevail through two months of ever-present adversity and ultimately complete their climb on Trango Tower, despite all the hardship that was heaped upon them.

Using optimism as a tool works because of the fact that the biggest obstacles we face are not the cliffs or mountains before us, but instead the beliefs we hold inside of us.

Using optimism as a tool works because of the fact that the biggest obstacles we face are not the cliffs or mountains before us, but instead the beliefs we hold inside of us. Thus, in finding a way to remain optimistic and sustaining a belief that the goal is still attainable, we prime the unlimited powers of our imagination, free will, and human spirit to propel us onward.

 ### *Become a Reverse Paranoid*

Often in climbing we become paranoid with fearful thoughts that undermine our ability to act with focus and resolve. This third strategy for overcoming obstacles turns this tendency on its ear to make us become what I call *reverse paranoid.* Here's how to do it.

No matter what speed bumps or apparent barriers you encounter on the way to your goals, believe that the universe is conspiring toward your success, and that what you want, wants you. In this way, view the obstacle as a signpost directing you toward a better course of action, instead of becoming obsessed with somehow breaking through the obstacle itself. Don't miss the clues for success that are hidden within every adversity—most likely the path forward requires a modified strategy, rather than simply trying to muscle through via your current approach.

Most important to becoming a true reverse paranoid is controlling your emotions (as covered in chapter 6) and using optimism and your imagination as both a shield and weapon. While many people who encounter adversity become drama queens or kings of pain, you must temper your emotions and resist the common tendency to exaggerate your current problem or challenge. Your brain will magnify whatever you focus on—focus on drama and you'll get more drama, whereas if you focus on optimistic, solution-oriented thoughts, like a good reverse paranoid climber, you'll eventually find a way to prevail!

Utilizing this tactic creates what Albert Einstein called "a new level of thinking"— an essential requirement for solving serious problems or making a major breakthrough. A good example of this is Hans Florine's quest to maintain hold of the speed climbing record for *The Nose* of El Capitan. Over the last eighteen years, Florine has set and lost

Table 8.1 *Chronology of Speed Climbing Records for*
The Nose *of El Capitan*

May 1990	—	8:06 Schneider/Florine
May 1992	—	4:22 Croft/Florine
October 2001	—	3:59:35 Potter/O'Neill
October 2001	—	3:57:27 Herson/Florine
November 2001	—	3:24:20 Potter/O'Neill
September 2002	—	2:48:55 Hirayama/Florine
October 8, 2007	—	2:45:45 Alex and Thomas Huber
July 2, 2008	—	2:43:33 Florine/Hirayama
October 7, 2008	—	2:37:05 Florine/Hirayama

the record numerous times as the total time for speed climbing this thirty-four-pitch route has been chipped down from eight hours and six minutes to just two hours and thirty-seven minutes (see table 8.1 for *Nose* speed climbing records).

When Florine first took hold of the record (8:06) in 1990, he surely felt that he was climbing as fast as he possibly could. Yet eighteen years later he's lopped off more than five hours, or 68 percent, from his time. How is this possible? It happened because events conspired to lead Florine to the new record, by way of other climbers improving upon his record, bringing new strategies to the fold, and fostering Florine's imagination and motivation to keep returning to the climb with a new level of thinking. The watershed moments, then, were not so much the days that he established a new record, but the days that other climbers improved upon his records. Instead of accepting defeat, Florine was able to view the faster ascents of other climbers as a "conspiracy" to bring him to climbing *The Nose* even faster. Without this reverse paranoid, can-do attitude, Florine would have never been able to marshal the energy and commitment to keep returning to the scene of the climb.

You, too, can use reverse paranoia to help propel you through adversity. Begin by viewing problems or setbacks as opportunities for growth, precursors to success, and triggers that will escalate your technical skills, your physical abilities, and—most important—your ways of thinking. With this perspective you will come to accept that adversity is part of the organic process of self-development and, in doing so, you will tap into the same power that fuels great climbers such as Hans Florine.

Develop Hanging-On Power

The next strategy for overcoming adversity is to develop what I call hanging-on power. This is a learned tenacity to persevere despite great physical pain and mental stress, whether the challenge is a hardest-ever redpoint, an extremely long and trying day climb, or a multiday push up a big wall or mountain. Hanging-on power has surely played a role in many of climbing's greatest ascents, as well as the breakthroughs of countless "average climbers" who have succeeded in pushing out their boundaries and hanging on to complete a personal-best ascent.

Some famous examples of mental hanging-on power being transformed into material achievements include Sir Edmund Hilary and Tenzing Norgay willing themselves to the first ascent of Mount Everest in 1953; Warren Harding's twelve-day first ascent of *The Nose* of El Capitan in 1958; Tony Yaniro's multiday effort to free climb *Grand Illusion,* the world's first 5.13c, in 1979; Todd Skinner hanging on to his dream to free climb the *Direct Northwest Face* of Half Dome, despite going through half a dozen climbing partners during the two-month process; Lynn Hill's tenacity to do the then unimaginable, a free ascent of *The Nose* of El Capitan, in 1993; Chris Sharma returning again and again to throw himself at an unclimbed route until one day he hung on to complete *Realization,* the world's first 5.15a; and Tommy Caldwell hanging on to complete the world's hardest big-wall climb with his 2004 all-free ascent of *The Dihedral Wall* (5.14a, Grade VI) on El Capitan.

The beauty of hanging-on power is that you have unlimited potential to wield its power. Developing this mental attribute, however, takes many years of progressively exposing yourself to greater challenges that stretch your mental and physical ability to continue or hang on. All of the remarkable climbers named above had a long record of suffering and sacrifice in the process of extending their reach beyond their current grasp. As an aggregate of all their efforts and an extension of their willpower, it was immense hanging-on power, perhaps more than any other mental or physical skill, that brought their dream climbs to fruition.

Don't internalize bad results. Find reasons that you can and should continue onward, and then push forward with determination and optimism as your sword and shield.

In striving to develop your own hanging-on power, you must force yourself to regularly take one more step or do one more move than you have before. While your old habit may have been to extrapolate current difficulties to justify backing off a climb, ending a workout, or whatever, you must learn to will yourself to do another set of pull-ups, climb one more bolt, or jam a few moves higher, despite physical discomfort and stopping thoughts. As detailed in chapter 4, this process of incrementally extending your boundaries recalibrates the brain's central governor and strengthens your willpower. And by challenging yourself in this way week after week, year after year, you'll develop Herculean hanging-on power that will empower you to perform beyond the apparent constraints of genetics, age, or your absolute technical ability.

Legendary Yosemite climber Royal Robbins alludes to the importance of hanging-on power in saying, "One of the things I learned was the importance of tenacity—that hanging on and not saying die until you're really beaten causes you to win a lot of the time. I learned that if you keep trying, even if you think you're not going to make it, then that increases the chance of success enormously. And even if it doesn't increase it enormously, if it makes a marginal difference, that marginal difference is all the difference in the world."

 ### Assume a Philosophical, Forward-Looking Perspective

This final strategy for coping with adversity is to assume a philosophical perspective when faced with an insurmountable hurdle or when caught in the shadow of an epic mountain experience. Not all adversities can be overcome by means of hanging-on power or through exploitation of any other coping strategy covered above. Sometimes the endgame is in, disaster has struck, or the door is closed on achieving your goal.

In both our climbing and nonclimbing lives, there will be times when a situation is beyond our control. For the typical Type A semi-obsessed climber who places high value on achievement, it can be exceedingly difficult to accept that a situation is beyond her control, and harder still to accept a permanent failure or tragic outcome. When faced with such adversity, the only effective coping strategy is to recognize that, while you can't change what's happened on the outside, you are capable of changing on the inside.

Embracing the facts of the adverse situation and coming to peace with the outcome is the first step. The second step is to shift your focus from dwelling on the situation and thinking *If only this hadn't happened* to a grateful, forward-looking perspective of what you still possess and can achieve in the future. Embracing this enlarged future-oriented perspective may take some time, but in doing so the adversity of the past will shrink from your conscious mind, as will the attendant negative emotions.

When Tommy Caldwell cut off his finger with a power saw, he could have slipped into a depressed state of thinking that his climbing career was over. Instead he came to accept the accident and not fight it (he had his doctors remove the portion of his finger that was reattached, since it was of no use in climbing), and he directed his focus and energies onto training harder and smarter than ever before. About his challenges Tommy says, "It's made me tougher . . . and with the kind of climbing we do now, being tough is important." Thus, Tommy reframed the accident into an event that would make him a better, tougher climber!

Much more tragic and life changing was a mountaineering accident that I witnessed up close. In January 1982, my best friend and main climbing partner, Jeff Batzer, was caught with fellow Lancastrian Hugh Herr in a blizzard atop a tall ice climb on New Hampshire's Mount Washington. Blown down the other side of the mountain in a whiteout, the pair was stranded for four days in arctic cold with no supplies of any kind. As they descended into unknown territory on the mountain's back side, Hugh slipped into an icy stream and developed hypothermia and frostbite by the end of the second day. The pair huddled under a large boulder and pine boughs, life sublimating from their bodies, for three subzero (Fahrenheit) nights. Jeff managed to make a final effort on the third day, wading through chest-deep snow in frigid conditions, in the hope of finding help or a trail out of the wilderness, and thus he suffered extreme frostbite on his fingers and legs. (Due to the swelling of his frostbitten feet, Jeff could only get one boot on this third day; he placed one of his mittens over his bare left foot so that he could crawl through the snow looking for a way out.) Miraculously, a sport snowshoer named Cam Bradshaw stumbled upon the lost climbers while out for a backcountry workout. Bradshaw alerted the rescue teams, who were then ending their search on the other side of the mountain, and the two climbers were extricated from the mountain's flank, only hours from death, as the sun set that fourth fateful day.

The endgame of this epic tale is that both Jeff and Hugh suffered life-altering frostbite. Within two years, Hugh—having lost both legs below the knee, but with no damage to his hands—was back into climbing and soon established *Stage Fright,* at the time one of the nation's most serious routes at 5.12d X. My dear friend Jeff was not so lucky in terms of a return to hard climbing, since he had sacrificed his fingers (he lost all five fingers from his right hand) and a leg to frostbite in his heroic effort to find an escape from their snowy, frigid prison cell. Amazingly, it was the tracks Jeff made through the deep snow on the third day, while hunting for a way out, that Cam Bradshaw discovered and then followed back to the climbers' huddle—so without Jeff's heroic efforts the previous day, both he and Hugh would have perished on the mountain.

Still, Jeff found a way deep inside to deal with the tragedy and move forward in his life with great passion. As in the strategy described above, Jeff dealt with the unchangeable facts of the accident with an intensely philosophical and spiritual viewpoint. Just a week after the rescue, he scratched out a short letter to me with his partially frostbitten left hand. He wrote, "When death is only an onion-skin thickness away you worry most if you are ready for God to take you. Then secondarily you think of only the people that are extremely close to you; nothing else matters."

Jeff's near-death epiphany is the ultimate bottom-line conclusion we should all embrace—that despite all of our goals, aspirations, dreams, and desires, it's our closest friends and family members that matter most. Undoubtedly there have been other stranded mountaineers who have come to this realization just moments before perishing. Thankfully we have their lessons to learn from, and we can make a conscious reality check of "things most important" when we begin to take climbing—or our adversities—too seriously.

A brief epilogue to this story: Today Jeff Batzer is a Christian pastor and counselor extraordinaire; Hugh Herr is a college professor and developer of advanced prosthetic limbs.

Tips for Overcoming Adversity

- **Exercise your mental agility and become a spin doctor!** Use your imagination to find a reason why the negative situation could actually be a positive. How might the lesson or learned toughness you gain from a setback help you in the future? Be flexible in your thinking and make a game out of trying to transcend the setback or block. Use mental gymnastics to stay positive and prevail despite the current problems, and you will prevail more often than not.

- **Use optimism as a tool.** Yes, you must accept the brutal facts of a bad situation, but analyze the data and make course corrections. Don't internalize bad results; instead strive to have amnesia to past results and let a sense of optimism overwhelm you. Find reasons that you can and should continue onward, and then push forward with determination and optimism as your sword and shield.

- **Become a reverse paranoid.** No matter the problems you face, believe that the universe is conspiring toward your success, and that what you want, wants you. In this way, view obstacles as signposts that will direct you toward a better course of action. Find Einstein's "new level of thinking" and the solutions and ideal outcome will likely be yours.

- **Develop hanging-on power.** Progressively subject yourself to greater and greater challenges that safely stretch your mental and physical limits. When pushed to your limit, strive to hang on for one more move, one more pitch, or one more day.

- **Assume a philosophical, forward-looking perspective.** This is the most important coping strategy of all, and it will guide you through moments of insurmountable adversity or when the door is closed on your mega goal. Come to peace with the unchangeable facts of the situation, and then shift your focus to a forward-looking and larger life perspective.

- **Take a personal inventory and recognize all that you still have to be grateful for.** With the support of your closest friends and family, plot a new course toward exciting new goals that transcend your previous ambitions.

Problem-Solving Strategies

Inherent to the process of pursuing your goals is a never-ending need to solve problems. As part of your daily endeavors, there will be numerous minor problems or conflicts to resolve. In moments of adversity, however, you will encounter more significant problems to transcend. The effectiveness of your goal pursuit will then depend on your ability to solve small problems on the fly and develop novel strategies to overcome larger hurdles.

It's appropriate, then, that I conclude this chapter on overcoming adversity with five mental strategies for enhancing your problem-solving skills and becoming more effective in your actions.

Focus on Finding Solutions, Not the Problem Itself

The brain naturally magnifies whatever you focus on, so it's absolutely essential that you focus on possible solutions, and not dwell on the problem itself. If you think about your lack of progress toward the intended goal and let a situation overwhelm you, it will poison your mental state and create physical tension. Your burgeoning thoughts of failure will ultimately become a self-fulfilling prophecy.

Conversely, you can best engage in problem solving and expedite the process by remaining calm, centered, and solution-oriented. Begin by using the relaxation and centering strategies detailed in chapter 6 to maintain optimal mental and physical states for creative thinking and action. With a calm focus, an open mind, and only a moderate level of pressure to perform, you can best imagine and test possible solutions. Ultimately, you want to assume a demeanor somewhat similar to that of a child solving a puzzle—awareness of passing time, outside distractions, and self will drop to the background as a single-pointed focus and enjoyment of the problem-solving process takes over. Suddenly possible solutions will begin appear, and the problem will soon be overcome.

 ## *Use Failure as Part of the Problem-Solving Process*

As I alluded to earlier in this chapter, it's essential that you embrace failure as part of the learning and problem-solving process. This is very difficult for most people, however. What's your modus operandi when you fall off a route: Do you get upset and keep trying the same sequence over and over, or do you remain positive and open-minded, and test alternative sequences? Obviously it's the latter approach of embracing and learning from failure that is best for unlocking a solution and passing quickly through a crux section.

It's vital, then, that you develop the character trait of being able to accept and use failure as part of a larger strategy to succeed. Assuming that a climb is safe, go up and try different sequences knowing that it's okay to fall or hang on the rope in testing out possible solutions. Be willing to discard failed solutions—even if it's the so-called correct beta—and move on try something different, with the feedback and lessons of your failed attempts still in mind. Most important, you must never extrapolate your current struggles into the future, nor entertain thoughts of utter failure. Trust that a solution—and success—will be realized given patience and persistence.

Beth Rodden exemplified this ideal in persevering through forty days of adversity and apparent failure in establishing America's hardest trad pitch, *Meltdown* (5.14c), in Yosemite. Beth states that *"Meltdown offered so many opportunities to give up: the impossible-seeming crux, the [waterfall] spray and snowmelt, injuries, and weather. I almost took them, but instead I decided to learn from each."*

Chunk Down the Problem into Manageable Parts

It's natural to feel overwhelmed and to lack confidence when faced with a problem or task so large that you can't imagine yourself overcoming it. Fortunately, you can diminish overwhelm and recapture confidence by chunking down the challenging situation into more manageable parts.

Common climbing examples of chunking down an impossible-looking challenge into possible-looking parts include breaking down a big wall to a series of three- to five-pitch sections, segmenting a sport climb into parts between good rests, and working a hard boulder problem one move at a time. In each case, the goal is to focus on solving one chunk at a time—this makes the climb much less overwhelming to work on, and your success in solving individual chunks will create a success gradient that grows confidence.

When working through the individual chunks, avoid becoming obsessed with any single section. Beating yourself up on, say, the second chunk of a six-chunk route is self-defeating, since even if you eventually solve this chunk, you'll be **Your brain doesn't know what you can or cannot do until you tell it. So never prejudge solutions or your capabilities!** too mentally and physically wasted to put in meaningful work on the other sections. Therefore, it's best to move on to working other chunks upon the onset of frustration or any judgmental self-talk, such as *I can't do this* or *I'll never figure this out*. If allowed to burrow into your subconscious, such judgments will coalesce to form the basis for reality.

Long-term achievement of a formidable goal (where short-term failures are inevitable) demands mental agility as well as the ability to trick yourself into persevering in the face of adversity. Breaking down a climb into a series of more manageable chunks and setting yourself up for several small wins is a most effective strategy.

 ### *Leverage Your Imagination and Intuition*

As you learned in chapter 2, the brain has two hemispheres—the left hemisphere, which generally presides over logical, practical, language, mathematical, and related matters, and the right hemisphere, which dominates in creative, artistic, intuitive, situational, and imaginary matters. The majority of people tend to be left-brained, and in the intense situations common to climbing, it can dominate with obsessively logical and linear ways of thinking. The result is that many climbers find it difficult to be imaginative and intuitive, as they succumb to racing thoughts, tunnel vision, and reactive decision making. I can think of countless times I've fallen on routes because I was thinking in a linear fashion and with blinders on that prevented me from finding a key hold, solving a tricky sequence, or locating a subtle rest position.

You can free your mind and best leverage your endowments of imagination and intuition by fostering a relaxed, centered state. Chapter 6 provided you with a few methods of creating a centered state before a climb and regaining center while on a climb. Your task, then, is to increase your state awareness and to be self-disciplined in modulating your state to support effective problem solving. Individuals with high-strung, Type A behavior must be especially aware of succumbing to the tendency of rushing up a route with narrow vision, a closed mind, and without summoning imaginative and intuitive input. Seeing the big picture and imagining all the possible approaches and sequences on a climb is a skill you must develop through conscious effort. Make it your goal, then, to balance logical, practical thinking with intuitive, creative thought, and you'll come to solve problems quickly and with minimal expenditure of mental and physical resources.

 ### Don't Prejudge—Trust That a Solution Can Be Found

The biggest block to problem solving is judgment. Self-talk like *Others use this sequence, so that must be the best way,* or discounting a novel solution to a problem that flashes into your mind without trying it first, is a form of self-sabotage. It's vital that you not limit yourself this way—your brain doesn't know what you can or cannot do until you tell it. So never prejudge solutions or your capabilities!

The best problem solvers are both creative and uninhibited. They never hesitate to try a novel solution that's entirely different from the known sequence or the apparent solution to the problem. You can foster these skills by ignoring the apparent solution—the one that's not currently working for you—and attempting a few completely different, or even ridiculous, ways around the problem.

On a problematic climb, try a variety of body positions, foot flags, and lunges, and don't ignore less positive holds like Gastons, side pulls, and pinches. Eliminate the seemingly must-use hold, or at least try using it with the opposite hand. Search for unchalked holds that might reveal a new sequence, and keep a constant watch for footholds that are off the main line of the route—a single missed foothold or high step can make the difference between "impossible" and "possible."

In solving non-climbing-move problems, you similarly need to brainstorm less-obvious solutions and consider what other resources you can bring to the task. Ponder what unconventional approaches you might apply to the situation—throw away the normal way of going about things and see if you can invent a completely new method of meeting the challenge or solving the problem. Furthermore, consider what new human resources you can tap—sometimes the fresh perspective and ideas of a coach or partner will give birth to a novel strategy or solution.

Most important, persist and never grow weary—always keep the faith that there is a solution to be found. As Abraham Lincoln famously put it, "Always bear in mind that your own resolution to succeed is more important than any other one thing."

Problem-Solving Tips and Success Strategies

- **Focus on problem solving, not performance.** Strive to remain relaxed, centered, and curious—enjoy the problem-solving process and allow a solution to evolve organically.

- **Be willing to fail (and in safe situations fall) as you ascend the learning curve.** View failed attempts as part of the problem-solving process, and be sure to never internalize or extrapolate failed attempts.

- **Break down big problems or hurdles into manageable parts.** Reduce overwhelm and the fear factor by reducing your problem or project to smaller, workable chunks. Feel your confidence grow as you solve each section.

- **Leverage your imagination and intuition to find novel solutions.** Strive to bring both creative, intuitive (right brain) and analytical, practical (left brain) power to work for you. When all else fails, try something ridiculous—sometimes the winning solution is the very thing you write off as not possible.

- **Trust that a solution will be found with patience and persistence.** Never prejudge the outcome or question your ability. Your own resolution to success is the most important factor in determining whether you will eventually solve the problem.

CHAPTER NINE

Improving Concentration and Focus

Some of the deep pleasure we experience in climbing comes by way of exercising a profound level of control, in a potentially dangerous situation, that is rarely possible in the other often chaotic aspects of our life. The strong attraction—perhaps even addiction—to climbing that many of us develop may then be as much about a quest to feel fully in control as it is a desire for adventure and challenge. In a perfect climbing situation, we find adventure, challenge, and total control coming together to produce a transcending sense of competence and an unparalleled feeling of being fully alive.

Becoming a master climber requires that you first become a master of your mind.

This relationship between being in complete control of a situation and feelings of competence and pleasure allows us to understand a major reason why we sometimes feel the opposite emotions of being frustrated, anxious, and unhappy (in climbing or everyday life). This discontent results from situations that overwhelm our ability to concentrate, induce fear, and make us feel out of control. Mental training to enhance concentration and manage fear, in challenging situations on and off the rock, is therefore essential in order to maximize experience, enjoyment, and absolute performance.

An alternative path-of-least-resistance strategy for gaining this sense of control in our lives is to reduce our exposure to potentially stressful situations that might challenge our ability to exert control over concentration and fear. For example, instead of engaging the world without boundaries, some people favor couch-potato activities such as watching TV and playing video games, since they foster a sense of total concentration and being in control (this explains why watching TV is a pleasurable and potentially addictive activity). I'm sure you would agree, however, that watching TV provides a rather shallow pleasure compared with the rush of going climbing. This is because TV watching offers no opportunity for personal growth, novel physical experience, or realizing our great potential to create and achieve.

Given this perspective, you can see that it would be self-limiting to avoid challenging and potentially fearful situations. Instead you need to pursue novel

Lisa Rands cruising up **Crazy Legs (V9), Rocklands, South Africa.** ANDY MANN experiences that will mentally and physically engage you and provide an opportunity for personal growth and maximum experience. Your goal, then, is to break free of the common tendency to play it safe by avoiding challenges and to embrace select opportunities to stretch your abilities, risk with calculation, and reach for worthy goals, despite the fact you will sometimes feel fearful and lacking control. This is, of course, the essence of recreating in the mountains—you willingly submit yourself to the potential for adversity and you welcome fearful and potentially dangerous situations, because you know that climbing offers a rich experience and sense of aliveness that you can't find on flat land.

In exposing yourself to such challenging situations, you must come armed with the mental skills to maintain concentration and manage fear in the face of difficulty or adversity. To aid your journey, this chapter serves up twelve powerful strategies for improving concentration, while the next chapter will provide fourteen must-know techniques for managing fear. It's a fact that concentration and fear management are two areas that mental training can fortify and elevate. Like physical skills, however, mental skills need to be learned and neuronally grooved with regular practice. It's therefore important that you strive to leverage your concentration and fear management abilities in all aspect of your life. In doing so, you will come to achieve and experience far more than you can currently imagine, both on and off the rocks!

> **In climbing, a focused mind joins you to the rock like a fifth appendage.**

One last comment before digging deep into this most elemental section of *Maximum Climbing*: There is nothing inherently wrong with the coach-potato activities alluded to above, it's just that excessive indulgence will shortchange you of much wonderful life experience. Some distant future day you will draw your last breath, and I guarantee that your final thoughts will not be a wish that you had watched more TV or done more Web surfing. More likely your thoughts will narrow to the joyful times that you engaged in family activities and stretched your boundaries in exploring this world of wonder.

Overview of Concentration

In climbing, a focused mind joins you to the rock like a fifth appendage, whereas an unfocused mind weighs you down like a heavy pack. Your pursuit of maximum climbing, then, demands that you develop the ability to create and maintain a focused mental state, despite whatever distractions or adversity you face.

Legendary extreme alpinist Mark Twight describes how such a highly focused state affected his climbing. "On certain routes," he says, "I achieved a mind/no mind state of mystical connection to the mountain so powerful I knew I could not fall or make mistakes. I could read my partner's mind. I was not affected by gravity. I lost myself on those days. I became the mountain."

No matter whether your preference is bouldering, cragging, or alpine climbing like Twight, training to improve your concentrative abilities will gradually lead you to experience a similarly distinct and advantageous mental state.

The opposite of concentration is distraction, and this explains why many climbers have a tough time sustaining concentration. There are myriad of possible distractions, both external and internal, that can sever your concentrative link to the moment as you climb. Looking at activity on the ground or checking your belayer, wrestling with your fears, or pondering the outcome of the climb will all break concentration and degrade performance. Learning to block out distractions is therefore central to improving your concentration.

In its essence, concentration is about being fully engaged and mentally in the moment. In the sections that follow, you will learn more about how mental focus works and what concentration killers you need to avoid. You will then learn four mental training exercises for strengthening your concentration, as well as numerous focusing techniques to employ as you climb.

Four Aspects of Concentration

Concentration is defined as the ability to direct focus and maintain attention on an object, sensation, or thought. There are four aspects of concentration that a climber needs to develop: task-relevant focus, situational awareness, targeting and zooming of focus, and endurance of focus.

- **Focus on task-relevant cues.** This is the ability to selectively target attention on relevant information, sensory stimuli, and environment cues in executing a task. A few examples of task-relevant concentration in climbing include focusing on critical holds, a planned sequence, and proprioception, while not allowing focus to stray to nonrelevant cues such as activity on the ground, environmental noise, and the like. Task-relevant focus is best trained through targeted skill-training drills and repeated practice or rehearsal of serial skill execution, as in working a boulder problem or route for redpoint.

- **Situational awareness.** This wide-angle focus enables you to size up the large-scale situation and, if necessary, react to outside forces that will affect your performance. Some of the outside factors you need to be aware of in climbing are changing weather conditions, other climbers you might encounter en route, time constraints (daylight remaining), and the attentiveness of your belayer. Novice climbers tend to have good situational awareness (although interpretation of the information may be poor due to lack of experience) and a corresponding lack of task-relevant focus. The goal, then, is to improve both aspects of focus, along with the capability to switch and zoom focus at will (per next item).

- **Targeting and zooming focus.** Perhaps the most important aspect of concentration is being able to acutely switch the target of focus as needed to optimize skill execution, sequence and route planning, and risk management. Never do you want to be so focused on a specific task that you fail to recognize critical environment cues that affect your strategy or safety. Consequently, you want to develop the ability to zoom from wide-angle focus, when searching for holds and determining strategy, to a single-pointed focus when executing a hard move. Your concentration must also be flexible in attending to both external and internal cues; in particular, you must be able to focus attention inward to recognize proprioceptive cues in executing a dicey move and to assess and mitigate physical tension and fatigue. Such targeting of focus is a master skill that is developed by consciously flexing your focus during practice sessions and when rehearsing a difficult climb. Table 9.1 reveals the four types of attentional focus that you must learn to switch among with ease and utmost awareness.

- **Endurance of focus.** Finally, there's the hardman capacity to maintain unbroken concentration during a long, hard sequence or in repeated bouts of severe climbing over an arduous day on a big wall or mountain. Examples of this include holding a tight focus for the duration of a maximal ten-move boulder problem, sustaining near-constant focus for a fifteen-minute redpoint or one-hour on-sight ascent, and being able to summon intense concentration pitch after pitch on a major wall climb. Mental endurance is often tested late in the day when fatigue and environmental conditions conspire against you. At these times you'll discover if you have the willpower and mental endurance to keep climbing, make correct decisions, and adjust strategy as needed. This essential capability is gleaned over the course of many trying experiences in the steep and, in particular, from times when you dare to extend yourself beyond previous limits.

Table 9.1 *Four Types of Attentional Focus*

		DIRECTION OF FOCUS	
		External	**Internal**
WIDTH OF FOCUS	**Wide**	Scanning for holds and visualizing sequencing. Monitoring other climbers, the weather, and objective dangers.	Monitoring various muscles and bodily functions while climbing. Thinking about general feelings of fatigue. Scanning body for tense muscles while at a rest position.
	Narrow	Focusing on a hold to grab, lunge to, or step on. Placing protection or examining the quality of a gear placement.	Focusing on a proprioceptive cue or your center of gravity. Mentally rehearsing a move. Concentrating on your breathing or targeting a specific muscle for relaxation.

Enemies of Concentration

Researchers have compared successful and less-successful performers and determined that the ability to maintain concentration is a primary discriminating factor. The best performers were less likely to be distracted by irrelevant stimuli or to succumb to worry and outcome-oriented thoughts. So in your quest to improve concentration, it's a good first step to increase your awareness of the enemies of task-relevant focus as well as common targets of misplaced concentration. Following are six common concentration killers or targets of misplaced focus.

1. **Focusing on mechanics of well-learned skills.** Skills and climbing moves that you possess high competence in (autonomous learning stage) should be turned over to the preconscious mind. Focusing on execution of well-learned movements often results in mechanical, lower-efficiency movement and diverts concentration from other task-relevant targets.

2. **Dwelling on internal feelings and sensations of fatigue.** While you must monitor internal conditions by occasionally turning your focus inward, dwelling on such internal feelings will rob external focus and inhibit performance. A common trait of hardman (and -woman) climbers is the ability to dissociate from the fatigue and pain of an exhaustive workout or climb. It's a fact that in focusing on the strain and deepening fatigue during a hard climb, you magnify these feelings and open the door to powerful stopping thoughts. Dissociating from such non-injury-producing "good pain" and dismissing phantom stopping thoughts empowers you to transcend previous limitations and achieve the uncommon.

3. **Entertaining nonproductive self-talk.** Vocal and subvocal self-talk is an inherent and almost ever-present feature of our conscious minds; however the nature and quality of this self-talk is not always in our favor. Negative self-talk is a powerful concentration and performance killer, because it directs attention inward to fretful or fearful thoughts. Therefore, it's essential that you direct positive, productive self-talk that helps maintain focus, aids execution, and sustains motivation. Strive to direct positive self-talk in all you do, and it will become a powerful ally in your toughest times.

4. **Focusing on the past.** The essence of effective concentration in sport is being fully engaged in the action of the moment. If you look into the rearview mirror and engage in thoughts of past failures, or other irrelevant events, it will quickly diminish or derail your performance. So in engaging the vertical extreme, it's essential that you remain in the present and only reflect on past experiences as is briefly necessary for strategic planning and managing risk.

5. **Focusing on the future.** Projecting into the future and pondering a possible performance outcome will thwart task-relevant concentration and impede your performance. Worse yet, in entertaining future-oriented thoughts of failure you generate pressure and anxiety that makes this unwanted outcome more likely! Controlling concentration and climbing your best therefore demands that you detach from outcome-oriented thinking and engage the moment completely.

6. **Visual and auditory distractions.** We live in an era of ubiquitous distractions, rampant ADD (attention deficit disorder), and almost unlimited potential for electronic and social engagement. Possessing a quiet, in-the-moment mental state can be exceedingly difficult to attain and maintain if you allow all this interference to reach your brain. The first step to developing better concentrative skills, then, is to endeavor to systematically eliminate distractions in all aspects of your life. In climbing, strive to eliminate possible distractions before you engage the route, and aspire to become a master at blocking out distracting people and sounds as you climb. As a final note, I want to stress that your mental state can benefit greatly by eliminating some of the things that hinder concentration in your nonclimbing hours. What electronics can you turn off (or discard) and what other actions could you take to reduce non-task-relevant stimuli and other distractions? The payoff is the gift of improved mental clarity, concentration, and self-awareness.

What Are Your Concentration Killers?

List the things that commonly disrupt your concentration during everyday activities and in climbing. If necessary, close your eyes and visualize yourself in a recent climbing situation in which you struggled to remain focused and in the moment. What thoughts, sensory stimuli, people, or other environmental conditions made it hard for you to maintain focus?

List Distractions in Everyday Situations

_____

_____

_____

_____

_____

_____

List Distractions While Climbing

_____

_____

_____

_____

_____

_____

Techniques for Improving Concentration While Climbing

Knowing the importance of concentration to effective risk management and optimal performance, it's essential that you step onto the vertical stage armed with techniques to fortify mental focus. Developing unbreakable concentration, however, takes a long-term commitment to gather and maintain focus every time you climb. In fact, improving concentration requires a comprehensive effort to reduce distractions and properly direct focus in all aspects of your life. You can't just turn on a high level of concentration while you climb; you must also learn to wield your concentrative powers at work, at school, and in doing all other important tasks.

Here are six techniques for enhancing and maintaining concentration before and during a climb—although you can also apply these strategies in the quest to improve your focus in everyday activities.

 ### *Deal with Potential Distractions Before You Climb*

The first and most obvious step to improving concentration while you climb is to preemptively deal with possible distractions before you even start up the route. For example, knowing that noise on the ground or a talkative belayer often disrupts your concentration while leading, you can address this matter as part of your preclimb ritual. Express to your belayer (or spotter) the importance of his attentiveness, and kindly ask other climbers to limit their movements and noise until you complete the boulder problem or climb.

Same goes for trying to marshal maximal focus at work, school, or elsewhere. Turn off cell phones and nix any distracting background noises; predetermine that you won't check e-mail or deviate for any reason from the task at hand until a certain point in time; and since your eyes often lead your focus, go somewhere that shelters your eyes from environment distractions or other movements.

An interesting research finding is that listening to classical baroque-style music helps deepen concentration and improve focus, especially when faced with a large amount of information to process.

Dissociating from such non-injury-producing "good pain" and dismissing phantom stopping thoughts empowers you to transcend previous limitations and achieve the uncommon.

The musical pulses common to baroque music, such as Bach, have been shown to affect brain waves in a way that may enhance creative thinking, problem solving, concentration, and learning. Some university professors now play baroque music in the background during lectures and tests, and countless others (including this author) have discovered the benefits of playing classical music while writing, reading, and studying, as well as during mental-training exercises such as visualization.

What about other styles of music—do they have the same positive effects on concentration? Perhaps. While faster-paced music and pop songs with lyrics do hold great potential to change your mental state and engage you in the moment of the music, they tend to make concentration on complex tasks more difficult. For example, I'm sure that you can sing along with a song on the radio (or talk on the phone) when driving in steady traffic on a familiar road. In trying to navigate chaotic traffic in an unknown city, however, I bet you have found it sometimes necessary to turn off the radio (and cease a conversation) in order to concentrate your complete attention on figuring the next turn and staying alive. The same is almost certainly true in climbing or performing any other complex task—subjecting your mind to engaging music or conversation will degrade concentration, whether you recognize it or not.

Use Rituals to Narrow Focus

Use of preparatory rituals is a natural, and powerful, way of narrowing focus before you climb (or engage in any important activity). By engaging in a sequence of steps and procedures in the hours and minutes leading up to a climb, the conscious mind is given a series of operations on which to target focus. For example, going through a progression of physical warm-up and stretching activities followed by a familiar sequence of preparing your gear and examining the route, the mind becomes engaged in task-relevant processes and is less likely to stray toward external distractions or internal, nonproductive thoughts.

In this same way, you can develop rituals to help focus your mental state in a wide range of life activities. Given the complexity of the world we live in and the ease of getting distracted, using rituals that deflect distractions and narrow focus will not only improve your concentration in all you do but also elevate your mental state in a way that increases the effectiveness of your actions. It should be no surprise, then, that peak performers in sports, business, and elsewhere habitually employ well-refined rituals to narrow focus and shelter their eyes and ears from irrelevant cues and potential distractions.

 ## *Use Self-Talk to Direct the Conscious Mind*

Earlier you learned the harmful effects of negative self-talk to your conscious state and ability to concentrate. It is obvious, then, that proactively directing positive self-talk is an indispensable tool for maintaining a focused, effective mental state. Examples of beneficial self-talk include simple instructions such as *Relax, Stay in the moment, Keep breathing, Focus on footwork,* and *Soften the grip,* as well as encouraging statements like *I can do this move, I love adversity, Keep going, Hang on,* and *One more move.* By filling your conscious mind with copious positive self-talk, it makes it difficult for outside distractions or negative thoughts to enter your stream of consciousness.

An important distinction in directing effective self-talk is that you never state the effect or outcome that you don't want to happen. Saying to yourself, for example, *Don't feel nervous, Don't fall, Don't blow this move,* or *Don't feel scared* brings the unwanted outcome into your conscious mind and thus makes it more likely that you will experience the very state or outcome you hope to avoid. This is often called the pink-elephant effect, since if you say to yourself, *Don't think of a pink elephant,* you will instantly see a pink elephant in your mind's eye! Such reverse polarity self-talk might be viewed as a form of self-sabotage, and it's actually a common bad habit of internal dialogue for many people. Make it your goal to forge a new habit of thinking. Strive for a greater awareness of your self-talk as well as better quality control in the words you speak to yourself.

Keep Your Eyes on Task-Relevant Targets

Whether concentration narrows or divests in a given moment often depends on where your eyes are pointing and what you choose to focus your vision on. Suppose you are lead climbing and glance to the rock or ground below you—in shifting your eyes downward, you open the door to visually engaging some distraction on the ground or perhaps even pondering the exposure of your current perch. In doing so, you sever task-relevant focus on the move at hand, in addition to blocking out important proprioception of body tension, muscular tension, and your center of gravity. The performance impact of this lost focus is decreased efficiency of movement, increased mental tension and anxiety, and an unfortunate increase in the chance that you will lose your nerve, pump out, or fall.

The best climbers avoid this cascade of distractions by locking their vision onto task-relevant targets and allowing their vision to stray only when they are at a good stance, rest, or ledge. Knowing this master skill, you gain a powerful insight on how to gather and maintain focus as you climb—direct your eyes only at objects that are relevant in the moment! Specifically, your eyes should target only the holds you are about to engage, the gear you are placing, and the rock immediately around you. Make this your modus operandi—and avoid straying eyes as you climb—and you will discover a new level of concentration that quickly boosts your climbing performance.

One vital task-relevant target that many climbers fail to focus enough on is foot placements. A common problem is focusing the eyes and mind on finding handholds, and allowing the feet to find the holds with only quick glances or peripheral vision. Once again, you can learn an important lesson by observing how elite climbers turn their faces and lock their eyes on each foot placement. Rarely do they feel for holds; instead they see each hold as a target and place the foot onto the target's bull's-eye (that is, the best part of the hold). This entire process might only take a second or two, but it's a distinct step in the process of performing each move with utmost precision and economy.

Perhaps you are now thinking that you can make this process of targeting each foot placement into an excellent practice drill. Absolutely—do it! To best improve your footwork with this drill, see each foothold as a target onto which you narrow your focus, observing it vividly, and then place your foot precisely on the best part of the hold. Similarly, you can go beyond just seeing a handhold as a place to grab by consciously zooming your vision onto the details of each hold. By seeing the unique shape, angle, depth, and texture of each hold, you will be able to engage it with optimal positioning and minimal force.

One final tip: When you are struggling to maintain concentration on a route, simply narrow your visual focus to the hand- and footholds before you. Pause for a moment, and direct a tight, yet relaxed focus on the hold you're about to engage next. Observe the minutest detail of the hold and marvel at its novelty. This simple five-second exercise will erase distractions and create a powerful focus to continue climbing onward with high efficiency.

Keep Your Thoughts in the Moment

Keeping your thoughts in the moment, detached from judgments and thoughts of outcome, is an immensely powerful Zen-master-like mental state. It's important to recognize that your body can only be in the present, so the invaluable mind–body synchronization that gives birth to peak performance is only possible when your mind is also in the present moment! Thinking about anything in the past or future makes mind–body integration impossible and peak performance elusive.

Engaging in meditation, or using the Singular Focus Climbing Drill (see page 166), before you climb is an excellent way to quiet the mind and get in the moment.

Concentration is about being fully engaged and mentally in the moment.

When you quiet your mind and eliminate distractions, your attention will naturally focus on the most important matter of the moment. On the rock, this single-pointed focus will shift effortlessly from hand- to foothold, or to gear placements and risk management, as needed. In being in the moment, the potential outcome of the climb, as well as people around you, wield no power to distract—you will climb onward as if you are the only person in the world.

 Use Willpower to Narrow Focus Despite Adverse or Imperfect Conditions

Leveraging willpower to narrow your concentration flies counter to the core concept that focus must gather naturally (as a result of eliminating distractions and quieting your mind), yet it is sometimes possible to will focus in adverse situations or when a deadline or competition outcome is on the line. This rare occurrence is the stuff of master climbers who are subjected to an acute or onerous situation in which they must direct intense focus in order to prevail or even survive.

A classic example of this is when an elite climber summons laserlike focus to complete a project climb on the final date of a trip or in flashing the final problem to win a competition. Chris Sharma has done this many times, in somehow being able to simultaneously tap into the energy and urgency of the situation while also detaching from the pressure to perform. In more than a decade of participating in bouldering competitions, Sharma has on-sighted more final routes than any of his peers—and he's also been able to apply his laserlike focus to send cutting-edge rock routes like *Jumbo Love* (5.15b), a mind-boggling 250-foot overhanging pumpfest that currently may be the longest, hardest route in the world.

No doubt there are many elite solo rock climbers and alpinists who similarly razor-sharpen their focus to prevail in their high-stakes endeavors. Think of Alex Honnold performing his unbelievable free solo ascent of the *Northwest Face* of Half Dome, or a mountaineer like Ed Webster pulling together the mental focus and will to survive in descending unknown territory on Everest with frostbite and virtually no equipment or food. Extreme situations will sometimes bless a climber with almost unlimited ability to focus and endure, and it just might be enough to "miraculously" survive an impossibly harrowing predicament.

Tips for Enhancing Concentration

- **Deal with potential distractions before you climb.** If necessary, ask your belayer or spotter for compete attention, and don't be shy about asking other climbers on the ground to limit their movements and noise until you complete the boulder problem or climb.

- **Use preclimb rituals to narrow focus.** Capture mental concentration—and seal off distractions—by engaging in a preparatory sequence that includes your physical warm-up, stretching activities, racking your gear, scoping the route, and the like.

- **Proactively fill your conscious mind with copious positive self-talk:** *Relax, Stay in the moment, Keep breathing,* and *Focus on footwork,* along with encouraging statements such as *I can do this move, I love challenge,* and *Hang on for one more move.*

- **Limit your eye focus to task-relevant targets.** Focus your vision only on the holds you are about to engage, the gear you are placing, and the rock immediately around you.

- **Keep your thoughts in the moment.** Use meditation, breathing exercises, and the Singular Focus Climbing Drill (see page 166) to quiet your mind and get in the moment.

- **Use willpower to narrow focus despite adverse or imperfect conditions.** Accept the reality of the situation, dismiss unproductive thoughts, and lose yourself in focused action.

As you grow in experience and mental skill, you too may someday find yourself in a situation in which you can will intense, sustained focus in order to prevail. Perhaps it will be in wielding the focus needed to send a competition final's route as the crowd howls, although it will more likely be in an outdoor climbing venue where you must summon peak concentration to succeed on a project before the weather turns or your road trip ends. Or perhaps you'll someday find yourself marshaling focus in extricating yourself from some big-wall or alpine ordeal. Whichever of these situations you someday find yourself in, you must accept the reality of the situation—yet dismiss worries and paralysis by overanalysis—and act with complete trust that you possess the maximum climbing skills, experience, and willpower to see yourself through.

Six Mental-Fitness Exercises to Improve Concentration

Concentration requires mental strength. Just as in strengthening a muscle, you need to exercise the mind to improve focus. Here are six mental-training drills that you can put to work, beginning today!

Second-Hand Clock Drill

This is a great—and surprisingly difficult—drill for developing laserlike focus and a still mind. You can also use this drill as a measure of your concentrative abilities; record the length of time you can maintain pure focus (as described below) and see how much you can improve with training. Here's how to do it.

Get an analog watch, stopwatch, or small clock (any timekeeper with a second hand will work) and sit down in a comfortable position in a quiet, distraction-free room. Close your eyes, take a few deep belly breaths, and let go of all thoughts and concerns. Now open your eyes and tightly focus your vision on the second hand as it ticks around the face of the clock. When the second hand reaches the twelve o'clock position, let your mind go completely blank with all mental energy locked on the second hand. See the hand tick second by second and think of nothing but the exact spot of the second hand. Chances are that your thoughts will quickly stray elsewhere—the moment an outside thought enters your mind, note the location of the second hand. How many seconds did you maintain complete focus on the second hand without a single outside thought? Chances are you only made it five or ten seconds before your singular focus was broken. That's the typical result for most people, and it reveals how extremely difficult it is to maintain single-pointed focus.

As a focus-training procedure, perform the Second-Hand Clock Drill about twenty times in a row, and do this sequence several days per week. Gradually, you will learn to quickly narrow your thoughts to a single point and apply this capability to other activities, such as climbing or studying. And never stop training—concentration is one area with limitless potential for improvement!

 ### *Singular Focus Climbing Drill*

This climbing drill is best used when practice climbing on a route a couple of number grades below your maximum ability. The goal is to climb a whole route by focusing solely on one aspect of movement. For example, try to do a route with your complete focus on just hand placements. Find the best way to grab each hold, use the minimum amount of grip strength necessary to hang on, and feel how your purchase changes as you pull on the hold. Place as little focus as is safely possible on other areas such as your feet, balance, belayer, and the like. For now, let these areas take care of themselves—allow your intuitive sense to determine foot locations and balance points.

Chances are, you'll find this focus-training drill to be quite difficult. Your thoughts will naturally wander to other tasks or even be drawn to distractions on the ground. If this occurs, simply redirect your focus to the predetermined task—in this case, the handholds. It is this process of becoming aware of your lost focus and returning it to the critical task that you are after. Sharpened awareness of lost focus is tantamount to improving your concentrative abilities.

Repeat this exercise two or three times, but change the focus each time—say, onto foot placements or center-of-gravity placement. Use this drill twice per week, and strive to increase the length of time you can maintain a singular focus. This helps build mental endurance, which can make all the difference in the world when you're bouldering or lead climbing near your limit.

Pinpointing Your Focus for a Climb

Use this exercise to quiet your mind and narrow your focus just prior to beginning a climb. After completing your preclimb ritual and being put on belay, assume an extended posture (shoulders back and chest out), close your eyes, and place the fingertips of your dominant hand against the rock face. Your fingertips should be touching the wall lightly (not gripping a hold), and your hand and arm should be completely relaxed. Now take three deep belly breaths, inhaling through your nose to a count of five and exhaling through your mouth to a count of five to ten seconds. Let a wave of relaxation wash across your body, and then narrow your focus to the tips of your fingers touching the rock. Concentrate singly on the sensation of your fingertips on the rock—you should begin to feel the thermal energy moving from your fingers to the rock (on occasions when the rock is hotter than your body, you will feel thermal energy conducting to your fingertips). Maintain a relaxed, singular focus on the energy exchange between your fingertips and the rock for anywhere from thirty seconds to a minute or two. If your focus ever wanders, simply redirect it to your fingertips. Soon your mind will become completely still, as all of your focus is pinpointed on the tips of your fingers. Upon reaching this state, open your eyes and begin climbing.

Attention-Shifting Drill

A critical aspect of concentration is being able to shift single-pointed focus to different task-relevant cues. Here are three ways to train your ability to redirect attention between difficult targets.

The first training method is to sit down, relax, and listen to a song on your iPod or stereo (using headphones is ideal in order to help seal off the outside world). With your eyes closed and body relaxed, narrow your focus to a single aspect of the song; for example, begin by listening to the thumping of the bass drum. Dwell only on the bass drum sound at the expense of listening to other aspects of the song, and it will soon become the dominant feature of the song. When this happens (or after about one minute), switch your focus to another instrument, such as the guitar chops or vocal harmonies. Once again, create a single-pointed focus onto this one aspect of the song; then after a minute switch to another instrument. Continue changing the target of your focus every minute or so for the length of two or three songs. Eventually you may discover that your focus is getting fatigued—yes, mental training can be tiring!—as you increasingly find yourself listening to all aspects of the song instead of a single feature.

Another training method is to sit alone in a room and to lock your focus onto a different object every couple of minutes for a total of ten to fifteen minutes. For example, begin focusing on a photo or picture on the wall; for about two minutes, look at only this picture and think about nothing else but the uniqueness of the picture. Observe minute details as you direct your eyes to different parts of the image. Should your thoughts wander elsewhere, simply acknowledge the lost concentration and return your focus to the picture. After two or three minutes, shift your focus to something completely different, such as the feeling of your breathing. Close your eyes and concentrate on the air flowing in and out of your lungs. Think of nothing else but the sensations of your breathing. After a couple of minutes, shift your focus again, this time focusing on the sounds you hear outside your apartment or house. Explore the sounds that you hear, noticing subtle differences in timbre, volume, and rhythm. Maintain your auditory focus for a few minutes, then open your eyes and pick another object on which to focus your vision. Repeat the above sequence a few times until you get mentally fatigued or bored.

The final way to train attention shifting is by consciously targeting focus as you climb. Initially you'll want to do this on a submaximal climb, but you'll quickly discover that you can do this on a maximal route and improve your performance to boot! Here's what to do: Focus your eyes and thoughts on the single most important task at a given moment, then shift your visual and mental focus as each new hold is encountered and as your body position changes. This is obviously a very dynamic mental drill since your focus will need to change every second or two as you encounter new foot- and handholds, interpret proprioception, and assess your changing fatigue and mental state. Imagine your focus targeting these different areas like the flickering beam of a laser-light show. Most important, however, is to lock your complete attention on that single most important task of the moment—really see the hold and feel your body position. With practice, the process of targeting and redirecting focus will become largely subconscious; and on the rare occasions when your focus does wander away from the task of climbing, you will quickly recognize this loss and redirect the focus to the best target of the moment.

 ### Two-Minute Breath Focus

This simple drill may be the hardest of all, and it's a great method of developing Zen-master-like focus. Sit down in a comfortable chair in a quiet room. Relax your muscles and feel yourself sink into the chair. Next, let go of all active thinking and focus your awareness on your breathing. Since most of us have active mind, this can be difficult—but try to let any outside thoughts pass, as your attention is centered on your breathing. Feel your belly moving as you take slow, deep belly breaths. Concentrate on the feeling of air flowing in and out of your lungs, and soon your mind will become very still. When void of outside thoughts, begin counting your breaths. Think of nothing but the feeling of your breaths and the number of breaths you have taken. If your mind wanders, return to zero and begin counting again.

Your goal is to count ten breaths without your mind wandering. At a rate of five slow, deep breaths per minute, it will take you about two minutes to take ten breaths. As you will discover, it's extremely difficult to maintain a single-pointed focus on your breathing for two minutes.

This breath-counting exercise is great for gathering your focus at the base of a climb. Proceed through the steps above; when your mind becomes completely breath-focused and still, stop counting and let your focus follow your breath out of your body—this will open your awareness to the rock before you. At this point you will possess both a quiet mind and uncommon awareness of your surroundings, which is an ideal mental state for beginning to climb.

 ### *Practice Single-Tasking*

This final focus-training drill is for use in your everyday life, and it flies counter to the exceedingly common practice of multitasking. Use single-tasking when you have an important task to work on; for example, studying, working, or engaging in an activity with a child or significant other. Detach from all other people and any possible distractions by turning off your phone and silencing the room (except, perhaps, for some baroque music).

Now engage in the specific task, whether it's locking your focus on your studies, getting lost in your work, or playing with your child. Strive to maintain this intense focus for at least thirty minutes without interruption. Chances are, you will discover that time elapses at a surprisingly fast rate, but also that you have enjoyed and accomplished more than you would have expected. Make single-tasking a regular feature of your daily life (as I have) and I guarantee that you'll discover a higher level of happiness and achievement than the multitasking masses.

Remember, multitasking is only an effective method when dealing with relatively simple tasks. Trying to multitask activities with greater complexity almost always has a negative effect on the quality of execution as well as long-term outcomes. This helps explain why obsessive multitaskers are generally overwhelmed in their daily lives and often ineffective in undertaking a major task, despite what seems like a major, albeit unfocused, effort.

Managing Fear

As ironic as it may sound, there is nothing to fear about fear. Fear is simply a genetically encoded protective response. Unlike animals, which respond to fear with either fight or flight, humans are endowed with the ability to evaluate fearful situations and respond with proactivity. We must then view fear as nothing more than a tool that we must learn to use to our benefit. Through experience and mental control we can develop the courage to act in the face of unreasonable fears and, just as important, learn to heed legitimate fears and act intelligently in these risky situations. Reinhold Messner aptly summarizes this vital concept in stating that "Courage and fear are equally valuable halves of an indivisible whole, to be held in balance. Whoever pursues fear as a stigma and courage as an ideal will not live long."

In your quest for maximum climbing, it's essential that you honestly answer this question: *Is fear your master or are you fear's master?*

Your answer to this question may be the single most revealing predictor of your future climbing achievements and what riches (or tragedy) you will find in the mountains. The best—and longest-living—climbers don't aspire to eliminate fear; instead they strive to eliminate the fear of fear. With the wisdom that comes from experience and exposure to fearful situations, maximum climbers learn to embrace fear and enjoy the sense of aliveness that it gives them. They treat fear as a companion that advises them, and they act with courage and prudence to proceed and succeed despite fears, or to retreat and live to climb another day.

Perhaps nothing is more elemental to climbing than fear. Becoming a maximum climber, then, requires that you learn to understand and manage your fears.

The goal of this chapter, then, is to increase your awareness of the fears you will face in the steep, and to give you the tools to conquer phantom fears and use legitimate fears. If you are looking for a way to eliminate fear altogether, you won't find it here. The delusional "no fear" mentality has no place in a serious sport like climbing, and those who internalize and worship at the no-fear altar may someday soon end up in a hospital—or worse.

Nathan Weldon taking a big whipper on **A Virgin No More (5.12d), Penitente Canyon, Colorado.** ANDY MANN

Write Down Your Common Climbing Fears

Write down all the fears you've encountered in climbing over the past year or two. Think back over a wide range of situations and explore the fears you have experienced, regardless of how ridiculous or petty they may seem now. Review past difficult climbs, adverse situations, and times you seemed to hit a barrier or stall point in the pursuit of a goal. What fears might have been holding you back? If you can only uncover a few fears, then dig deeper. Consider other areas of your life outside of climbing, since everyday fears often cross over to become climbing fears. Try to identify at least ten or twelve fears or fearful situations.

_____   _____

_____   _____

_____   _____

_____   _____

_____   _____

In recognizing that fear is a friend, and not a foe, you can begin an effective study of understanding and managing fear. The first step in this process is to gain a clear handle on your most common fears, big and small. In this way you are empowered to deal with them once and for all.

After completing the exercise above, you now want to classify each fear as either a fear of **falling,** a fear of **injury or death,** a fear of **failure,** a fear of **embarrassment,** or a fear of an **unknown.** If it's not clearly apparent, write down next to each entry which type of fear is at play. You can now page ahead to learn the numerous fear-management strategies for each of these common fear types.

Fear of Falling

The number one fear-related question I receive, through my Web site, coaching, and in giving climbing performance seminars, is how to overcome the fear of falling. This most fundamental fear is, of course, not a fear that you want to overcome absolutely. The goal, then, is to manage the fear so that you can climb upward in dangerous situations or look for less risky alternatives (perhaps even retreat) when the fear of falling is a legitimate warning.

In learning to lead climb, we have all experienced the almost paralyzing effect that fear of falling can have on us. Our muscles tense up and our concentration is shattered as this fear becomes our master. Moving upward while in the clutches of this fear is not only difficult, but also quite unenjoyable, stressful, and effortful—it often feels as if we are climbing with a heavy weight on our back. The effects of fear, then, are not much different from having sandbags hanging from your harness. This explains why novice leaders tend to climb mechanically and pump out quickly—they are hauling a great fear load up the route with them! More experienced leaders, who are better at managing their fears, haul fewer sandbags up the route with them; and on their best ascents, they carry no additional fear load because they have fully managed fears.

Learning to manage the fear of falling rarely "just happens," however—it's a skill that is developed by exploring, and willfully challenging, the fear in a variety of climbing situations. Therefore, you must progressively expose yourself to climbs that require you to summon both greater courage and better fear and risk management. In using the five following strategies, you will gradually glean the confidence and wherewithal to press onward despite the fear of falling; in doing so you'll discover a new level of climbing. No, you will never be completely liberated from the fear of falling (at least I hope not!); instead you will become an expert fear manager who hauls little or no fear load up a route.

Distinguish Between Reasonable and Unreasonable Fears

The single most powerful fear management strategy is to determine whether the fear you are feeling is *reasonable* or *unreasonable*. This is largely an intellectual calculation based on your experience and knowledge of the safety system (spotting or belaying). Most climbers with at least a few years' experience should be capable of correctly assessing whether a fear is reasonable and legitimate or not. Less experienced climbers should obtain input from a more experienced climber or coach to make the right determination as well as gain the wisdom to make autonomous assessments in the future.

Examples of unreasonable fears include the fear of taking a lead fall onto bomber gear and the fear of falling from a moderate-length boulder problem with a crash pad and attentive spotter in place. Some of the reasonable falling fears, which should be heeded, include the fear of taking a ground fall, the fear of falling with a ledge or protruding rock feature in the fall zone, and the fear of falling off a highball boulder problem or onto a rocky landing zone.

Not all falls, however, can be classified as either absolutely reasonable or unreasonable. For example, the reasonable fear of taking a dangerous fall from moderate moves (which you would not likely fall from) could be viewed as unreasonable! Furthermore, the probability that you will fall and the danger of the potential fall is often an unknown that depends on variables such as rope stretch and whether or not a marginal piece of gear will hold. It's in these situations that less experienced climbers should err on the side of prudence, whereas veteran climbers can often intuit the right call and act accordingly.

Lynn Hill, one of the greatest free climbers of all time, uses this very process of distinguishing reasonable from unreasonable fear. She states, "I take calculated risks. I decide whether a move is reasonable or not. If I decide yes, then I don't think about the consequences of a fall. Instead, I think positively about what I need to do to get the move."

Take Practice Falls

I occasionally hear an experienced climber, with hundreds of ascents under his belt, complaining that he still wrestles with a severe fear of falling even after many years of climbing. I explain to him that you don't learn to expertly manage the fear of falling simply through experience at climbing—you become empowered to challenge the fear of falling through experience at falling!

Consequently, engaging in occasional practice falling is an essential part of becoming an effective fear manager. Practice falling will benefit you in a couple of important ways. First, it teaches you to trust the belay system and thus dismantles ridiculous fears such as that of the rope breaking or a bolt failing. More important, it teaches you how to fall—learning to relax your body, stay upright, and avoid catching your foot on the rope or rock while falling are all critical skills that will become largely unconscious through practice. Finally, taking practice falls will gradually override the innate fear of falling in safe situations (when the gear is solid and the fall will be clean). In time, these skills will wire into your brain, thus empowering you to make the right choices in climbing upward despite the fear of a fall, and enabling you to react instantly in managing a fall when it happens.

Taking practice falls is best done in the controlled setting of a climbing gym, although you can also do it at a sport crag. Practice on a somewhat overhanging sport route that's void of protruding holds; use a good rope, double-check your knot and harness buckle, and employ an experienced belayer. Start off by taking a few short falls with a bolt location near your knees—with rope stretch this will result in about a 5- or 6-foot fall. When you become comfortable taking these short falls, climb a bit higher so the bolt is somewhere near your feet. Depending on the amount of rope between you and the belayer, this will result in a medium-length sport climbing fall of about 10 feet, give or take. Practice taking these short- and medium-length falls at least once per week for

All the climbing in the world won't get you past the fear of falling—only in falling will you come to manage this fear.

a few months and you will gradually come to accept these falls as the no-big-deal that they are (when gear is good). Some climbers progress to taking practice falls with the bolt a few feet below their feet; these longer sport climbing falls can total 15 to 20 feet depending on the amount of rope stretch and belayer "give." These longer falls should always be practiced on routes that overhang between twenty and forty-five degrees past vertical, so that they are "air falls" with no chance of hitting the rock hard or catching a foot on the rope.

The long-term effect of taking practice falls is that you will be able to detach from the fear of falling in safe situations and climb free with little or no fear load. Still, you will occasionally come upon situations where a fall looks to be completely safe, yet for some reason it's making you feel a little scared (perhaps the fall will yield a bit of swing, or it just looks weird). In such a case, you would benefit greatly by taking a single test fall in order to experience what it will be like—this will erase the fear you are feeling, because it's not knowing what the fall will be like that you fear, not that act of falling itself.

The tactic of taking a test fall is not an option when on-sight climbing, so an alternative strategy here is to take a few mental practice falls. In your mind's eye visualize what a fall might be like from the apparent crux position. If you can visualize a clean, safe fall (based on the data you have available and similar past experiences), you will greatly diminish the fear of falling in on-sight ascents.

In the end, addressing the fear of falling is a long-term endeavor that will take you months or years, not days or weeks, to come to manage. It's a step-by-step process that requires both the willingness to take practice falls, as well as the courage to push yourself to the limit and take real falls when climbing for performance.

 ## Change Your Interpretation of the Fear Response

The sympathetic nervous system (SNS) of the human body is designed to kick into action at times of stress, modulating various bodily functions in preparation for fight or flight. It should not surprise us, then, that the brain prepares us for the stress of climbing by triggering numerous physiological changes such as accelerating heart rate and blood pressure, increasing breathing rate, slowing digestion, and increasing perspiration rate, among other responses. These physical changes are accompanied by a release of adrenaline that helps increase energy, muscle tension, and focus.

In a complex sporting activity such as climbing, the aforementioned fight-or-flight responses may diminish performance and might even be viewed as counterproductive, except in rare situations such as needing to sprint from an avalanche or rockfall. Fortunately, the effects of the SNS are not an all-or-nothing response. A big part of state management is learning to control physical reactions to stimuli and climbing situations. The expert climber learns to control the flight-or-flight response, and thus optimize muscular tension, heart rate, and breathing for the task at hand. Consult chapter 6 for numerous state management strategies.

A big factor in controlling the fear of falling, then, is learning to interpret and modulate your physical response to fearful situations. In stepping up to a climb—or in engaging a scary-feeling crux—the butterflies, sweaty hands, cotton mouth, and muscle tremors that you feel are signs that your SNS is kicking in. It's vital to recognize that these feelings are a natural response to the stressful situation you're in; they are not a stop sign or signal to retreat.

By consciously acknowledging efferent effects of the SNS and taking countermeasures, such as slowing your breathing and shaking out your muscles, you control the physical response and prevent an eventual escalation to a full-fledged fight-or-flight response. Conversely, worrying about and focusing on the worsening physical response—your cotton mouth, sweaty palms, sick stomach, and trembling muscles—is tantamount to letting go of the reins and opening the door to a cascade of performance-killing physical responses.

Becoming familiar and comfortable with the range of physical responses you experience in climbing is the ultimate goal. With increasing experience in the steep and dedicated practice at proactively managing your physical state, you will come to control and leverage your SNS to maximize your performance. Feeling butterflies and getting scared are natural parts of climbing that we must embrace and manage, not try to avoid. The legendary Jeff Lowe underscores this idea in passionately stating that "I like to be pushing the edge of my control but always staying in control. I like the heightened concentration that comes from that slight tension between fear and control and just feathering that edge and making sure you're on the safe side of it."

 ### Use Self-Talk and Breath Control

One thing that's interesting about the fear of falling is how the fear factor can change dynamically as you ascend a route, and sometimes even fluctuate wildly from move to move. For example, fearful thoughts can invade your consciousness when running it out on lead, but then vanish in an instant upon reaching a good hold or gear placement. Knowing the dynamic nature of fear, you must accept that moments of acute fright are part of the game. Fortunately, you can temper a rapid rise in the fear factor via positive self-talk and breath control.

As detailed in chapter 6, self-talk is a power tool for narrowing concentration and controlling your state; and it's similarly useful in dealing with the fear of falling. For example, you can diminish your fear, as you climb into a crux sequence or run it out above good protection, with self-talk such as *Relax, this is safe; Focus on the feet; Keep breathing; Flow and stay centered.* Furthermore, you can prevent distracting thoughts and help maintain confident focus with mantralike, repetitive self-talk, such as *Relax and flow, relax and flow, relax and flow.*

Another powerful strategy to down-regulate fear and tension is to take conscious control of your breathing when entering a difficult sequence or hanging on to finish a long pitch without falling. Knowing that the fight-or-flight response results in shallow rapid breathing, which is not ideal for climbing, you can consciously direct beneficial deep, belly breathing. Maintaining slow, deep breathing on all but the hardest moves (which might require holding your breath for a moment or directing bursts of forced exhalation) will slow rising physical tension, increase blood oxygenation, and help break the mind–body feedback loop of fear and tension that can quickly snowball out of control. Take advantage of every rest position to check in on your breathing (are you inhaling through your nostrils and exhaling slowly through your mouth?), and you will best maintain an optimal performance state.

Feeling butterflies and getting scared are natural parts of climbing that we must embrace and manage, not try to avoid.

Fear of Getting Hurt or Dying

It's an old adage that "there are old climbers and bold climbers, but there are no old, bold climbers." The accuracy of this adage depends on your definition of *bold*, however. I know many bold climbers who expertly manage risk; hence, they will likely become old, bold climbers. I also have known a couple of bold climbers who didn't properly manage risk or took unnecessary risks for the sake of an adrenaline high or the quest for higher awareness or some feeling of ultimate liberation. Sadly, both are no longer with us—one died free soloing, and the other perished in a rope jumping accident.

The difference between the bold, still-living climbers and the bold, deceased climbers is in heeding the fear of getting hurt or killed (and not ignoring it), and using prudent risk management strategies (and never throwing all caution to the wind). Of course, no amount of risk management can ensure your complete safety—heck, you could even die in some accident or random crime if you stayed home! So your goal must be to balance taking reasonable risks in exploring this world of wonder with heeding fears via risk management strategies and occasional retreat. The bottom line, then, is that we must accept that fear and the risk of death are inescapable parts of climbing. As Yvon Chouinard succinctly put it: "There can be no adventure without risk to life and limb."

> **No amount of risk management can ensure complete safety—we must accept that fear and the risk of death are inescapable parts of climbing.**

Learning to assess the real risk of a climbing situation, and then acting to temper the fear response and manage the risk, is the pith of the matter. In the sections that follow we'll examine the processes of evaluating the legitimacy of your fears and using fear as a tool to help direct effective risk management.

 ### Evaluate the Legitimacy of the Fear

It's a common experience among climbers that certain routes, especially those with great exposure and unfamiliar terrain, trigger a high fear load that overwhelms the ability to remain relaxed, focus, and climb effectively. Rising emotions and a racing mind magnify the fears that often key off an imagination run wild with scenarios of getting hurt, stranded, or killed. This wrestling match with escalating fears often grinds your progress up the route to a halt. Retreat then ensues, ironically, before any real adversity is encountered.

As exemplified in this story line, an imagination running wild with fearful thoughts and unlikely scenarios can be extremely disempowering. The first strategy for managing the fear of injury or death, then, is to determine whether your fears are legitimate or not.

It's my experience that many of the acute fears found in the steep are merely illusions. For example, consider the fear you feel when climbing an extremely exposed expanse of rock or when you have to trust a single, nonredundant piece of gear (as in jumaring or rappelling). Assuming that you have solid protection in leading up the exposed terrain, or in knowing that your rappel anchor and rope are sound, then the fear is an unfounded phantom of the mind.

However, there will certainly be times when such acute or mortal fears are founded. For instance, fearful thoughts in preparing to climb an R- or X-rated pitch, solo a route, or ascend into bad weather in the mountains are all legitimate and should never be dismissed. Instead, you must acknowledge the fears and make a calculated risk assessment based on past experience (more on this in a moment).

Ultimately, the key to this fear management strategy is to determine whether the fear of injury or death that you are feeling is *reasonable* or *unreasonable*. In some cases, a black-or-white objective assessment is possible—for example, in dispelling the fear that a new rope or bolt might fail. Quite often, however, deciding the legitimacy of an acute fear is a subjective call, as in deciding whether a piece of gear that you placed will hold a fall and in intuiting your chance of falling in the given situation.

As in all acts of fear assessment and risk management, the novice climber is less likely to make the proper call (and more likely to be fooled by phantom fears and to miscalculate risk), whereas the experienced climber can operate nearer the edge thanks to her wealth of experience. Thus, each fear experience is part of the risk-assessment educational processes, as well as a powerful reality check for acknowledging both your own mortality and the value of life. Wolfgang Güllich summarized this idea well in writing that "Only conscious confrontation with thoughts of death can lead to more awareness of life. Thoughts of death teach us to appreciate life. Whoever forgets the face of death in the process is lost."

 ### Use Risk Management to Shift the Odds of a Safe Ascent in Your Favor

Climbing can be serious business. I've seen the proof in the form of bloodstained ground, broken limbs, mummified fingers, and a contorted corpse resting among cliff-base boulders.

Obviously, many of the fears we encounter in the steep are very real and should never be written off as illegitimate (as in misusing the previous exercise). Proactive risk management is the only viable pathway to managing legitimate fears and climbing onward. While an extensive study of risk management strategies is well beyond the scope of this book (there are other Falcon how-to books that address gear and safety measures), I will touch on six mental strategies for addressing risky, fear-inducing situations.

- **Proactively manage the most obvious dangers.** Many climbing risks and fears can be tempered, or even reduced to near zero, through use of modern climbing equipment and safety protocols. Compared with the gear and safety procedures of my formative days (the late 1970s), today's state-of-the-art tactics and gear can make many climbs a near walk in the park in terms of real risk to life and limb. Still, pilot error can lead to disastrous outcomes. Thus, appropriate training and vigilant adherence to all protective protocols is essential to maintain the high standard of safety we have come to expect in modern climbing.

- **Anticipate what-if scenarios and predetermine solutions.** Central to good risk management (in anything) is the anticipation of unexpected situations, hazards, or setbacks that you might encounter and how you would respond in each situation. In lay terms, this is called planning ahead. Addressing what-if scenarios before you climb will reduce the fear load you haul up a route as well as empower you to redirect fearful energy into focused action. The ability to transmute nervous energy into productive power is a hallmark of all elite climbers.

- **Determine if you can handle the worst-case scenario.** In imagining possible what-if scenarios, you will likely come up with a worst-case outcome that may be unmanageable or represent total failure. The question you must ask yourself is: *Can I handle and accept this worst-case scenario should it happen?* On a boulder problem, the worst-case outcome might be merely a failed attempt; in the case of free soloing, however, it could be death. (Most worst-case outcomes are somewhere between these two extremes.) By willfully accepting the worst-case scenario, you become liberated to act with full commitment, whereas deciding that you can't accept a worst-case outcome will compel you to modify your plans or find another climb. Each of us has to make our own determinations, based on our value systems and beliefs. Legendary climber and author Pat Ament shares his belief system, with regard to free soloing, in stating, "What I stand to gain from free soloing seems—no is—infinitely less than what I stand to lose."

> **The ability to transmute nervous energy into productive power is a hallmark of all elite climbers.**

- **Actively discern between "no fall" and apparent "safe fall" situations.** Perhaps the most important analysis you can make while on a climb is whether a fall would be safe or dangerous at any given moment. Making an accurate judgment requires experience in similar situations, knowledge of safety systems and quality of protection, and the ability to visualize fall trajectory and distance. While engaging a crux sequence that could possibly cause you to fall, you will be empowered to "go for it" and risk the fall when you recognize it as a safe-fall situation. In judging a particular section of a climb as no-falls territory, however, you must acknowledge the potentially serious consequences of falling and engage in measured decision-making as to whether you should climb onward with caution or retreat to safety.

- **Listen to your gut instinct when risk is incalculable.** Calculated risk management, as a protective system, breaks down in the many climbing situations that possess inherent uncertainty and immeasurable risk. There are only two reasonable tactics to apply in these situations. The first tactic is to always retreat when faced with incalculable risk, while the second tactic is to proceed with your intuitive sense in command of the wheelhouse. Clearly, the when-in-doubt-retreat tactic is the safest and most appropriate for a beginner. If you are to frequently realize the maximum climbing experience and discover the full majesty of the mountains, however, you must develop and learn to trust your intuitive sense in order to climb onward despite ambiguities and uncertainties.

A climber's gut instinct, or what I refer to as intuition, is a sixth sense that is developed and sharpened with experience. Novice climbers therefore possess little ability to intuit themselves through a risky situation—they would be wise to follow a more experienced climber upward or retreat to safety. Expert climbers, having logged thousands of hours in the steep, possess a well-honed intuition that can guide them through almost any imaginable situation. For example, master climbers such as Peter Croft and Ed Viesturs can move quickly and confidently through harrowing terrain, rife with unknowns, guided by their intuitive prowess. Most of us possess more modest intuitive capabilities, yet we must learn to trust this mystical power as we gain experience and pursue greater challenges.

- **Assess how your experience and abilities match up to the inherent risk and size of the challenge.** Accomplishing to the best of your ability, while still appropriately managing risk, is a tenuous balancing act to say the least. The goal is to suss out the margin between overestimating your abilities (and risking injury or death) and playing it too safe (and unnecessarily limiting your achievement) due to an overestimation of risk. Finding and operating in this delicate margin becomes even more difficult as fear and tension cloud judgment and intuition. It's therefore essential that you attempt to objectively assess the match-up of your experience and abilities versus the inherent risk and size of the challenge before you start up a climb. Figure 10.1 reveals that peak performance will most often be found when you select a climb with a level of challenge and risk that's roughly proportionate to your technical capabilities and risk management skills.

Table 10.1 Risk–Ability Matrix

	Underestimate Risk		Overestimate Risk
Overestimate Ability	Great danger	Overreach	Overreach
↕	Danger	**Peak performance zone**	Underperform
Underestimate Ability	Danger	Underachieve	Underachieve

Underestimate Risk ⟷ Overestimate Risk

Fear of Failure

Fear of failure wields tremendous power over climbers who possess an unbending need for success. Ironically, the fear of failure tends to produce failure because it leads to a tight, timid approach while trying not to blow it. There are many good examples of this in mainstream sports; think of the way a football team often gives up the winning score when, late in the game, they shift into the so-called prevent defense; or the moment when a pro golfer, in trying not to blow a critical shot, tightens up and misses a makeable putt.

In climbing, a try-not-to-fail "prevent defense" results in tentative movement and apprehension in making tenuous or dynamic moves. Furthermore, the fear of failure leads to second-guessing sequences, doubting your ability, and focusing on the possibility of failure. This mental tension manifests itself as shallow breathing, overgripping of holds, jitters, and tense, inefficient movement. Before long, the very thing you are trying to avoid finds you.

Great climbers, while proactive in managing risk, do not attempt to manage outcome in this way. Renowned highballer Jason Kehl explains his Zen-like approach: "I think it's better to not have an idea of the outcome; just going and seeing what happens—not fearing failure or success."

Ultimately, it's in climbing for yourself—win, lose, or hanging from a quickdraw—that you will feel most happy and indeed climb your very best.

The good news is that since the fear of failure is completely self-imposed, it can be eliminated! Following are three strategies for killing this fear at its roots.

 Acknowledge Your Preparedness and Experience

Whereas novice climbers, enamored of the process of learning to climb, possess scant fear of failure, more experienced climbers often assume a more outcome-oriented mind-set and thus empower the fear of failure to strike at their soul. Fortunately, by consciously reviewing your preparedness, training, and experience, you can largely extinguish this fear.

Apply this coping strategy when you are scoping and roping up for a climb. Begin by taking a mental inventory of your recent training as well as your many climbing successes. Next relive in your mind's eye a few similar routes that you have prevailed on in the past. Finally, return your thoughts to the comfort of preclimb rituals that have proven many times to be precursors of a successful ascent.

Just as important, you must banish any thoughts of previous failures (on this or other routes) and wash from your consciousness the what-if adversities and worst-case scenarios that you imagined as part of your risk-management preparations. If necessary, counter these worrisome images with a few crisp, confident thoughts of what is probable and realistic based on past experiences and your investment in training. Then, as you step up to engage the rock, narrow your focus to the holds before you and dwell only on process-oriented thoughts.

Focus on Process as You Climb

Fear of failure is born from an outcome-oriented mind-set that constantly ponders the odds and consequences of success versus failure. Therefore, you can defeat this fear by focusing on the process of climbing and never letting your mind wander to possible outcomes.

Concentrate on the things immediate to your performance, such as precise foot placements, relaxing your grip, moving quickly on to the next rest position, and such. You can accentuate this laserlike focus by sharpening your visual awareness of the holds and wall features before you. Notice the slight variations and imperfections that make each hold unique, and strive for optimal placement of every hand and foot. If you capture your attention in this way, there will be little room in your consciousness to think about success or failure.

Anytime your thoughts begin to shift away from process orientation, immediately respond by redirecting your thoughts to your breathing. If possible, pause and take a deep breath or two—feel the air rushing in and out of your chest, and your focus will immediately return to the present moment. Once accomplished, return your focus to climbing with a quick study of your current hand- and footholds. This will get you back into the optimal process-oriented mind-set.

 ## Accept All Possible Outcomes Before You Begin Climbing

A more global approach to permanently eradicate the fear of failure is to simply adopt the attitude that it's okay to fail. By willingly accepting this fate (if it should even happen), you totally eliminate the fear and become empowered to climb unhindered and with full commitment. Embracing the potential of a negative outcome doesn't mean you aren't going to try your best or that you want to fail. Instead this position simply places you in a frame of mind from which you can give it your all without reservation.

Of course, gracefully accepting failure is easier said than done for some people. You can only assume this mind-set by consciously detaching your self-image from your performance. This can be difficult in the setting of a well-populated crag, since strangers tend to make first judgments of others based on what they see on the outside (appearance and performance).

Your goal, then, must be to recognize that your true friends will like you regardless of your performance, and that the opinions of strangers are not relevant. Whether or not you can completely embrace this mind-set is a measure of maturity and self-confidence—make developing this attitude part of your maximum climbing program. Given a long-term effort at assimilating this way of thinking, you will gain mental prowess and free yourself from the chains of needing to perform for others. Ultimately, it's in climbing for yourself—win, lose, or hanging from a quickdraw— that you will feel most happy and indeed climb your very best.

Fear of Embarrassment and Criticism

Fear of embarrassment and criticism can be one of the most debilitating for a climber. It's also the most unnecessary, since it's totally self-created—the result of a pathological need to be accepted and praised by others. While it's indeed a nice feeling to be liked, basing your happiness on the opinions of others is an absurd concept when you really think about it.

We all get into climbing for the pleasure and challenge it gives us, yet some climbers gradually shift to a mind-set that they must climb well to gain the acceptance and praise of others. The reason this happens is because climbing has become both a social activity and a media-covered sport. In choosing to climb in a group environment or in seeking media pub, you set up yourself to potentially succumb to both peer pressure and outside expectations. Obviously, the easiest way to eliminate this pressure is to avoid a group setting for climbing and to instead head to the boulders or crags alone or with just your partner.

Let's examine two more strategies for eliminating the fear of embarrassment and criticism.

 ### *Learn to Use Failures and Criticism in Your Favor*

Reinhold Messner, one of the greatest performers on this earth's highest stage, long ago came to the conclusion that "So long as I am criticized by older and younger climbers, I am reassured. I know I am on the right path and making progress."

It's a fact that anytime you step onto a public stage of any kind, you expose yourself to the potential for criticism and public failures. With the growth of climbing as a sporting activity—with crowded climbing gyms and crags alike—it's now hard to escape the eyes and opinions of others in recreating in the steep. As long as you are climbing for yourself with no concern for what others think or say, all will be good inside your head. When you begin to listen to and care about the comments of others, however, you open a Pandora's box of potential effects to your psyche.

For a professional climber who puts himself on a public stage, some form of acute criticism is inescapable; a thick skin is therefore indispensable! For the rest of us "average climbers," however, criticism is likely less acute and infrequent. Still it's important to briefly analyze criticism (and our failures, for that matter) in a search for any valid clues for improvement that they might contain. For example, in hearing someone comment about your bad footwork or "drama" while leading, consider these criticisms as legitimate clues for improving your climbing. As for unfounded criticisms from peers or strangers, recognize that their critical comments merely reveal their own weak character and poor self-concept.

As described in chapter 2, there are two basic types of people in the world: critics and doers. What's more, you can only be one or the other—compulsive criticizing and passionate doing are mutually exclusive character traits. Name a great climber—Caldwell, Honnold, Sharma, or Hill—and you are naming a passionate doer. Add your name to the list!

Take on a Bigger Perspective—You Are Not Your Failures!

The global strategy for eliminating the fear of an embarrassing performance is to always view your climbing from the big-picture perspective rather than on a climb-to-climb basis. Begin by judging yourself based on your climbing track record of the past few months or years; surely you've had some successful days on the rock to feel good about. Realize that an occasional bad-performance day is inevitable—even the best climber in the world has off days!

Drop the facade, pretense, entourage, and image-caring attitude and you'll discover both a new level of performance and a truer joy in climbing sans pressure to perform.

In terms of what other people will think of you, recognize that your friends know the big picture of your climbing record, and they will not think any different of you because of a down day (and if they do, they are not true friends). As for the expectations of others: Forget about it! The burden of others' expectations is a heavy weight to haul up climbs. You can't possibly climb your best with this mind-set; or as philosopher Jiddu Krishnamurti put it, "As long as you are trying to be something other than what you actually are, your mind wears itself out."

The bottom line: Drop the facade, pretense, entourage, and image-caring attitude and you'll discover both a new level of performance and a truer joy in climbing sans pressure to perform.

Fear of the Unknown

One of the most unrecognized fears—and one that at times effects nearly every climber—is fear of the unknown. Unlike the fear of falling or the fear of failure, which tend to be in your face, the fear of the unknown is more subtle and often sabotages performances covertly.

Fear of the unknown is actually multifaceted, comprising fear of ambiguity of outcome, fear of unknown aspects of the climb (gear, crux location, objective dangers, and such), and fear of pain, among other things. The common thread running through all of these fears is a lack of control. The outcome, availability of gear, objective dangers, and pain of performance are all outside the control of the climber. The aggregate fear load of all of these unknown factors can become so large—especially for individuals with control-freak tendencies—that advancing up the climb or mountain becomes overwhelmingly stressful and taxing.

As the weight of ambiguity grows during an ascent, a climber does have one action she can take to regain complete control: Retreat from the climb! In quitting the route, and returning to the ground, all uncertainty instantly evaporates. The ultimate unknown, which is that of the climbing outcome, becomes known by the very choosing of the climber.

Fear of the unknown runs deep in many novice and intermediate climbers, and it is likely to blame for many halfhearted (failed) efforts and obvious instances of self-sabotage. Veteran climbers are less likely to be shut down by this fear, since they've grown to accept the many ambiguities of climbing via the courage born from vast and diverse mountain experiences. Furthermore, these veterans have come to recognize that adventure and ambiguity are inseparable and that complete control is impossible when recreating in the mountains. Peter Croft supports this sentiment in expressing that "adventure is something I can take an active part in but that I don't have total control over."

Getting a solid handle on the fear of unknowns is obviously a long-term proposition, since it requires gaining experience in a wide range of climbing situations. There are, however, several fear management strategies that I will impart on the following pages, the simplest of which is to fall in love with the unknown!

 ### Accept and Welcome the Unknown

In pushing personal boundaries and confronting the unknown, it's common to ponder the benefits of a retreat instead of pushing into the discomfort zone. Acknowledge such a mental battle—between your desire to do adventurous things and your primal instinct to avoid discomfort and fear—as being a normal part of the process. It is something that you can work through and acclimate to in time. To this end, constantly remind yourself that the unknown is one of the most wonderful things about climbing.

If you wanted the known, you would have stayed home. Now that you're at the cliff base or in the mountains, however, it's time to embrace the mystery of the unknown. So instead of stressing out about whether you will succeed or fail on the climb, embrace the idea that a great challenge is before you and it's time to make a proud effort despite the unknowns. Do actively engage in whatever risk management actions are necessary, but let the ambiguity of the route's actual danger level sharpen your senses and focus. Finally, hold no solid expectations as to how much effort or energy you have to give to the climb; allow the route to draw out the best in you, and perhaps you'll discover resources heretofore unknown!

In committing to the magical mystery tour of the steep, you embark on a truly marvelous process of challenging fears, expanding your mind, and revealing unknown potentials.

The bottom line: You must begin to accept a moderate level of uncomfortable ambiguity and nervous energy as the price of admission for the adventure you desire. (A sense of high anxiety and dangerous unknowns should never be accepted without serious consideration.) In committing to the magical mystery tour of the steep, you embark on a truly marvelous process of challenging fears, expanding your mind, and revealing unknown potentials. And in climbing upward into the unknowns of wild places, you prospect for novel life experiences that no flatlander will ever discover. Retreat, and you miss out.

Anticipate and Prepare for Unknowns

The quickest way to deflate fear of the unknown is to find out (and make known) some aspect(s) of the unknown affair. For example, in watching a heart-pounding, palm-sweating scary movie, you can relieve much of the discomfort by asking somebody how the movie will end (or if the protagonist will survive the current horrors). The effect of this spoiler is twofold: It lowers your fear level, but it also reduces the excitement of the movie.

Similarly, you can take the edge off your anxiety of the unknowns in climbing by preparing for as many possible unknowns as you can anticipate beforehand. A few examples of preparatory actions you can take to reduce unknowns includes acquiring a very accurate topo of the route (very helpful for a complex multipitch route), getting beta on gear requirements or crux sequences (if you don't mind giving up the opportunity for an on-sight ascent), and sussing out the descent ahead of time (or asking other climbers for guidance) if there's a chance it will not be obvious or difficult to figure out in the dark.

The more information you can gather ahead of time and the more you can anticipate unknowns of the ascent, the less distracted and fearful you will feel as you climb. Certainly there are some climbers who feel that obtaining such beta spoils the adventure and perhaps even lowers the stature of the route. One of the great beauties of our sport, however, is that there are no official rules to follow—we each can use whatever tactics we choose, as long as they don't affect other people's experiences or permanently alter the climb in some way.

Take Control of Your Self-Talk and Imagery

Thoughts and mental images are precursors to the deep and growing fears that many climbers experience. Consider that you can't experience a fear-induced state of high anxiety and physical tension without first engaging in a sequence of scary thoughts or mental images. The essence of this fear management strategy, then, is to simply fill your mind with productive self-talk and process-oriented imagery so that there's little room remaining for your imagination to wander off into the twilight zone of delusional fears.

As described earlier, self-talk is a powerful tool for keeping your mind engaged in the action of the moment. Vocalizing or subvocalizing targeted statements, such as *Focus on precise foot placements*, *Relax and breathe deeply*, and *Keep moving to the next rest*, makes it difficult for fearful thoughts of the route's unknowns to invade your consciousness. Likewise, it's helpful to actively engage in mental imagery in which you see yourself successfully moving upward, finding gear placements and rest positions, and enjoying the challenge of solving the rock puzzle above.

One of the core concepts of this book is the power of the intimate mind–emotion–body connection, and how you can control your state and performance by consciously directing your thoughts in productive ways. Seizing control of your thoughts in tough situations, by engaging in self-talk and imagery, is a giant step toward developing the mental toughness common to hardman and elite climbers the world over.

Tips for Assessing and Managing Fears

- **Analyze your fears to determine if they are real or imagined.** Take action to mitigate the risk(s) associated with your legitimate fears. Strive to become a master of risk management, and you will be able to reduce a wide range of fears including the fear of falling, getting hurt, and the unknown.

- **Overcome imagined fears with reason—know that these phantom fears are bogus.** Fill your consciousness with productive, positive, process-oriented thoughts and dismiss all other illusionary fears that might surface.

- **Eliminate the fear of failure by acknowledging your preparedness and training.** Take a mental inventory of your training, planning, and past successes, then lose yourself in your proven preclimb ritual and get climbing!

- **Challenge the fear of falling by taking practice falls.** All the climbing in the world won't get you past this fear—only in *falling* will you come to manage this fear. Take a few practice falls (on safe routes) at least once per week during your first couple of years as a lead climber, and you will lose the fear of taking reasonable falls.

- **Change your interpretation of the fear response.** Some butterflies and nervous energy are natural before an important performance—acknowledge this and use the energy to enhance your focus and commitment, rather than letting it scare you.

- **Use self-talk and breath control to remain in a centered state.** Direct positive, process-oriented self-talk and strive to maintain steady, deep breathing throughout your ascent. Check in on your breathing, and renew focused self-talk at every rest position.

- **Focus on the process of climbing, and detach from the possible outcomes.** Concentrate on the things immediate to your performance, such as precise foot placements, relaxing your grip, and moving quickly onto the next rest position. Let the climb unfold one move at a time.

- **Actively discern between "no falls" and apparent "safe fall" situations.** Feel empowered to climb aggressively onward—and risk falling—when you assess a climb, or crux sequence, to be a safe-fall situation. (Subvocalize to yourself: *Go for it, it's safe to fall!*) In identifying a particular section of a climb as no-falls territory, however, you must acknowledge the potential consequences of falling and engage in measured decision-making as to whether you should climb onward with caution or retreat to safety.

- **Adopt the attitude that it's okay to fall (assuming a safe fall) and that *Falling won't bother me, I'll just get back up and give it another go.*** By willingly accepting this fate (if it should even happen), you totally dissolve the fear of falling that weighs down so many climbers.

- **Accept that feeling some fear and experiencing occasional failure are part of the climbing process.** Adventure and fearful feelings are inseparable, just as failure and learning go hand in hand. If you love climbing, then you must learn to accept some degree of fear and failure. Trust that with increasing experience (and patience), these fears will wane.

- **Leave your ego, pretense, and need to succeed at home.** Strive to regain your beginner's mind-set, when you loved climbing simply for the sake of climbing, irrespective of performance. Refuse to let the pressure to perform—or your fears—ruin your enjoyment of each climbing experience. Love climbing unconditionally.

CHAPTER ELEVEN

Mind Programming
and Behavior Modification

Whether you recognize it or not, you are a mind programmer. Every waking moment your thoughts and mental images, and your decisions and physical actions create new synaptic connections and solidify (or degrade) existing neuro-associations. For your ever-malleable brain, the only constant is change.

The focus of this book's instruction is on taking greater control of the processes of neuro-association and neuroplastic change (physiological changes of the brain) in order to become a better climber. Preceding chapters have provided dozens of practical techniques for improving self-awareness, concentration, clarity of thought, and fear management, among other things. This chapter will arm you with powerful mind-programming strategies to improve conscious and unconscious brain function and increase performance in all you do.

In the first section we'll examine proven techniques, such as mental rehearsal, visualization, and affirmations, to effect change on the brain. Such mind programming can help you learn new climbing skills, preprogram an on-sight ascent, improve

Advancing to the next climbing level demands that you think and act differently than you have up to this point.

climbing technique and tactics, and elevate your redpoint ability. The latter half of the chapter will examine several cognitive-behavioral techniques to help you modify limiting behaviors and challenge undesirable tendencies and habits.

While only a primer on the subject of cognitive-behavioral science, this chapter will underscore the great power you possess in terms of programming your brain–behavior connections and directing your life. Ultimately, you create your future every day when you decide what you want, and how you will think and act. What you imagine and think to yourself not only dictates your present actions but also programs your brain and future outcomes. Yosemite big-wall pioneer Royal Robbins aptly applies this concept to climbing in stating that "Before the deed, comes the thought. Before the achievement, comes the dream. Every mountain we climb, we first climb in our mind."

Lauren Lee redpointing **Only Entertainment (5.13b), Eleven Mile Canyon, Colorado.**
KEITH LADZINSKI

By learning to better channel our muscle and brain power—and tap into new reserves—we can achieve beyond our current comprehension on the rocks, mountains, and beyond!

Reading this book is a significant step toward realizing a new level of cognitive and motor skill, as well as new heights in your climbing. Ultimately, however, it's your dedication to learn and apply the individual mental-training exercises that determines how great an impact brain training will have on your future.

I believe that we each possess a vast reservoir of untapped brain power; additionally, we all waste a portion of our current brain resources on low-value pursuits and ineffective thinking. Thus, by learning to better channel our muscle and brain power—and tap into new reserves—we can achieve beyond our current comprehension on the rocks, mountains, and beyond!

Programming Your Mind for Peak Performance

Preceding chapters have shown you how thoughts and mental imagery are precursors to action, and you've learned many techniques to target thinking to enhance the quality of your actions. The mind-programming strategies revealed on the pages that follow take this concept to the next level—you will learn how to use mental imagery and verbal affirmations to wire your brain to better execute a physical skill and follow through on a desired course of action. Such mental training not only makes the conscious mind more familiar with a specific movement or task, but also programs the unconscious mind by firing related synapses and creating neuro-associations that will guide future behavior and execution of complex motor skills.

The use of mind-programming techniques as a method of enhancing self-regulation and physical performance can be traced back to the Russian space program and Eastern Bloc Olympic training programs of the 1950s and 1960s. It was Russian sports psychologist Alexander Romen who showed, through electromyograms, that mental imagery triggers electrical impulses in muscles. This suggested that the mental rehearsal and visualization of physical skills triggered the same neural pathways as physical exercise, and thus it had practical use for preprogramming a sports skill or any other important routine.

Not until the 1980s did Western countries grasp the power of such mental training, perhaps spurred on by a study of Russian athletes training for the 1980 Olympics. This study compared the performance of four groups of athletes, each engaging in different amounts of physical and mental training. Group 1 engaged only in physical training for the Olympics; Group 2's training sessions were a combination of physical and mental training at a ratio of three to one, respectively; Group 3 equally split their training time between physical and mental training; while Group 4's training comprised 75 percent mental training and 25 percent physical. In comparing the four groups just prior to the Olympics, Group 4 showed the most improvement and Group 3 the second most. No doubt, this remarkable finding compelled athletes in many other countries to include copious mental training in their preparations for competition.

Upcoming you will learn several applications of mind programming that are guaranteed to improve your climbing. Specifically, we'll examine the power of mental rehearsal, visualization, physical simulations, and affirmations as preparation for skilled movement and as pathways to greater confidence and higher overall efficacy.

Mental Rehearsal

Mental rehearsal, a most basic form of mental imagery, is a well-researched cognitive-behavioral method widely used among climbers. It involves the simple process of reviewing a sequence of moves soon to be performed and considering risk management steps to be taken.

For example, in standing at the base of a climb you would talk through the sequence—*Right hand goes here, then the left hand goes there*—and imagine a possible sequence of gear placements (and then rack your gear accordingly). Engaging in this form of mental preparation increases your familiarity with the holds, sequence, and protection, and thus empowers you to move more quickly and accurately, as well as to anticipate risk and protect yourself more effectively. Simple mental rehearsal does little to preprogram the unconscious mind and neuromuscular system, however; visualization is the power tool to use for this (more on this in a bit).

Here are two excellent applications of mental rehearsal for climbers.

 ### Preclimb Mental Rehearsal of Sequences and Protection

Preclimb mental rehearsal is an exercise of your visual acuity, imagination, and familiarity with the full breadth of climbing moves. Obviously, vast climbing experience is essential in order to accurately "read" the holds, moves, and body positions of an upcoming climb. Less experienced climbers can most quickly develop this important skill by using mental rehearsal before every route and by occasionally engaging in guided imagery with a more experienced climber or coach (see the next exercise to learn more).

The goal of this mental exercise is to identify all the critical holds and as much of the sequence and protection as possible. Based on past experience you try to imagine body positions, rest positions, and gear placements, as well as potential fall trajectories and how the rope and gear (or spotter) can be best positioned to protect you. Mentally, this process involves open-eye imagery in which you "see" yourself moving on the rock, placing gear, and perhaps even falling (in order to determine the potential danger of a fall). Such mental rehearsal is an essential part of risk management as you imagine what-if scenarios and anticipate responses.

For big-wall and alpine climbers, mental rehearsal expands into a much more complex and lengthy task of developing an overall ascent–descent strategy. The mental rehearsal can be aided by examining a climbing topo or route photo (to rehearse the ascent strategy), talking to other climbers who have done the route (to gather beta), and even using Google Earth to capture a three-dimensional mental image and gain a sense of "knowing" with regard to a somewhat unknown approach and descent (a tool that I've found to be both helpful and inspiring in preparing for a major climb).

Guided Imagery for Beginners

Guided imagery is an excellent learning tool. The most common use of guided imagery is for an expert climber (or coach) to help talk a less experienced climber through the mental rehearsal of a route. Standing at the base of the climb, the coach helps the student see the holds, likely sequence, and path of the route. Effective guided imagery should include clear descriptions of proper hand and foot placements, body positioning, center-of-gravity placement, and protection locations or clipping positions. The best guided imagery will also include descriptions of the subtle proprioception of doing an unusual or crux move. For example, he might say, "Shift your hips over your high-stepping right foot and feel your center of gravity settle over that foot; at the same time let your arm muscles relax and feel tension fall on the bones of your straight arms."

A coach can also use guided imagery to teach proper visualization to a novice climber and to prepare a competition climber for the novel setting of an upcoming event. In a quiet room, the student should relax, close her eyes, and visualize the exact sequence of the climb or competition situation as described by the coach. The coach should provide vivid details that draw the senses of vision, touch, hearing, and proprioception into play. After a few sessions of such coach-guided imagery, the climber will possess enough knowledge of proper mental rehearsal and visualization technique to effectively engage in these preparatory techniques on her own.

Visualization

You have just learned the benefits of mental rehearsal, a widely used method of mapping out a sequence before climbing. Less commonly used, except among elite climbers, visualization goes far beyond the simple task of locating holds and mentally rehearsing a sequence in that it actually provides you with a practice ascent via the virtual reality of your mind's eye. Thus, while mental rehearsal helps you see a sequence, visualization actually allows you to *experience* the sequence!

Numerous studies have shown that vivid visualization provides many of the same benefits of physical practice and training. One study observed similar brain activity in subjects who sat at a piano and imagined played a sequence of notes as those who actually played the sequence of notes on the piano. Another study compared a group doing a finger exercise and a group that just imagined the finger exercise. The physical group performed sets of fifteen maximum contractions, while the other group vividly visualized the exercise and the sound of a coach shouting at them "Harder, harder, harder!" After four weeks of training, the group doing the physical exercise increased their strength by 30 percent; the group engaging in only imagined training amazingly increased theirs by 22 percent!

The likely reason for the improvement is that vivid visualization fires brain neurons specific to the physical activity with the same motor programs and neural pathways being activated. And since your imagination can transport you out of the present moment, you can imagine a past or future climb to strengthen or even create task-specific neuronal activity, respectively.

To be effective, however, visualization must be vivid and multisensory. Incorporating tactile feel of rock, the kinesthetic (proprioception of what moves feel like) and auditory sense (hearing slow breathing and carabiner clips), and metacognition (what you will think in certain future predicaments) makes visualization a profoundly realistic mental experience that embosses the brain in ways similar to the actual physical experience. The result is a mental blueprint for quick, accurate execution of moves, increased confidence and concentration, and a déjà-vu sense of feel for moves that you've not before climbed.

Let's continue our study of mind programming by learning the two primary modes of visualization: dissociated and associated.

- **Dissociated visualization** involves seeing yourself from the perspective of an outside observer. You watch yourself investigate and climb a route from that observer's point of view. As used in mental rehearsal, you can effectively use dissociated visualization to mentally test body positions, sequences, and risk management strategies from an on-TV perspective before beginning vivid associated visualization to preprogram an ascent. This mode of visualization is also best for reviewing a past poor performance that you hope to improve upon. As a

---

Table 11.1 *Important Components of Effective Visualization*

Dissociated Visualization (mental rehearsal using "observer's" perspective)	Associated Visualization (mind programming via "virtual" climbing)
• Identify hand- and footholds, and then imagine possible body positions and moves by projecting an image of your body onto the rock.	• See yourself grabbing each hold and carefully placing each foot from the perspective of the climber.
• Imagine gear placements, the rope path, and possible problems with rope drag that may arise.	• Feel the texture of handholds and feel the quality of foot placements.
• Imagine possible fall trajectories and swing; determine if there's any potential to hit a ledge or other object should you fall.	• Feel climbing movements and proprioception of changing body positions.
• Imagine climbing strategy, as well as risk management what-if scenarios.	• Hear steady, deep breathing and the reassuring sound of the rope clipping into carabiners.
• From a bird's-eye view, imagine the path of the approach and descent from the climb.	• Feel your muscles relax at shakeouts.
	• Experience the pleasure of focused movement.
	• Feel the emotion of a successful ascent.

detached observer, you can replay the movie and objectively view the mistakes or falls without reliving the possibly unhappy emotions of the situation.

- **Associated visualization** provides a "through-your-own-eyes" perspective— you might call this "virtual climbing" since you are visualizing the sensory experience of the climb in your mind's eye. Such associated visualization is ideal for preprogramming a future ascent: It activates the brain's motor programs and neural pathways in a way that's similar to actually climbing the route.

Given this remarkable array of benefits, you can see why going beyond simple mental rehearsal and becoming proficient at visualization is essential for climbing your best. No doubt, you already engage in some simple visualization in your daily life, perhaps without even knowing it. For example, when you think about the best way to drive across town, you likely see the key turns or landmarks along the way in your mind's eye. Visualization is also used "effectively" by people who worry a lot—part of their worry ritual is wild visualization of some future event that may or may not happen to them (or some loved one). This form of negative visualization is especially painful and depressing when experienced from an associated perspective.

Every mountain we climb, we first climb in our mind.

Following are four ways to use visualization to improve your climbing. You can best master this powerful mental tool with daily practice that expands the use of vivid visualization to other areas of your life.

Visualization to Enhance Learning and "Climb" While Injured

Visual imagery is part of the coding system that helps humans understand movement and learn skills. The natural tendency for many people, however, is to visualize with rather vague sensory detail and in a dissociated mode. You can enhance and accelerate learning by creating vivid, multisensory, and associated mental movies of practicing a move or sequence as if you were really executing the physical skill.

Specific examples of applying this to climbing include: visualizing every tiny detail of movement and feel in climbing a hand crack; visualizing the explosive arm and leg movements and kinesthetics of making a lunge movement on a boulder problem you are working; and visualizing all the movements and experiencing the proprioception of executing a crux sequence on a project climb. By entering a calm, relaxed state (use the relaxation exercise on page 106) and repeatedly running these vivid mental movies, you groove the neural pathways for successful, effective physical execution.

If you climb for enough years, you will at some point likely find yourself laid up due to some type of injury. Whether you are out for a few weeks due to a finger injury or out for the season with a more serious problem, you can still exercise the brain's motor programs and fire neural pathways with regular visualization. Spend thirty minutes a few days per week vividly visualizing various exercises and climbing routes, and you certainly will be better off than if you did nothing at all during your break from climbing.

Preclimb (or Pre-Action) Visualization

One of the most powerful applications of visualization is to transport yourself to a place you've never been before in order to practice some unrehearsable task. Applied to climbing, this is an invaluable tool before an on-sight attempt on a boulder problem, rock climb, or alpine ascent, and ahead of a climbing competition.

Since you have no firsthand experience, it may be difficult to create an accurate movie from the associated perspective. Therefore, you'll want to begin visualization in the dissociated mode and attempt to work through as much of the experience as possible from this detached, overview perspective. Create images of your body on the rock performing moves, dropping in gear at the obvious placements, and hanging out at what appear to be good rest positions. Visualize any hazards unique to this climb—where a lead fall might be dangerous, what you can do to minimize the risk, and so forth.

As you develop a game plan and gain comfort in the situation, you may be able to associate and live out the experience as if it were happening in the present moment. Try to feel the moves and see the sequence play out as if you are successfully ascending the route. In aggregate, this breadth and depth of visualization preprograms your unconscious mind with neurological tracks for proper technical execution of the climb, and it prepares your conscious mind with strategy and confident feelings that will help you challenge the fears and unknowns of the situation.

In competition climbing, good visualization skills might mean the difference between winning and finishing in the middle of the pack. Since many events allow only a brief preview period, you will only be able to create a "rough-cut" movie, including the basic route path, location of the obvious rests, and whatever you can glean about the moves or sequence. Even if you can't decipher a sequence (or if you didn't get a route preview), you can still take a mental picture of the wall and competition setting, and project yourself climbing with grace and confidence to the cheers of the crowd. Most important, strive to eliminate any self-defeating and distracting images that cross your mind, and foster a calm mental state from which you can climb your best.

Visualization to Enhance Projecting

Projecting is the process of working a difficult boulder problem or route, usually over a period of days or weeks, in which you repeatedly practice the climb and perhaps even train for a certain physical demand of the climb. Mental training is also an integral part of the process; when done properly, it can accelerate learning and hasten realization of a successful ascent.

Most people begin the projecting process by exploring the climb via rappel, toprope, or liberal hangdogging on lead. In gathering data about the climb, you can employ dissociated visualization to mentally test possible moves before you try them for real. Eventually you will unlock a sequence of doable moves to hopefully connect for a successful redpoint ascent. The problem is that most project climbs are so physically rigorous that you are limited to only a few redpoint attempts per day. This is where associated visualization excels. If used properly, it can lift you to send the route sooner than you might expect.

The key is to embrace the training strategy of the top Russian athletes in the 1980 study described earlier. These most-improved Olympic athletes engaged in mental and physical practice at a ratio of three to one, respectively. Thus, for every physical attempt you make on a project climb, you should ascend the route three times in your mind's eye.

Since you know all the moves—how they look and feel—it's essential that you engage in associated visualization and strive to experience all aspects of doing the climb. Leave no detail out of your mental movie: See each hand and foot placement in vivid detail, feel each move and finesse of body tension, experience each clipping position (hear the carabiner clip), feel deep, steady breathing, and subvocalize the positive self-talk you use to coax yourself through a crux move. Make the movie positive and perfect in every way, and always conclude with the sight and feeling of reaching the top.

In addition to using associated visualization of your project between attempts, you should also run these vivid mental movies on your rest days. Such mental training is arguably more important than doing physical training exercises, since it is far more specific and actually fires the same neurons as doing the climb for real.

You can obtain the greatest programming of your unconscious mind by engaging in visualization while in a highly relaxed state. The unconscious mind is most accepting when the brain is in the alpha state that develops just before falling asleep. Knowing this, you should mentally climb your project routes as you lie in bed just before falling asleep. Perform a few minutes of progressive relaxation (page 106), then begin your associated visualization. Try to foster a still, distraction-free mental state in which there's no activity other than the mental movie playing in your mind's eye. Ideally, you'll drift off to sleep during your third or fourth mental ascent of the project climb.

As a mostly weekend-only climber, I have effectively used weekday visualization to increase my chances of sending a project during brief trips to the crags. A most memorable example was working on the first ascent of *Diamond Life,* a route at the New River Gorge that would become West Virginia's first 5.13 climb. Over the course of three weeks, I worked the route a few times each weekend and then climbed the route dozens of times more in my mind's eye during the weekdays at home in Pennsylvania. This strategy enabled me to send the route on a cool, crisp late-October day back in 1987. Interestingly, I can today still remember the entire crux sequence—further evidence of the power of mind programming via visualization!

Visualization in Problem Solving and Possibility Thinking

Einstein famously pointed out that "your imagination is a preview of life's coming attractions." It should be no surprise, then, that visualization is an integral part of planning to reach future goals, solving complex problems, and creating novel products, ideas, and achievements.

The power of your mind to take you to places you've never been is quite amazing and profound. You can investigate solutions, invent things, test novel actions, develop goals, and—as Messner put it—"move mountains in your mind." It's important to recognize, however, that future-oriented visualization goes far beyond daydreaming (which tends to be vague, wishful, and lacking any real intention to act) in that it is highly targeted, purposeful, and frequently coupled with physical action. The outcomes of daydreaming versus those of purposeful visualization are unmistakably different—daydreaming produces little or no tangible benefit or achievement, whereas visualizing with intention yields a track record of achievements (and failures), inventions and innovations, and lives changed.

You can put future-oriented visualization to work in all aspects of your life, not only by visualizing what you plan to do in the next moment, but also by projecting your imagination weeks, months, and years into the future. For example, invest some time each day into visualizing the pathway to the goals you set in chapter 7. Actively experiment and modify your mental pathway and strategy for reaching these goals—such long-term visualization must be kept dynamic and changing, not set in stone, since there will undoubtedly be twists and turns in your real

---

Tips for Enhancing Performance with Visualization

- **Use dissociated visualization (observer's perspective) for route finding, imagining possible sequences, risk management, and reviewing failed attempts.**

- **Use associated visualization (climber's perspective) to mentally climb the route.** Feel the ascent evolve, including all physical movements and thought processes. The goal is to mentally practice—virtually experience!—all aspects of doing the climb.

- **Make associated visualization as bright, detailed, and multisensory as possible.** Relax and don't rush through it—your goal is to visualize a complete ascent with no interruptions.

- **Keep your visualization positive.** Quickly nix any negative images that surface, such as visions of yourself struggling or falling.

- **Engage in visualization in a quiet area free of distractions.** To maximize programming of the unconscious mind, precede visualization with progressive relaxation, or engage in visualization training just before falling asleep when the brain enters the receptive alpha state.

journey toward the goals. To this end, use your long-term visualization as "thought experiments" in which you test different strategies and permutations of action.

One thing to avoid in future-oriented visualization is dwelling on the risks and possible negative outcomes the future may hold. While mental planning must include what-if scenarios that anticipate potential risk and your subsequent countermeasures, you must not allow your visualization to degrade into a brainstorming session of reasons not to act. For instance, if you primarily visualize yourself failing on some future route or in competition, you not only preprogram this possible outcome but also destroy your self-confidence in the process. Similarly, you must balance thought of the risks of action with images of the potential rewards of acting in pursuit of your goals. Finally, remember that it's human nature (pursuant to the innate survival instinct) to overestimate risk and the chance of failure when planning to step into the great unknown of the future. Use the fear management strategies provided in chapter 10 to challenge these imaginary fears, and use optimism as a tool to deal with uncertainty and potential unknowns.

Physical Simulation

One of the best methods of grooving motor skills, developing neuro-efficiency, and building confidence is to engage in a highly specific physical simulation that fires many of the same neuropathways as the target task. Two applications of physical simulation are training on a simulator climb that closely mirrors the project climb, and simulating the approximate setting and protocol of an upcoming competition. Let's take a closer look at these two training strategies.

 ### Build a Simulator of a Specific Skill or Sequence

Simulator training dates back at least to 1960, when John Gill began training for the small, pebbly *Thimble* route in the Needles of South Dakota. To simulate the difficult pebble pinching, Gill climbed the wall of a gymnasium by pinching nuts and bolts sticking out from the wall! Famous Colorado climber Jim Collins used route simulators to help train for cutting-edge first ascents of *Psycho Roof* and *Genesis* in the late 1970s.

With the advent of indoor climbing walls, developing a training simulator became a relatively simple matter. You can select a section of wall with a similar angle to your project climb and then mount holds of the same size in the approximate configuration of your project route's crux. Pumping out several laps, a few days per week, on this simulator will groove motor programs, develop schema, and build highly specific strength. Furthermore, this form of blocked practice will shift more technical aspects of move execution to the preconscious mind, thus freeing up more conscious bandwidth to focus on the most critical elements of movement. Given these many benefits, it should be a no-brainer to employ simulator training to help make your next project a reality!

A final point: You can also use simulator training to accelerate learning of a set of skills. For example, you can build a theme boulder problem that isolates a specific skill, such as backstepping, hip turning, or deadpointing, that you'd like to improve.

You can also make an adjustable crack board or visit a gym with different-size cracks to develop specific crack climbing motor programs.

Simulate a Competition Situation

Mainstream sports teams frequently engage in practice with simulated competition settings and situations, such as a football team practicing a two-minute drill with artificial crowd noise blasting away at the field. Serious competition climbers would be wise to similarly engage in mock competition practice.

The goal is to mimic an upcoming competition as closely as possible, including exactly timed climbing and rest intervals, background noise and distractions, and incorporating all the other rules of the event. In preparing for a bouldering competition in which you will attempt to climb a series of five problems in specific time intervals, for example, you would execute a series of increasingly difficult routes in a way that mirrors the competition format. Your goal is to go through all the preparations and climbing rituals just as you will on competition day. The payoff for such a realistic competition simulation is that your brain (conscious and unconscious minds) will have a blueprint for effective action, thus yielding a confident *I've been here before* feeling and an optimistic familiar sense in engaging the climb.

Affirmations

As learned in chapter 9, affirmations and mantras are effective tools for narrowing focus and directing the conscious mind. Nearly fifty years ago Bulgarian psychiatrist Georgi Lozanov demonstrated that repeating specific words and phrases could also be used to condition human response. Lozanov showed that repeated self-talk, in the form of affirmations stated in the first person, could alter physiological functions, mental health, behavior, and learning.

The key is to saturate the unconscious mind with brief, positive statements of intention and belief. Repeating affirmations, while in a state of deep relaxation and mental stillness, transmits these messages to the unconscious mind where they will eventually be acted on as real and true. Here's how you can use affirmations to program your unconscious to assume a more positive, productive, and resourceful state.

Program New Habits and Beliefs with Bedtime Affirmations

First, determine what mental quality or aspects of your self-image you'd like to modify in order to enhance your day-to-day attitude and effectiveness. Boil down the desired affect or trait to a short phrase that is very specific, positive, and present tense, and then make it personal by adding an *I am* at the beginning of the phrase. A few examples of well-structured affirmations include: *I am a strong, confident, and capable climber; I am patient, disciplined, and on track toward my goals; I am mentally tough and physically strong; I am calm, confident, and energized to act.*

After creating a brief, specific, and personal affirmation (or adopting one of the four affirmations listed above), repeat the affirmation fifty to one hundred times

Summary of Mind-Programming Techniques

- **Use mental rehearsal before every climb and important task.** Use dissociated mental rehearsal in deciphering route sequences, developing climbing strategy, and risk management planning.

- **Engage in vivid visualization to program the unconscious mind for all your climbs and goals.** Regularly visualize the pathway to your mega goals, and use visualization before every major climb. Associate with the mental movie—*see* the action in vivid color and *feel* the motion and emotion of the process.

- **Utilize simulator training to build task-specific skills and strength.** Physical simulations will better prepare you for a competition as well as condition your muscles, motor skills, and mind for the specific demands of a project climb.

- **Use affirmations to create an optimal mental state and unconscious behavioral forcing.** The words you think and speak direct your conscious and unconscious minds, so repeat positive, empowering statements first thing in the morning, at bedtime, and throughout the day.

each night as you are falling asleep. You do not want to actually keep count of the affirmations; instead just slowly repeat them in your mind as you drift off to sleep. The affirmations will best penetrate and program your unconscious mind if you are in a deeply relaxed state, so it's advantageous to perform progressive relaxations (see page 106) before you begin.

Affirmations are also powerful for establishing an optimal state as your day begins. Upon waking, crowd out of your mind any negative thoughts (*I'm tired, I don't feel like getting up and climbing right now,* or whatever) with a brief, positive affirmation that will set the stage for a great day. Create an inspiring affirmation that will put you in an optimal mental state each morning, and then use it daily. Or you can use one of my two favorite morning affirmations: *I'm excited and energized to live this day to the fullest,* and *This is the day that the Lord has made, I will rejoice and be glad in it.*

Like many forms of mental training, use of affirmations provides a gradual conditioning effect that may not become noticeable for some period of time. However, faithfully use your affirmation each night as you fall asleep and upon waking in the morning, and trust that it will benefit you greatly in the long run. Some future day, as you confidently prepare for or top out on a climb, you will discover that you possess the empowering quality or trait that you have been affirming. On this day of realization, resist the thought that you can now cease your bedtime affirmation and instead leverage the fact that your past affirmations have worked to compel a renewed commitment to use a modified or new affirmation every day.

Modifying Limiting Behaviors

Bridging the gap between you and your goals requires learning new skills, taking effective actions, and eliminating limiting behaviors. While you are undoubtedly passionate about learning to climb better, chances are you possess some habits or behaviors that limit your effectiveness and covertly sabotage your performance. The focus of this section, then, is to identify and eliminate behaviors that hamper— or perhaps even cripple—your ability to think, act, and climb with maximum effectiveness. Left unchecked, such limiting behaviors weigh you down like invisible sandbags, robbing you of physical energy, straining your thought processes, and quelling your spirit.

A central theme of this book is that your thoughts play a most fundamental role in how you respond to life's events and challenges. Some of us take on challenges with a repertoire of well-honed analytic skills (to quickly and effectively size up problem situations and craft responses), confidence, strength, and persistence. Others shrink from challenges, perhaps because they lack those very qualities, all of which involve positive, higher-order thinking. The very good news is that for the vast majority of us, the thought processes involved in effectively analyzing situations, planning, and performing effectively are modifiable. With hard work we can improve ourselves. We can achieve goals we might have thought impossible, and we and those around us can experience newfound happiness and fulfillment.

Self-improvement begins with improving your metacognitive ability (self-awareness of your thoughts) and refining your internal dialogue. Once you've taken control of your ways of thinking, you can modify or delete limiting behaviors by learning to solve problems (instead of wallowing in them), change bad habits (instead of allowing them to sabotage you), challenge fears (instead of avoiding them), and compel intelligent action toward your goals (instead of backpedaling at the first sign of adversity).

As you delve into this section on behavior modification, it's important to recognize that real change requires strong, focused efforts, not unlike cranking through a maximal crux move. Change requires that you challenge your old reactive ways of responding by taking a firm hold of the moment between the stimulus (a presenting problem or challenge) and your response to it. The crux of this process is to stretch out this interval between stimulus and response—call it the *moment of decision*—so that you can intelligently interpret the situation and then leverage your hierarchy of values and goals to formulate a most effective response (see figure 11.1).

This moment of decision is a human endowment that far too many of us fail to use effectively. For example, by responding to a stimulus instantly or impulsively, without rational thought, we risk behaving in ways that may have unfavorable consequences. Think about incidents of road rage, impulsive eating or buying, substance abuse, gambling, and so on. While rapid responding is particularly adaptive in some rare situations (for example, instinctively ducking away from rockfall or running from an avalanche), overly reactive responses most often produce ineffective, even counterproductive responses. The master skill you want to develop is the ability to resist a reactive response and to seize the moment of decision in

Figure 11.1 *The Moment of Decision*

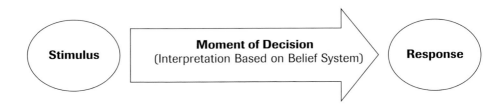

Between stimulus and response, humans have the freedom to pause and choose their response based on rational thought and personal values.

order to think and respond most intelligently to a stimulus. Possessing this skill will empower you to best respond to the many small decisions you make throughout the day, as well as in major watershed moments of decision that may have life-changing impacts.

This section on behavior modification employs techniques that would fall under the general psychological classification of cognitive-behavioral therapy (CBT). While CBT has been used effectively in the treatment of phobias, depression, attention deficit disorder, and other psychological problems, it has also been used extensively in sports psychology and other areas of self-improvement. This chapter is not intended to address or provide psychotherapy; please consult a licensed psychologist or psychiatrist if you feel you have psychological concerns that need to be addressed. Some of the tenets of cognitive-behavioral therapy are:

- Emotions and behaviors are moderated (influenced) by your thoughts and need not be held hostage by external variables such as people, events, and expected outcomes. Therefore, you must change your ways of thinking if you want to change your feelings and the quality of your actions.

- Becoming upset about negative situations and outcomes is most often counterproductive. By responding to undesirable situations with stoic calmness and skilled analysis, you put yourself in a better state to act with intelligence and economy.

- Since many emotional and behavioral reactions are learned through life experiences, they can also be unlearned and changed through planned experience. The key is to learn to seize control of the moment of decision—to objectively interpret events and intelligently select your thoughts and course of action.

- Thoughts and thought patterns should be treated as hypotheses, not fact, and they should be questioned and tested to determine validity. This inductive method encourages you to base your thoughts on fact, rather than subjective feelings.

- Changing your ways of thinking, feeling, and acting is hard work. Real, lasting change requires disciplined *mental training.*

On upcoming pages I will reveal numerous cognitive-behavioral techniques for overcoming procrastination, increasing motivation, breaking patterns of negative thinking, diminishing bad memories, dismantling bad habits, overcoming unproductive emotional states, lowering stress, and changing limiting beliefs. It's important to recognize, however, that change is rarely quick or easy—there are no quick fixes, despite what some self-help books or infomercials might imply.

While we can benefit from the positive stimulation of external sources, like this book, ultimately we all must grow and change from the inside out. Rewiring our brains and developing new ways of thinking is hard cerebral work that requires daily mental training fueled by a compelling reason to change. So always keep your goals in mind and, as Saint Augustine said, "Pray as if everything depends on God, and work as if everything depends on you."

Identifying Limiting Behaviors

In the space below, or in your training notebook, list patterns of thought and behaviors that limit your effectiveness in climbing and other important everyday activities. Consider the situations and challenges you face in climbing and other activities of importance and write these in the left column. Next, determine what thoughts hinder you in these situations/challenges; what reactions disempower you; and what habits or tendencies rob you of energy, focus, and time (which could be better invested in working toward your goals). Write these down in the right column. Finally, consider this: Is there one area or aspect of your life that you feel must be changed? If so, write that area of change on the bottom line. Now read on, and think of how you can use the various techniques detailed on the pages that follow to modify these behaviors and embark on a new trajectory toward your goals.

Situation/Challenges

Thoughts/Reactions/Habits

_____ _____

_____ _____

_____ _____

_____ _____

_____ _____

_____ _____

_____ _____

Ending Procrastination, Increasing Motivation, and Changing Your Ways

I'm sure you've heard the saying that, "The definition of insanity is doing the same things over and over and expecting different results." Surprisingly, though, many of us are practitioners of this "insane" way of acting. We go to the gym and crags (or live our lives) with the same modus operandi as last week or last year, and expect things to change or improve. We willingly bask in the comfort of training the same ways, climbing at the same areas, and partnering with the same people, even though this is a fundamentally flawed strategy for improving in climbing and reaching our goals.

Similarly, some people struggle with procrastination as they put off working toward the goals they have set and the future life experiences they desire. There is great comfort in remaining within the margin of what is known in the present, whereas exploring beyond the margin brings risk of stress, discomfort, and fear of the unknown. While they may still envision breaking free and reaching for something greater, they find the gravitational pull of their present world as too strong to overcome, too comfortable. Consequently, many people gradually fall into the trap of willingly accepting the status quo as "good enough."

If any of this sounds familiar, you are about to discover a pathway to change! No longer do you need to be limited by the past, your lack of motivation, or the fear of change. By employing the techniques that follow, you will quickly overcome the inertia of your current ways and embark on a new and exciting journey toward your goals.

 Make Action (or Change) a Must by Imagining the Pain of Inaction (or Not Changing)

Procrastination, lack of motivation, and acceptance of status quo are habits of inaction that develop over time. Since these tendencies were learned at some point in childhood or adulthood (there's no such thing as being a born procrastinator!), they can also be unlearned given a serious effort. There's a fondness these days in talking about change, yet real change never comes until the "change" shifts from rhetoric and slogan to an actual modus operandi. The key to making this shift is finding a strong enough reason why change is essential. Saying that you'd like to change isn't going to cut it—you need to decide that change is a *must* and that you will live each day with the intention to engage in acts of change.

Associate pain with inaction and pleasure with taking action.

The best way to gain leverage to embark on a path of change is to shift from the paradigm of always considering the risk and discomfort of change to instead considering the risk and pain of not changing. You can create massive leverage for change by asking yourself these questions: *What are the long-term consequences if I don't change, and how do they compare with the short-term risk and effort of initiating change? What dream climbs might I never experience and what things might I never accomplish if I don't change? How might changing some aspect of my life and elevating my personal effectiveness have a positive impact on the lives of those around me?*

In answering these pointed questions, you can rationally see that you may very well lose out on opportunities that life serves up or, perhaps worse, experience more pain in the long term by not acting! Thus, you create two powerful new associations: *Taking action is pleasurable* (since it will move you toward your goals), and *not acting results in a sense of loss or is painful* (since inaction means you will never reach the goals you so much desire). This simple tactic is the secret of peak performers the world over who exhibit an amazing bias for action—they associate pain with inaction and pleasure with taking action. By doing the same, you will depart on a new path toward uncommon success and experience!

 ### Set Small Goals to Build Lasting Motivation

If you struggle with motivation to train or go climbing, then you'll never reach your mega goals or experience maximum climbing. While setting big goals tends to incite motivation, some people discover that their mega goals create a sense of overwhelm that can subdue their motivational energy. Even highly accomplished veteran climbers occasionally experience motivational doldrums—even burnout—as a result of lack of improvement, boredom with their current climbing routine, or overtraining. So regardless of your ability, I can guarantee that you will occasionally encounter motivational troughs. Here are three techniques to arouse motivation and maintain forward motion toward your goals.

- **Decide that you will only do a brief workout or take an easy climbing day.** Brief lapses in motivation can happen to anyone at any time, as a result of low physical energy, a stressful day at work or school, or an emotional life event. Such temporary motivational troughs affect us all from time to time, and they are something that you must resolve to push through. The trick is to somehow prod yourself to go to the gym for a light workout, a short run, or a brief climbing session. By willing yourself to engage in just an abbreviated workout, you naturally change your physiology and thus your mood and energy level. Your thoughts turn from *I don't feel like doing anything . . .* to *I feel great—man, did I turn that funk around!* You may even continue on to complete a full-length workout or climbing session.

- **Set a series of short-term goals that you can reach for each workout or week.** More persistent motivational troughs are best overcome with a written to-do list of skills to learn, routes to send, or physical benchmarks to reach. Such performance-related benchmarks are like a metaphoric carrot that you reach for each day. The most common type of performance goal is a desired climbing grade to achieve. This month it may be to climb 5.10; next month it may be to boulder V4; next year it may be to redpoint 5.12. Similarly, you can set training goals that will pique motivation to achieve the physiological changes you desire. For instance, you might set a goal to do ten pull-ups or to lose five pounds. Training goals are most effective if they are concrete and measurable, as opposed to a less specific goal such as to improve flexibility. Over many weeks of training, you will see tangible progress toward your performance benchmark, and this will elevate your motivation even more.

- **Completely change your routine, or take a few weeks off to do other things.** A severe bout of low motivation—when you feel burned out or perhaps even ponder quitting climbing—can develop as a result of a stagnant climbing routine, a long-term performance plateau, or a loss of inspiration to engage in the same forms of climbing. The solution is to make a radical formulaic change in your climbing by changing your partners, the places you climb, and perhaps even your climbing preference. For example, if bouldering has been your focus in recent years, decide to transform yourself into a competent lead climber. Act on the belief that there is a world of amazing routes to experience if you commit to applying your bouldering prowess on the sharp end of a rope. Imagine all the great climbs and maximum climbing experiences that await you, and a renewed passion for climbing—and supercharged motivation—will be yours!

 ### Engage in Feed Forward Visualization

Many people get stuck in the trap of mainly viewing their lives from the perspective of the present (with the crisis, stress, and other urgencies of the moment); when they do envision the future, they only see the potential risks and pain that might be encountered. Of course, taking action toward long-term goals will be difficult, perhaps impossible, given a mind-set ruled by the drama of the moment and fearful visualization of future.

Just as asking yourself the right questions is empowering (as in the first exercise), so is visualizing the right images. Here's a powerful visualization exercise that I call Feed Forward. Every day, preferably in the morning, close your eyes and visualize the future and all the amazing potential that it holds. Gradually let your mental imagery settle into a clear, vivid picture of one of your important goals. With a vision of the goal completed, begin to work backward in time toward the present moment and, with all your imagination, figure out what single step you can take *today* to move you toward that future vision. Once you identify that single step, open your eyes and take it!

Summits are achieved by a small group of individuals who possess a bias for action and a love of the journey (both outside and within).

This mental exercise works because it helps you identify a specific action that you can take right now to move measurably toward a major goal. By comparison, people who procrastinate often do so because they tend to focus on a task as a daunting whole. While beginning each day with a vision of the finished goal provides a good reminder of why you must act, the process of taking effective action demands a more myopic vision. The process of pursuing any goal mirrors that of climbing a mountain—you must narrow your focus to taking one effective step at a time in the uphill direction. Use the Feed Forward exercise to help you determine what step you can take today.

In summary, pursuing big goals requires disciplined thought, a resolve to act, and the willpower to push on through adversity. Ultimately, summits are achieved by a small group of individuals who possess a bias for action and a love of the journey (both outside and within). You can become one of those people!

Eliminating Negative Thinking

Negative thinking seems like an epidemic these days, as evidenced by the ubiquitous criticism and complaining we experience in the media, at work and school, and in many social settings. Given that thought is a precursor to action, you might come to the generalized conclusion that negative thinking is what causes many people to be ineffective in their lives and perhaps even leads some people to fall victim to alcoholism, drug use, overeating, or some other method of altering their state.

In addition to giving birth to action, our thoughts determine our subjective reality. Every moment of every day, we have the choice to interpret our current situation and events in a positive or negative way. Amazingly, the choices we make often determine our reality, like a self-fulfilling prophecy. This is a remarkably simple yet immensely powerful truth.

One profound outcome of this simple truth is that life can become an amazing adventure with unlimited potential—if you can habitually find positive interpretations for events and situations. Alternatively, life can devolve into a depressing, nihilistic journey if you come to interpret most of life's events in negative ways. The bottom line: By directing positive, productive ways of thinking, you open the door to a life with great potential for achievement, experience, and wonder.

Chapter 6 provided detail instruction on how to take control of your state and develop an ideal mental, physical, and emotional platform from which to perform. One of the most important methods was to supplant negative thinking with positive thoughts, ideas, and visions. Following are three more specific techniques to help you combat negative thoughts and create a more productive and happy mental state.

 ### Thought Stopping and Thought Parking

All it takes is a single negative or unproductive thought to break your focus and degrade your ability to think and perform effectively. Furthermore, one stray bad thought can make you lose your nerve on a climb or cause you to botch a sequence and fall. It is therefore imperative that you have the mental muscle to eliminate an unwanted thought the very instant it enters your mind—to let it linger may very well lead to a cascade of negative thinking that will completely ruin your mental state and performance.

There are two simple, yet highly effective techniques to overcome a negative thought the moment it enters your consciousness. These two techniques, called *thought stopping* and *thought parking,* are ideal for use when you are in the midst of critical action that requires complete, unbroken focus. Let's take a look at each.

Thought stopping involves simply saying "Stop!" aloud whenever an irrational thought enters your mind. In lead climbing a safe route, for example, you might say "Stop!" whenever a bogus fearful thought enters your mind (such as questioning whether the rope, bolts, or your belayer will hold you); or you could say "Do it, do it!" when a thought of quitting enters your mind in the midst of a crux sequence. A training application of thought stopping is to say "Go, go!" aloud when rising fatigue causes thoughts of stopping to enter your consciousness. In each of these cases, your brief, pointed verbal statement will crowd out the negative thought, and thus help maintain focus and sustain physical performance.

Thought parking is an excellent technique to use when your mind wanders to topics or issues unrelated to the activity at hand. Let's say you are training or climbing, for example, and thoughts of school, work, or some personal relationship enter your mind. Or perhaps you are in the midst of a major climb, and thoughts arise regarding the implications of success or failure on this route. Entertaining these thoughts will transport you to the past or future as you explore the subject—yet training or climbing effectively demands that you engage the present moment with complete attention. The countermeasure is to consciously push aside, or "park," the thought to be dealt with later. Say to yourself "Not now!" and then push the thought beyond the margin of your action-oriented focus. Return your thoughts to the move or action at hand, and only revisit the parked thought when your activity has concluded.

Collapse Bad Memories

Reliving memories of ill-fated or painful past events is a most dangerous form of negative thinking. (Note that I am not referring to extremely traumatic events, like rape or war situations, that can stamp in physiological changes that present as post-traumatic stress disorder, or PTSD, and almost always require psychological assistance.) In replaying this negative experience in your mind's eye, you re-create all the emotion of the past situation and relive the pain and anxiety in the present moment. People who exhibit negative attitudes or emotions are almost always consumed by thoughts of past failures, missed opportunities, and undesirable, painful outcomes. Not only do these people think themselves into a downcast state, but they often ruin their chances of experiencing happiness and positive performance outcomes in the present moment.

As a climber, you will sometimes need to replay past epics or failed attempts as a way of leveraging past lessons and better managing risk in the present. When you must relive a poor outcome in this way, do so by visualizing the event from a dissociated, on-TV perspective. This way you can tap into the lessons learned without tapping into the bad emotions of the event.

On occasion, however, you may find yourself reliving a past failure or an unfortunate event in an associated state. This will rapidly trigger negative emotions, and put you in a poor state from which to perform. One of the biggest confidence killers and anxiety producers before beginning a climb is thinking back to a past failure and perhaps even projecting this negative outcome onto your current endeavor. Engaging in this thought process is a form of self-sabotage, and it's vital that you come to recognize this process at its onset and immediately take countermeasures to break the cycle of negative thinking.

Since we think and remember in pictures, you can take rapid control of negative memories by changing the content of the pictures you see. For example, when you discover that you are mentally reliving a bad event, immediately take control of the mental pictures and make them dark, out of focus, and small. By collapsing the mental image of the past event down to a small, dark, out-of-focus icon you immediately reduce the strength of the negative emotions the memory carries. Next, mentally compress the dark icon to tiny black dot—or even see it dissolve or explode into nothing. This process of collapsing a bad memory into nothingness begins a process of weakening your neuro-associations for this event. By collapsing the past memory in this way every time you experience it, you will soon weaken the memory to the point that it wields no emotional power over you.

Another countermeasure you can take, after collapsing the past memory, is to trigger a pre-created positive emotional anchor. In chapter 6 you learned to create a positive anchor that you can trigger at will to recall a positive, resourceful state. Use these two techniques, collapsing bad memories and triggering positive anchors, and you'll never again have to be a slave to bad memories that degrade your mental and emotional state.

 ### Surround Yourself with Positive People and Images

The most dangerous thing about negative thinking is that it's contagious. If you surround yourself with negative people who complain and criticize, it's almost inevitable that you will develop these tendencies as well. Likewise, by engaging in undermining thought, regularly visualizing negative outcomes, or entertaining worry, you allow these crippling patterns of thought to burrow deeper into your unconscious mind.

As detailed in chapter 2, your brain is a living creature with an appetite, and it is ever-learning and ever-changing. It should be overwhelmingly obvious, then, that you must vigilantly guard against negative thoughts and influences while constantly feeding on positive thoughts and images. One strategy for nurturing productive, goal-oriented thoughts is to hang inspirational photos, quotes, and a list of your goals in places that you will see them throughout the day. It's also advantageous to saturate your conscious and unconscious minds with empowering inputs at bedtime each night by reading inspirational and educational books for a few minutes before falling asleep.

Another invaluable resource are like-minded peers, possibility thinkers, mentors and coaches, teachers, parents, and any elder with wisdom to share.

Make it your approach to work, recreate, and socialize with positive, energetic people while avoiding the impossibility thinkers and complainers of the world.

Make it your approach to work, recreate, and socialize with positive, energetic people while avoiding the impossibility thinkers and complainers of the world. This is brain training at its best, because such a steady diet of fresh, positive, and novel inputs will drive neuroplastic change that literally makes you a smarter, more creative, and more effective climber.

Breaking Bad Habits

Bad habits of action wire in the brain just as good habits of action and skill do; and the more ingrained they become, the harder they are to break or, more correctly, unlearn. Regardless of whether the undesirable habit is negative thinking, smoking, or poor footwork on the rock, change is a gradual process that takes both a desire to change and the discipline to bring about change. No, breaking habits isn't easy, and rarely is it a quick process—the fast-change methods found in many self-help books rarely work.

Before I describe three methods for reprogramming unwanted behaviors, I want to stress the importance of not allowing bad habits to develop in the first place. Self-awareness of the learning process (as described in chapters 2 and 3) will empower you to take a more active role in the process of programming new skills and habits into your brain. The key concept to always keep in mind is that "neurons that fire together will wire together." So every time you get scared and grab a quickdraw, you wire this neuro-association and further ingrain this bad habit. And every time you get stressed heading into a crux sequence and allow your footwork to degrade and upper body to tighten up, you wire this behavioral reaction. Engage in these behavioral reactions repeatedly, as many climbers do on route after route, and you will develop bad habits of climbing that will plague you for many years.

With heightened self-awareness, however, you can take countermeasures when you begin to feel scared or stressed out on lead—rather than grabbing a quickdraw and allowing your footwork to degrade, you can direct deep breathing, shake out your arms, and focus more on your feet. In this way, you created a more effective neuro-association that will empower you to perform better in tough times. The master skill, then, is to become acutely aware of the learning and habit forming that is constantly ongoing in your climbing, and to play an active role in creating useful neuro-associations rather than unconsciously allowing unproductive, reactive associations to take root.

It would be advantageous to expand this proactive way of learning to all aspects of your life as well. The process of forming new neuro-associations that gradually give way to hard-to-break bad habits is exactly the same when you are at home as at the crags. If you overeat or drink excessively when you feel stressed out, this will eventually wire into a self-destructive habit. Similarly, if you react to harsh words or the criticism of others by getting mad and criticizing back, you will develop a potentially lifelong unproductive habit of letting other people pull your strings, thus diverting your focus and energy toward fighting back when it would be far more beneficial to remain focused on your goals and game plan.

The bottom line: Strive to develop iconic control of your mind, reactions (remember to pause between stimulus and response), and the learning process. Guard your sensory inputs, direct the learning of effective behaviors, and, when you identify an unproductive behavior, earmark it to be unlearned. Here are three strategies to help you do just this.

Supplant an Unwanted Habit with a New One

This first strategy works best with a newly acquired bad habit that has not been firmly wired into the brain with years of conditioning. Because this is a less deeply grooved habit, you may simply be able to replace the unwanted behavior by forcibly supplanting it with a new one. This supplantation process involves three steps: self-awareness of the undesirable habit (what stimulus triggers what response), knowledge of a more effective behavior, and seizing this moment of decision by willing yourself to replace the old behavior with the new behavior. Steadfast use of this supplantation process will often enable you to overcome an unwanted habit in a matter of days or weeks. Let's look at one example of supplanting an ineffective behavior in climbing, although you can adapt this technique to overwrite any number of other climbing or nonclimbing behaviors.

Let's examine the redpoint- and on-sight-killing behavior of grabbing gear or hanging on the rope at the first sign of stress or adversity on a lead climb. Assuming the climb is well protected and relatively safe to fall on, it's self-defeating to grab gear or "take" on to the rope when you could instead self-regulate your mental and physical state, shore up your technique, and perhaps willfully climb on to the top of the route without falling.

Applying the three-step supplantation process, you first need to develop self-awareness that the stimulus of feeling scared or pressed is about to trigger the response of grabbing gear or hanging on the rope. Next, you need to consciously think about or picture the more desirable behavior in this situation (taking a few deep breaths, relaxing your upper-body muscles, and shoring up your footwork and center-of-gravity positioning). The third step is to seize this moment of decision by choosing the new behavior over the old, and then becoming fully engaged in all aspects of the new behavior to the point that the possibility of engaging in the old behavior evaporates from your consciousness.

Choosing and engaging in the new behavior is indeed an exercise of willpower that, in addition to overwriting the old behavior, builds mental toughness. You can leverage self-talk, visualization, and any of the other mental tools that you've learned in this book to help bring about the new behavior. Say to yourself *Relax, Feel the feet, Keep climbing,* or whatever else it takes to follow through with the new behavior. Then, as you find yourself successfully engaging in the new behavior, give yourself kudos aloud by saying *Yes!, Good job,* or something else that's encouraging.

You can use this process of willfully supplanting old behaviors with new empowering ones with almost any new or evolving specific habit of action; for example, overgripping handholds or hand jams, allowing your footwork to degrade as you fatigue or get scared, overprotecting a traditional climb, or climbing mindlessly on toprope (not thinking out moves in advance and climbing with a strategic mind-set). The key is to nip the unwanted habit in the bud, before it becomes neurologically wired to the point of being an unconscious habit that will be difficult or impossible to break.

Use Zen-Like Awareness and Intention to Foster Change

Using willpower to consciously supplant a bad habit (per above) is ineffective for combating a well-learned behavior that is unconsciously triggered and not consciously realized until after the fact. Common climbing examples of often unconscious bad habits are scumming feet on a hard sequence, impulsively taking on the rope at the first sign of becoming pressed on a climb, and cursing or exploding emotionally after a failed attempt. Modifying such a deeply ingrained, instantaneous stimulus-response reaction requires a much different and more long-term approach. The technique here is to foster change on the unconscious level by combining Zen-like awareness with a persistent intention to allow change to occur, without force and anxiety, on its own schedule. Here's the five-step process to foster change.

1. Set an intention to change a specific habit. For example, *I intend to eliminate the habit of ineffectively scumming my feet across the rock when I struggle on a hard sequence.*

2. Since the habit is largely unconscious, strive simply to become aware of the habit after it's happened. Without judgment or self-criticism, observe that it happened, and consider what the ideal new behavior would have been and how it would have improved your efficacy.

3. Maintain the intention to change the behavior and continue to become aware of the ineffective behavior each time it occurs. Soon you will begin to notice the behavior as it is happening.

4. Eventually you will become aware of the unwanted behavior as it begins to occur, and thus you can choose to replace it with the more effective behavior. In the case of foot scumming, you will notice the very first time one of your feet begins to skid on the rock, and you'll instantly choose to refocus on placing your feet more solidly.

5. With repetition, and even earlier recognition and replacement of the old behavior, the habit will fade as a conditioned response. The new behavior will gradually wire into your unconscious.

Act Out the New Behavior or Quality You Want to Develop

This programming technique is based on the idea that if you walk, talk, and act as if you've already attained a new behavior, personal quality, or desired goal, you will rapidly begin to feel the part and act in congruent ways necessary to make it reality. A good sports coach exploits this technique in telling his players to "act like you've been there before," even though they are in a very difficult, novel situation. As a result of walking, talking, and acting as if they have been there before, their unconscious minds miraculously summon just the right resources to best deal with the difficult situation and maximize performance.

You, too, can use this technique in preparing for a difficult or stressful situation, or in trying to adopt a new behavior or modus operandi. Determine what qualities or MO would benefit you in the task at hand—maybe confidence, decisiveness, or even courage—then pretend as if you already possess the desired quality, and act accordingly. In doing this, you will rise to the challenge at hand and, in the long term, permanently develop the behavior or trait.

In addition to physically acting the part, you of course also want to think and feel the part. The more you can bring your mind, body, and emotions into a congruent, balanced state, the more you will actually become and exhibit the very behavior or quality you aspire to.

Employ self-talk, affirmations, and associated visualization as part of the process of acting the part, and you can quickly begin to create the new behavior or quality that you aspire to possess. For example, in trying to act the new behavior of being unafraid to lead a (safe) route, you would begin by vividly visualizing and feeling yourself ascend the route with confidence and courage. Then, just before starting up the climb, assume a confident, assertive posture with your shoulders drawn back, chest pressed out, and chin lifted up. Finally, direct copious self-talk as you engage the route—counter any scared feelings with statements such as *I'm calm and confident, I'm brave and strong,* and *I'm focused and in the moment.* While this self-talk might seem like lies, given your past struggles and old behaviors, decisively acting and affirming the part will create beneficial momentum and help sustain effort in the short term. More important, acting the part triggers the process of conditioning the new behavior, quality, or personal modus operandi in your unconscious mind.

While results are rarely instantaneous, they will be realized with a disciplined effort to consistently act the part. In time you will discover that you no longer have to act the part, because you now behave this way instinctually!

Changing Unwanted Feelings

Dealing with unwanted feelings, or even depression, is a complex topic that largely exceeds the scope of this book, although I do know of many cases in which climbing and other forms of demanding physical exercise has proved therapeutic.

This section provides a primer on the subject of changing unwanted emotions by examining two basic pathways to change: altering your physiology and changing your thoughts. Figure 6.2 (see chapter 6) reveals that you can modify how you emotionally feel by thinking new thoughts or acting in different ways. This explains why climbing is such a powerful method of changing how you feel—by its very nature, climbing demands that you narrow your thoughts to the complex task at hand *and* it forces you to alter your physiology as you engage in the strenuous process of moving over stone. Almost like a drug being injected into your system, it takes just a few minutes on the rock to completely change both your thoughts and your physiology and, thus, massively transform how you feel.

This powerful state-changing effect is exactly why many of us find climbing to be so pleasurable and perhaps even addictive. Unknowing, we may use climbing as a "drug" to modulate our feelings or to escape problems in our daily lives. The dilemma that we may eventually find ourselves in is that we can't climb every day, nor can we endlessly escalate our extreme activities in the quest of giving our brains and bodies the necessary stimulus to change how we feel. (There are a few famous examples of climbers who tried this, and they ultimately either died from their extreme behavior or quit climbing for the easier high—or escape—that alcohol or drugs provide.) We need healthy alternative strategies for changing how we emotionally feel, both in our everyday lives and for use during the occasional day of climbing when things aren't going as planned.

Following are two safe and effective methods of changing your emotional feelings. First we'll revisit the powerful state-changing faculties of the human body, then we'll examine how you can achieve a seismic change in your emotions simply by shifting your thoughts and modifying your belief system. Once again, I want to recognize that some people possess chemical imbalances in the brain that cause persistent or deep emotional troughs. If this sounds familiar, I urge you to engage a psychologist or psychiatrist.

 ### Change Your Posture or Engage in a Physical Activity

The simplest way of changing your state is to radically change your posture or to engage in an activity that will elevate your heart rate. If you don't believe me, do this simple experiment: Walk around for one minute with your shoulders curled downward and head hung low and observe how you feel; then lift your head and stand straight up with your shoulders drawn back and your chest pressed forward and walk around in this way for one minute. I'm sure you will notice a dramatic change in how you feel when in these two very different postures—slumped over you will feel weak and bleak, while standing erect with your head up you will feel energetic and optimistic. The upshot of this simple experiment is that something as simple as your posture can affect your emotions, desire to act, and potential to succeed. It's a fact that you can tell great climbers by the way they walk and talk—this is one trait of master climbers that you can safely model regardless of your ability.

Activating your body with exercise will similarly impart a dramatic change in the way you feel. One of the most interesting paradoxes in human physiology is how you apparently gain energy by working out. Thus, you can overcome a weak feeling or depressed state by forcing yourself to engage in some form of physical activity for a few minutes. Getting off the couch and beginning a workout is the crux of the matter, and it demands mental toughness and volition (so think about your goals!). After just a few minutes of exercise, however, your elevated heart and body temperature will yield an improving sense of energy and a surprising desire to keep going. The rub, then, is that if you can just get yourself to begin the workout (coax yourself by mentally committing to only a short workout), you will be transformed to a more positive, energetic state and very possibly continue on to complete a full-length workout. More important, you will have successfully extracted yourself from an unproductive funk, and you will likely go on to have a positive and pleasing day beyond the moment of the workout.

Change Your Interpretation of Events and Modify Your Belief System

Your belief system provides the framework with which you interpret events, and it's your beliefs about a specific event that determine your subjective feelings. One of the simplest ways to change how you feel, then, is to modify your belief system in ways that will allow you to interpret and react to life events more positively and productively. In evaluating your current belief system, you may discover that some long-held beliefs are not factually based, but instead simply opinions based on past experiences and old perceptions.

Update your belief system in ways that will better serve you, and you'll discover a wonderful new sense of liberation and possibility!

Create empowering beliefs that serve you, and dismantle beliefs that make you feel weak, listless, and unproductive.

In the end, there are very few absolute truths in life—the reality of a situation is usually a matter up for subjective interpretation. The most emotionally healthy, happy, and productive individuals are those whose belief systems empower them to choose a positive interpretation for almost any life event they encounter.

It takes mental toughness to challenge long-held beliefs in which you find comfort and familiarity. Change of any kind requires intense desire, effort, and a commitment to follow through in the ongoing process. For most people, modifying their belief system is a gradual process that takes time, and a continuing attitude that change is a *must*. To help expedite the process, here are four ways of challenging your old subjective interpretation of events.

- **Evaluate your mental filtering.** When in intense situations, you must resist the tendency to dwell mainly on negative feedback and outcomes while filtering out or ignoring positive results. Such mental filtering distorts the reality of the situation and is extremely disempowering. Instead you must see the full continuum of feedback—learning from your failures *and* being energized by your successes.

- **Limit or nix black-or-white assessments.** Few things in climbing (or life) are black or white; only your beliefs make them so. In falling from a climb, failing an exam, or even losing at love, it's easy to jump to the emotional conclusion that "I'm a failure." (I know, because at some point I've experienced each of these feelings.) Instead you must resist all-or-nothing assessments, and instead believe that the current situation is just a single scene in a long movie.

- **Assume the best, not the worst.** Some people see danger and failure at every turn, while others see opportunity and potential for success. Which mind-set do you most possess in climbing and life? Pause frequently to challenge thoughts of a worst-case outcome, and instead choose to use optimism as a tool (see page 143). Furthermore, knowing that your thoughts give birth to your reality, choose to focus on taking positive action in the moment rather than extrapolating current difficulties or past failures into the future.

- **View situations from a larger perspective.** In chapter 8 you learned the benefit of taking a mental inventory of past successes and life experiences—this exercise gets to the heart of your global belief system regarding the quality and meaning of your life. Never forget that you are blessed in many and unique ways, and you can best create positive emotions and a sense of well-being by viewing your life from a perspective that's much larger than your present situation.

In summary, the most productive and happy people choose their beliefs carefully, and so should you! Create empowering beliefs that serve you, and dismantle beliefs that make you feel weak, listless, and unproductive. Remember that beliefs are subjective and cannot always be logically assessed. The only litmus test of a belief's efficacy is whether or not it will help you live a more effective, happy, and peaceful life.

A classic example of such an empowering belief is French philosopher Blaise Pascal's famous wager. Pascal chose to believe that God exists, because in living with intense faith he had potentially everything to gain, and absolutely nothing to lose. Alternatively, choosing to not believe in God, Pascal would have had nothing to gain and potentially everything to lose. Obviously, Pascal's Wager is an immensely powerful belief that can affect how you feel every waking moment of every day.

Reducing Stress

Chances are there are occasionally times when you feel like your life is but a rat race amid a maze of stress-inducing situations. Perhaps even the things you do in the name of relaxation cause you to feel stressful. Consequently, you may sometimes dream of a life that's free of stress.

Stress, of course, is a part of life, and it's essential for growth and inseparable from the achievement process. Still, not all forms of stress are the same. The crux of this section is learning to actively discern between *good stress* and *bad stress.* Good stress is anything that comes as part of the process of personal growth. Just as you need to stress a muscle with exercise to make it stronger, you need to introduce some stress into your life in order to grow in just about any area. For example, beginning a new relationship is stressful; going to school or growing your career is occasionally stressful; even going climbing is frequently stressful. These areas are all sources of good stress, however, that you must recognize as such and persevere through. In doing so, you will become stronger and more capable in all the important areas of your life. The bottom line: Never give in to good stress—embrace it!

On the other hand, bad stress is what you feel in a situation that has no real benefit or in no way relates to a high value area of your life. Bad stress, left unchecked, will accumulate to the point of making you feel unmotivated, anxious, sick, or depressed. Once identified, you must immediately take action to eliminate bad stress situations from your life—typically they will not go away on their own. Following are three exercises to help you reduce stress.

Distinguish Between Good Stress and Bad Stress

Take a few minutes to write down all the things that have caused you stress over the last month. Think day-to-day if necessary to identify situations, activities, relationships, or anything else that makes you feel a significant level of stress. Next, go down the list and write good stress or bad stress next to each item. Remember that good stress has a silver lining, a potential for growth, or somehow serves a high-value area of your life (see page 96), whereas bad stress is a liability with no discernible upside potential.

_____   _____

_____   _____

_____   _____

_____   _____

_____   _____

_____   _____

Self-awareness to differentiate between the good and bad stress empowers you to persevere through times of good stress and to eliminate causes of bad stress. When you recognize that you are feeling good stress, acknowledge that it's your friend and, in fact, a sign that you are on the road to success. Constantly remind yourself, *Good stress is good!*

Conversely, view bad stress entries as the possible enemies of your current happiness and future success. Examine each bad stress item closely and consider what you can do to improve matters and lower stress; or use zero-based thinking (per below) to determine if you should permanently exit the situation.

 ### *Use Zero-Based Thinking to Eliminate Major Causes of Bad Stress*

Here is a powerful thought exercise. Ask yourself this: *Knowing everything that I now know, is there a project, activity, or relationship that I would not have gotten into in the first place?*

Often the bad stress in your life is tied to a job, activity, or relationship that you would not choose to enter again if you could start from scratch. Zero-based thinking involves imagining what you would do if you could start all over again—and then doing it! Granted, there are some situations in which you simply can't take a mulligan and start anew—perhaps you have a moral obligation to remain with some organization or relationship. However, there may be one or two stressful situations from which you can cut your losses and move on. Either way, it takes courage to honestly assess the importance of the situation, and then to make the right choice—stay and work to improve the situation, or remove yourself form the bad stress situation and move on with your life.

Use Relaxation and Meditation as an Antidote to Stress

Sometimes you can lower stress—and improve how you feel—on the spot with a few minutes of relaxation or meditation. Engaging in a few minutes of progressive relaxation (see page 106) is highly effective for lowering physical tension and reducing mental stress and anxiety. Similarly, deep breathing and meditation can go a long way toward attaining a more resourceful, lower-stress state for performing in an important situation. Follow the instructions for effective breathing and meditation found on pages 103 and 115, respectively.

Summary of Behavior Modification Techniques

- **Take control of the moment of decision.** Your future is largely determined in the moment between stimulus and response, so it's paramount that you stretch out this moment and leverage your values, goals, and wisdom in order to choose the best response in these critical moments.

- **End procrastination and increase motivation by visualizing your long-term goals and then identifying an immediate task to do or step to take toward that future vision.** Associate pain with inaction, and pleasure with taking a step, no matter how small, toward your goals.

- **Eliminate the poison of negative thinking and self-criticism.** Use thought stopping and thought parking to fend off distracting thoughts in times of action. Collapse bad memories and foster positive, productive visions. Surround yourself with positive images, music, and people.

- **Break habits that limit your effectiveness and rob you of achievement potential.** Supplant old habits with new empowering behaviors, and rewire your brain with a desired new behavior by acting out the new behavior or trait as if you already possessed it.

- **Take control of your emotional feelings.** Arouse positive emotions in the present moment by adjusting your posture and doing something physical to elevate your heart rate. Make permanent changes in emotions by rewriting your belief system—establish new empowering beliefs that allow you to interpret life's events with optimism and peace of mind.

- **Make stress work for you, and not against you.** Eliminate sources of bad stress by divesting from activities and relationships that offer no upside potential. Embrace the good stress of stretching your comfort zone and exploring your true potential in high-value activities.

Part Four

Maximum Climbing Training Programs

CHAPTER TWELVE

Mental-Training Programs

Just as physical exercise strengthens our muscles, mental training develops our brain in ways that will improve all aspects of our climbing and everyday life. Neuroscientist and brain-training expert Dr. Michael Merzenich says, "We choose and sculpt how our everchanging minds will work, we choose who we will be the next moment in a very real sense, and these choices are left embossed in physical form on our material selves." In other words, we are always mentally training, since our moment-to-moment thoughts and actions constantly change our brains and all that springs forth from them.

Unlike physical training, then, which you might do for an hour or two per day, mental training is an ongoing process throughout all your waking hours. While it may exhaust you just thinking about mental training all day long, what I'm talking about is simply striving to improve the quality and effectiveness of your thoughts throughout the day in order to foster a more productive state for pursuing your goals and enjoying life. The previous chapters have armed you with dozens of techniques for controlling your state, overcoming adversity, improving concentration, managing fear, and

Your brain is being trained, and thus changing, every single day whether you actively participate in the process or not.

much more—many of these techniques can be employed instantly when present conditions demand flexible, creative, and controlled cognition. Some of your biggest breakthroughs will result from consciously flexing your mental muscle in a wide range of nonclimbing situations throughout the day.

A significant part of your mental-training program must, of course, directly relate to climbing, as you engage in specific mental-training exercises during rest days and leverage mental-training strategies at the crags. Preceding chapters have detailed dozens of powerful exercises and strategies that you must first strive to fully understand, and then learn to apply with aptness and discipline. As Goethe put it, "Knowing is not enough; we must apply. Willing is not enough; we must do." Therefore, reading this book is just the first step in your journey to discover your true potential and open up vast new frontiers for experiencing maximum climbing.

The author on his New River Gorge arête classic The Gift of Grace (12b).
DAN BRAYACK

It's the never-ending process of mental training and the constant quest to challenge yourself mentally that will propel you to a higher and higher trajectory in all you do.

A final thought before I outline the mental-training program. Training your brain is in many ways a less tangible process than physically training your muscles. Furthermore, the results of mental training are largely subjective, measured by your quality of thought, movement, and experience rather than common objective metrics of physical training such as how many pull-ups you can do or how much weight you have lost. Consequently, it's remarkably common for people to give mental training only a brief try, or to dismiss it all together, because the training is "strange and different" and the results are not easy to measure. As you have learned in this book, however, the brain is the epicenter of all aspects of climbing performance, and therefore mental training is the ultimate—and most powerful— method of training for climbing. Knowing this, you must engage in a consistent, disciplined mental-training program and strive to exert mental control in all you do. Persist patiently in your training, and trust that the long-term cumulative effects of your efforts will yield a seismic shift in who you are and what you will accomplish and experience.

Now let's explore the structure of a mental-training program, beginning with an overview of how to integrate mental training with your ongoing physical and technical training. Next we'll examine how to incorporate mental-training exercises into your daily schedule, as well as how to employ mental training at the crags. The chapter then concludes with a short study of how to better use your brain in all you do, as you learn to dream big, inspire and be inspired, and find a sense of balance, harmony, and meaning in your existence.

How to Train Optimally

The pursuit of maximum climbing—whether you define it as realizing your climbing potential or maximizing your climbing experience—requires a long-term, disciplined effort to train optimally. While some climbers confuse *optimal training* with *maximum training,* you surely understand that the narrow-minded train-till-you-drop approach will not lead you to the promised land of your goals.

Optimal training is rarely about doing more training, but instead a matter of doing more of the right kinds of training. For a beginning climber, the right kind of training is usually to simply climb on a regular basis in order to maximize learning of climbing skills, both technical and mental. For an intermediate climber, however, right training must integrate frequent climbing of a challenging variety with supplemental physical- and mental-training exercises. At the elite level, optimal training becomes a most complex endeavor of identifying and eliminating subtle performance defects and constraints in each area of the performance triad (mental, technical, and physical). Ultimately, then, this final stage of the many-year maximum climbing journey is mostly about stripping away the things that are holding you back by eliminating technical inefficiencies, disengaging from distractions, overcoming fears, breaking counterproductive habits, eliminating the pressure to perform, reducing time wasted on low-value activities, and constantly refining your training to get the most out of every minute you spend in the gym.

If it's beginning to sound as if I'm promoting intense pragmatism as a virtue, then you are reading me correctly. What you think and do, each day of your life, changes both who you are in the present and who you will become in the future. To not live each day in a very pragmatic way would be a form of self-sabotage.

You must assume the mind-set of a sculptor whose work of art is never completed. From your first day to your last, you are refining skills, increasing efficiencies, and defining your form as an individual. This is a mindful process, but also a sort of secret journey within that both plumbs the depths of your being and explores beyond the margin of what is known. Doing this can be a wonderful lifelong endeavor, if you choose to become a climber for life. One of the many beauties of climbing is that with advancing age comes wisdom, efficiency, and a more thoughtful approach to climbing that all make the process even more sacred, gratifying, and profound.

Your journey toward maximum climbing is ultimately self-directed, yet you can accelerate the progress by leveraging the wisdom learned from this book and sage partners alike. To this end, let's delve into the subjects of the improvement curve and training efficiency.

Understanding the Improvement Curve

As in most areas of life, improvement in climbing is a dynamic and somewhat unpredictable process. There are growth spurts, or periods of rapid improvement, and there are plateaus in which no gains in ability are apparent. The most noticeable gains naturally occur during the formative stage as you learn and refine basic skills and assimilate information on all aspects of climbing performance. As depicted in figure 12.1, it's during your first year of regular climbing that climbing ability increases most rapidly as a result of steep gains in technical, mental, and physical capabilities. Simply going climbing a few days per week will yield near-maximal gains for most climbers. In fact, investing large amounts of time in fitness training or some form of cross-training, at the expense of climbing time, will retard improvement.

As you enter the intermediate stage—the realm of the mass of climbers—gains in climbing ability slow, and there are often periods of little or no apparent improvement. For many climbers, this stage of slowed improvement can trigger some level of frustration. Experiencing a performance plateau can also be somewhat perplexing since you are likely training harder and climbing just as much and in the same ways that produced steady gains in the past. It's in these times that you must recognize that advancing to the next level demands that you think and act differently than you have up to this point!

Breaking through a performance plateau demands that you engage in new forms of physical and technical training (see part two), as well as heighten self-awareness and mental skills (see part three). In examining the Improvement Curve (see figure 12.1), you will notice that physical capabilities plateau a number of times before reaching some ultimate, genetically determined limit. Furthermore, notice how gains in mental ability lag behind technical and physical gains (for the average climber).

Figure 12.1 *The Improvement Curve*

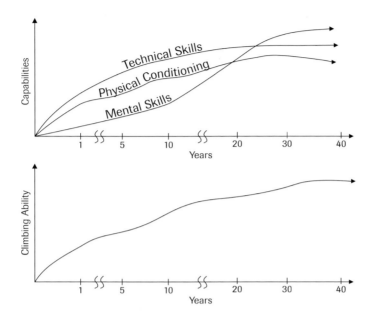

The top graph depicts theoretical changes in technical, physical, and mental ability over many years for the average climber. The bottom graph shows aggregate ability and maximum climbing potential increasing for three decades or more.

Thus, the two biggest keys to breaking the frustrating plateaus that are hallmarks of the intermediate climber are to experiment with new physical-training techniques (that target your unique physical constraints) and to begin a disciplined mental-training program (details upcoming!). No longer will "just going climbing" produce steady gains in performance—you now need to train smarter by exercising your mind and body in highly specialized ways.

After five to ten years of regular climbing, you will likely become a highly accomplished or elite climber. Despite many great achievements and maximum experiences, some individuals begin to lose interest in climbing at this stage because improvement becomes imperceptibly slow. Some climbers begin to train obsessively as if more strength were a panacea for all their climbing woes. This approach belies the fact that you can only get so strong—unlike your technical and mental abilities, which can improve almost indefinitely, your genes dictate a strict upper physical limit no matter how hard you train.

At this advanced stage, performance constraints are highly personalized. Some climbers are indeed physically limited due to ineffective training practices, while many others remain limited by technical defects and a wide range of mental handicaps. (The self-assessment evaluations in chapter 1 and in my book *Training for Climbing* can help you isolate your primary performance constraint; a climbing coach may also be helpful.) Of course, decision making and mental control come into play in almost every aspect of your training and performance as an elite climber; therefore the optimal training program for most elite climbers must include a heavy emphasis on mental training.

As you mature into a veteran climber with multiple decades of experience, you will experience a gradual age-related decline in your physical capabilities. Fortunately, you can leverage your technical wizardry and mental prowess to continue climbing at a very high level. Engaging in an age-appropriate physical-training program can greatly slow the loss of maximum strength and endurance that naturally occurs after age forty. The optimal training program for a performance-minded veteran climber, then, is to engage in regular physical training and to continue on the lifelong mission to eliminate technical defects and break through mental barriers. As illustrated in figure 12.1, exploitation of this comprehensive approach to training can sustain advances in climbing ability for thirty years or more. I know of numerous fifty- and sixty-something super-fit Zen Masters of Rock who still send at a very high level—many of them also profess to enjoy climbing every bit as much as they did in their younger days!

Embarking on a Smart-Training Program

Smart training is defined as training in a way that yields the greatest improvement on the rock given the time and energy you have available to invest in training. Your current yield is influenced by a number of factors. First, obtaining a high yield requires that you focus your efforts on training up your weaknesses (which of course demands self-awareness of current performance constraints). Secondly, your time spent training should be limited to that which is required to obtain the maximum results possible for a given session. Accordingly, training yield drops (not-smart training!) when training focus strays from targeting your weaknesses and when training becomes excessive to the point of providing little upside and tempting injury or overtraining.

Unfortunately, training yield is not something that you can easily calculate. Instead you must strive to be acutely self-aware of what you are doing in the gym, how long you are doing it, and what performance gains (or declines) you obtain week-to-week. Maintaining a training notebook is immensely helpful in determining critical cause-and-effect relationships. By reviewing the details of past workouts, you can often discover what training inputs are providing you with the greatest performance enhancement.

Central to your mission of maximizing smart-training yield is keeping your eye on the bull's-eye of your weaknesses. It's vital to recognize that your climbing constraints are a moving target. Quite often your target weaknesses of today will be different from those of last month or year. Once again we return to the importance of self-awareness—identifying new emerging performance constraints and modifying your training accordingly is a master skill that takes years to develop. Therefore, it would be advantageous to consult a climbing coach or retake the self-assessment in chapter 1 every six months or whenever you feel as if your training yield is dropping off.

Designing an effective physical- and technical-training program (and selecting the proper exercises and drills to perform) is obviously beyond the scope of this

Seven Absolutes of Effective Training for Climbing

1. **Unfit or novice climbers will improve no matter how they train as long as actual climbing is part of the program.** Climbing to learn skills will yield the fastest improvement, although any physical training (even ill conceived) will yield physiological changes that appear to help your climbing. This phenomenon has given birth to many anecdotal claims that "such-and-such training really helped my climbing," when it was in fact just the simple act of climbing that was responsible for the improvement.

2. **Upon achieving a reasonable level of general fitness, you must train to become specifically fit.** Excessive time spent cross-fit training is a misappropriation of precious resources. The principles of specificity and overload are paramount (see *Training for Climbing* to learn more). To be maximally effective, your training must address the specific performance constraints of your preferred type of climbing.

3. **More training effort is needed to improve physical fitness than to maintain a specific fitness level, yet too much physical training is harmful.** Thus, it's a fine line between training enough and training too much. Leveraging recovery strategies (see *Training for Climbing*) is essential for training optimally and avoiding the overtraining syndrome.

4. **You can only become so fit—and no fitter—as determined by your unique DNA.** Therefore, after years of extensive training and upon achieving a high level of physical conditioning, further performance gains come mainly from improving technique and the mind.

5. **Even after physical capabilities begin to wane (beyond age forty), you can continue to improve by refining technique and developing greater mental prowess.** Your potential to improve technically and mentally is almost limitless.

6. **Among the mass of climbers, it's not physical fitness that discriminates climbing ability, but mental and technical skills.** The notion that "getting stronger is the master key to climbing harder" is false. The best climbers put the complete puzzle together by training their minds, bodies, and techniques.

7. **In the final analysis, it's the brain that matters most in determining climbing performance.** Not only are motor skills and cognitive abilities brain-based, but maximum strength and stamina are directed by the brain's central governor. Therefore, the best training program for climbing is a brain-training program!

book (consult *Training for Climbing* or hire a climbing coach). Regardless of your information source or the program details, it's important to create a written plan of action that expresses an intelligent, long-term training strategy rooted in the principles of effective training (see "Seven Absolutes of Effective Training for Climbing"). You then need to exercise great self-discipline to follow through with the plan rather than returning to some comfortable old routine or training as your peers do. Frequently remind yourself that engaging in a haphazard or ad-lib style of training will yield mediocre results at best, and may even be counterproductive. As a general rule, you are often better off "just climbing" as training as opposed to launching into the darkness of a trial-and-error approach. The bottom line: Do your research, design what seems to be the most effective program for you, and then commit to executing the program long-term and making the necessary course corrections along the way to sustain a high training yield.

Smart training is obviously a very mental process, and I hope that this book will serve as an inspirational source of practical techniques, wisdom, and psychic energy that will serve you for many years to come. In closing this section, I want to stress the importance of time management in your smart-training endeavors and in living a most fulfilling life. We are all blessed with a fixed allotment of time, but there is no way of knowing how much time remains in our account. From this perspective we should all be compelled to make the most of the time we have—to obtain the greatest "smart-living yield," if you will. The goal is to live each day with passion and to invest our limited time and energy mostly into the activities and people that we value most.

Daily Mental-Training Programs

The central theme of this book is that you can maximize climbing performance—and experience—through a comprehensive brain-training program that produces highly efficient use of motor skills, maximizes physical capabilities and capacity, and fosters masterful command of wide-ranging cognitive skills. Given this broad purview, you can see that brain training is an ongoing process during all of your waking hours. Acting efficiently and thinking effectively aren't things you can just turn on when you're at the crags—mastery comes by striving to develop these abilities in all aspects of your daily life. Thus, your mental-training program is best viewed as a 365-day-per-year endeavor.

While the idea of mental training every day of the year might seem extreme—you would never want to physically train every single day—it's a indisputable fact that your brain is changing with every thought and action you take, so you really are brain training every day whether you consciously participate in the process or not. This is a critical distinction: Your brain is being trained, and thus changing, every single day whether you actively participate in the process or not! Therefore, if climbing is a top-tier personal value, then it would be impractical and foolish not to participate in the ongoing day-to-day training process. See "Brain-Training Exercises for Everyday Use" on page 247 for a list of ways to exercise your brain throughout the day, every day.

Clearly the biggest improvement will come if you address the whole person, not just the climber part of you. The mental skills you call into use at the crag—concentration, fear management, visualization, dealing with adversity, and such—are also vital mental skills for maximum living in the flatlands. So if you really want to become a mentally strong master of rock, you must strive to exercise thought control and to perform efficiently in all you do. As in climbing, perfection is unattainable in other areas of your life—but in striving to do your best you will perform uncommonly well, both achieving and experiencing beyond your expectations.

This has been my goal for many years, and I work each day to extend my reach despite occasional setbacks and failures, the evolving complexities of life, and the physical challenges that come with advancing age. But my life is rich and rewarding in many ways, and I'm still able to climb at a moderately high level despite an aging body lacking the raw power of my youth. Fortunately, the brain can often more than make up for this growing strength deficit. It's my wish that you can similarly grow and accumulate new experiences through all your future days by applying the concepts and strategies in this book.

Toward this end, the following pages will serve up a three-stage daily mental-training program. Depending on your current level of mental development, you might spend anywhere from a week to a several months executing the Stage One program. Stage Two is an intermediate mental-training program suitable for anyone serious about taking their mental game to uncommon heights—many climbers will continue with the Stage Two program indefinitely. The third and final stage is presented as a guideline for individuals who place climbing at or near the top of their hierarchy of personal values. At this highest level of commitment to climbing, the goals and challenges will be unique and therefore require climbers to develop novel training—and living—strategies.

Mental Training—Stage One

This is a streamlined entry-level mental-training program. No matter whether you are an experienced climber or total novice, I strongly encourage all readers to begin with a few weeks of the Stage One program as a kind of icebreaker into mental training for climbing. The time commitment for dedicated training is just ten to twenty minutes per day, although the goal is to increase awareness and executive control of thoughts and actions throughout the day.

Program Goals

- Learn principles of brain training outlined in chapter 2. Incorporate the brain-training tips on pages 44 and 247.
- Learn the principles of motor learning described in chapter 3. Utilize some of the nine practice strategies (see page 59) in each of your climbing sessions.
- Increase self-awareness of thoughts, emotional triggers, personal weaknesses, performance outcomes, and your hierarchy of personal values using exercises in chapter 5.
- Improve self-regulation of your mental, physical, and emotional state using exercises in chapter 6.

- Engage in long-term and weekly goal setting as described in chapter 7.

- Improve concentration and focus in climbing and nonclimbing activities using techniques detailed in chapter 9.

- Identify one limiting fear in climbing and another in everyday life; then challenge these fears using techniques described in chapter 10.

- Learn to use affirmations and visualization (see chapter 11) to modify your state, mentally rehearse a climb, and help maintain a focused, positive mental state.

- Identify limiting behaviors, and then pick one bad habit or behavior to modify using the techniques in chapter 11.

- Improve confidence, poise, and performance in your preferred climbing subdiscipline, while striving to expose yourself to the challenges of new forms and styles of climbing.

Self-Assessment, Learning, and Planning Activities

If you haven't already, take the ten-part self-assessment that begins on page 21. Identify your three or four lowest-scoring areas and earmark them to become the focus of your initial mental-training efforts. Re-read the chapters that address each of your weak areas, and consider which exercises and strategies you can put to work to improve in these areas. Begin keeping a training notebook or journal in which you can develop a written record of what you identify and intend to do. Next, review the hierarchy of personal values you developed in chapter 5; then proceed to chapter 7 and perform the goal-setting exercises.

Daily Mental-Training Exercises

Now let's examine what you can do every day to improve your mental fitness. The first and most important thing is to develop greater metacognition. Strive to regularly evaluate your thoughts and actions. What are you thinking and why are you thinking it? Are your current thoughts helping or hurting your state? How could you think more effectively? What are the immediate results of the actions you are taking? What course corrections can you make to improve your effectiveness? Will your current actions have some long-term unintended consequences?

Regularly evaluating your thoughts in this way allows you to identify self-limiting thoughts, inefficient or fearful ways of thinking, and perhaps even some bad habits or unwise actions that may be ultimately counterproductive or lead to unintended consequences. The things that you identify are the keys to making giant steps toward improving your personal effectiveness and advancing toward your goals—make challenging and changing these unwanted behaviors a *must!* Leverage the appropriate exercises in part three of *Maximum Climbing* to aid your journey.

Another daily goal is to engage in ten to twenty minutes of relaxation, meditation, or visualization (see table 12.1, "Stage One Mental-Training Program"). This is something you must put into your daily schedule. You might do it upon waking in the morning, during a midday break from work or school, or before bedtime at night. Make this ten- to twenty-minute routine sacred—under no circumstances will you skip this short but vital training period. This is where many people fall off the mental-training wagon. They view these subtle mental exercises to be less important than their physical training; so while they may be good physical trainees, they fail to follow through on their commitment to mental training, thus missing out on the potential windfall of gains. Developing the habit of doing your daily mental-fitness training is the single greatest indicator of your level of success in becoming a maximum climber!

Mental Training at the Climbing Gym or Crags

As physical as climbing often feels, we all know that it's the mind that matters most. Accelerating your improvement and achieving breakthroughs into new levels of difficulty are more about improving your mental game and technical mastery than getting stronger. It's essential, then, that you strive to become both more thoughtful in the process of preparing to climb and more mentally in control as you engage the rock. Here are a few Stage One methods for improving cognitive abilities at the climbing gym and crag.

First, it's best to arrive at the gym or crag with a mental game plan or written workout routine that will keep you on the path toward your goals for the session. At the gym, this list will guide you through a logical sequence of warm-up activities, climbing practice drills, roped sends and/or bouldering, and conclude with a series of supplement exercises that target your physical weaknesses. Similarly, your plan of attack at the crag would begin with a few warm-up routes, followed by the day's major event, whether it be working on a project or engaging in a high volume of submaximal practice climbing to accrue experience, foster economical movement, and train physical stamina. Regardless of the location of your climbing session, be it on a home wall, at a commercial gym, or a crag, it's fundamental that you have an intelligent strategy for action.

With regard to specific mental-training exercises, it's most important that you spend several minutes before each climb engaging in mental rehearsal and fear management strategies. It's also crucial that you evaluate your mental, physical, and emotional state before beginning to climb—are your thoughts, feelings, and arousal level optimal for climbing your best? In many cases they will not be, so you'll need to modulate your state using the self-regulating strategies detailed in chapter 6. All your preclimb preparations should be developed and refined into a powerful preclimb ritual that ends with you standing at the base of the climb in a relaxed yet energized and focused state.

As you engage the climb, you'll need to balance concentrating on the move at hand with concentrating on your internal state. Like watching two TV programs at a time by flipping back and forth between channels, you need to alternate focus between the process of climbing and the many internal matters of interpreting proprioception of movement, monitoring physical tension, managing fears, and maintaining focus despite environmental distractions. The best approach is to attend to the internal matters while at a good rest stance or clipping position, and then to focus mainly on the process of climbing when moving over stone. Every climb has unique demands, however, so you must develop the skill of intuiting the best balance of internal and external focus each time.

Table 12.1 *Stage One Mental-Training Program*

Below is an example of how you can incorporate the various exercises and strate-gies from parts two and three into a daily mental-training program. I suggest that you use this program as a starting point, then after a few days modify the program by substituting in a few different exercises that address your personal challenges and goals. Transpose this program into a training notebook, then each day check off the sections that you successfully completed. Keeping account in this way will increase motivation to follow through with your training, as well as keeping you mindful of what other exercises or strategies you might consider using.

Waking/Morning Mental Training

- Use positive, goal-directed affirmations to establish a positive mental state (see page 199).
- Review your plan for the day; decide how you can act most effectively to make steps toward your short- and long-term goals.

All-Day Mental Training

- Actively monitor and modulate your state to optimal levels for various daily activities. Alter your physiology to change how you feel (see page 108).
- Observe your thought quality; direct self-talk and mental imagery to override negative thinking (see page 111).
- Strive to respond positively and productively in adverse situations. Employ problem-solving strategies (see page 149).
- Identify limiting behaviors and determine which are most holding you back. Use strategies in chapter 11 to help you overcome these limitations.
- Use the brain-training techniques, detailed on page 247, several times throughout the day.

Climbing Mental Training

- Use mental rehearsal before every climb (see page 191).
- Use brain-training practice drills to develop skills and improve technique (see page 247).
- Use breathing and centering techniques before each climb and at each rest position (see page 103).
- Precisely identify the fears you feel—are they reasonable or unreasonable? Use strategies in chapter 10 to better manage these fears.

Evening/Bedtime Mental Training (10–20 minutes)

- Practice proper breathing techniques and the Progressive Relaxation Sequence (see page 106).
- Use visualization to replay a recent great climb move by move. Also use visualization to review new skills or to practice climb project routes in your mind's eye (see page 192).

Upon completing or retreating from a climb, it's essential that you replay the ascent in a dissociated state to identify what you did well and what you did poorly. In both success and failure, there are clues for improvement and lessons to be learned. To simply pull your rope, or pick up your crash pad, and move on to the next climb without first pondering the journey is to miss out on some of the learning and joy of each novel climbing experience.

Mental Training—Stage Two Program

This program is designed for someone who wants to make a more significant commitment to mental training. Before commencing with the Stage Two program, it's important to first engage in the less extensive Stage One program for an "acclimatization" period. Experienced climbers with past experience in mental training may proceed to Stage Two after just a week or so, whereas individuals who are new to mental training should continue with the Stage One program for a minimum of one month. By engaging in the Stage One program, you will develop a habit of daily mental training with a less ambitious routine, rather than risking overwhelm (and perhaps quitting) in doing the more extensive Stage Two program right out of the chute. The time commitment for Stage Two mental training is twenty to forty minutes per day, although the overriding goal is to become more mentally attuned in all you do throughout the day.

Program Goals

- Learn and incorporate the brain-training principles of developing skilled movement and maximizing strength, power, and endurance as detailed in chapters 3 and 4.

- Foster minute-by-minute awareness of your thoughts, emotional feelings, and physical state (see chapter 5) and become proficient at optimizing your overall state on the fly by using the techniques from chapter 6.

- Become an excellent goal setter and time manager. Plan your days and weeks in detail to focus mainly on high-value activities. Exercise self-discipline to follow through with your plans.

- Develop a habit of stepping it up in times of great challenge or when facing adversity. Become a master of the numerous strategies for problem solving and overcoming adversity as described in chapter 8.

- Foster an uncommon ability to narrow focus and maintain single-pointed concentration when working on high-value activities. Train frequently with the concentration-training exercises, and learn to maintain steady concentration while climbing using the strategies in chapter 9.

- Become the master of fear, instead of letting fear be your master, in all you do on and off the rock. Use the fear and risk management strategies described in chapter 10.

- Become proficient in using all the mind-programming strategies detailed in chapter 11. Use techniques such as visualization and affirmations before every climb; strive to expand use of these techniques to other high-value life areas.

- Identify one or two limiting behaviors, and then use the techniques detailed in chapter 11 to eliminate the performance drag that these unwanted behaviors create.

- Actively discern sources of good and bad stress in your life. Learn to embrace good stress and become proactive at removing sources of bad stress from your life.

- Strive to become "more mental" in all you do. Re-read this book frequently to become well versed in the many powerful mental-training exercises and performance strategies. Use these tools daily to elevate performance, improve attitude and poise, and maximize experience in all you do.

Self-Assessment, Learning, and Planning Activities

Take the ten-part self-assessment (see page 21) every six months to identify changing weaknesses and limiting constraints. In developing a comprehensive training program, it will also be beneficial to take the self-assessment test contained in *Training for Climbing*. Re-read the chapters, in both *Maximum Climbing* and *Training for Climbing*, that address each of your major weaknesses, and then develop a detailed program to train up these limiting constraints.

At least once per year, update your hierarchy of personal values (see page 96) and reconsider your mega goals. Perform a monthly gap analysis (see page 131) to refine the strategy for reaching your seasonal and longer-term goals. Evaluate your current level of commitment—is it sufficient for seriously pursuing your goals? Keep a training notebook or journal in which you detail your goals, training strategy, lessons learned, and goals reached.

Daily Mental-Training Exercises

The overriding goal of the Stage Two program is to become aware and in control of your thoughts from the moment you awaken in the morning until you fall asleep at night. In examining your thoughts, you want to determine whether they are helping or hurting you, both in terms of supporting a positive mental state and in directing effective actions that yield movement toward your goals.

Another vital part of the Stage Two program is improving your time management. Scheduling how you will spend the minutes, hours, and days of your week is essential to maximize your effectiveness. Conversely, use of the common making-it-up-as-you-go method of planning will lead to wasting much time in common low-value activities (social, passive entertainment, and such) and a decided lack of results in high-value activities. Some time should be spent each Sunday planning the week ahead—both climbing and nonclimbing activities. You must then develop the habit of following through on the game plan with great self-discipline. This will almost certainly mean fending off and saying no to any number of social invitations and opportunities to engage in low-value activities.

The capstone aspect of the Stage Two program is twenty to forty minutes of daily mental training. You can perform this training any time of the day as long as you can find a quiet, distraction-free location. You might do it first thing in the early morning while your house and mind are still quiet, or perhaps retire to the quiet shelter of your car over a lunch break at work or school, or wait until the late evening and perform the mental training as part of your quiet time before bed (as I do). Pick two to four mental-training activities from part three and train intently and without interruption (see table 12.2, "Stage Two Mental-Training Program"). You might perform certain exercises, such as the Progressive Relaxation Sequence and visualization, for ten minutes of every session, while you vary other exercises used according to need. For example, use the Second-Hand Clock Drill for a few weeks if you feel that your concentration is sometimes lacking.

Most important, make this twenty to forty minutes of daily mental training a sacred part of your day that will not be skipped for any reason. When you ponder skipping a session, remind yourself that changing your brain and elevating your mental prowess demands a consistent, focused, daily effort.

Mental Training at the Climbing Gym or Crags

As a passionate climber, it's at the gym or crag where you want to shine most and maximize experience. Thus, exerting a high-level of mental control in all aspects of the climbing game is a most important aspect of the Stage Two program.

Having engaged in the Stage One program for a few weeks or months, you should have a well-established habit of going to the gym or crag with a workout strategy or climbing-day game plan. Engaging in mental rehearsal and modulating your state before every climb should be as natural a part of your preclimb ritual as tying your shoes and chalking up. The goal of Stage Two mental training is to take your mental preparations to the next level by engaging in vivid, associated visualization, as well as thorough risk and fear management, before every major climb. By clearing out potential minefields of the mind, you can foster a deeper focus and mind–body synchronization before starting up the route.

Performing your best demands that you nix outcome-oriented thinking and let go of the need to succeed.

Upon beginning the climb, you must let go of the future-oriented mind-set of preparation and narrow your focus to the moment and move at hand. The crux of the Stage Two program is developing an acute awareness of your climbing efficacy in the moment; that is, having a clear, steady self-awareness of proprioception, proper sequencing, and your changing mental and physical state. While you may initially have to work at this process, the long-term goal is to make this self-monitoring and self-regulation process nearly preconscious and automatic. This way, your conscious mind can remain fully engaged in the process of climbing; only when you sense a lack of balance, growing muscular tension, or some other undesirable change in state do you briefly shift your focus away from the rock in order to make the necessary adjustments of mind and body. Ideally you want to limit these state checks to rest stances and clipping positions rather than making them in the middle of the crux sequence when a break in concentration might lead to a botched sequence or fall.

As your passion and performance grow, it's not uncommon to develop a psychological need to succeed and perform your best—after all, you expect to do

Table 12.2 Stage Two Mental-Training Program

Use this sample Stage Two program as a starting point for your daily mental-training program. Actively add or replace exercises from throughout the book to best meet the goal of training up your weaknesses and limiting your constraints on the rock. Transpose this program into a training notebook, then each day check off the sections that you successfully completed. This accounting of your mental training will increase motivation to keep with the program.

Waking/Morning Mental Training (5–10 minutes)

- Use positive, goal-directed affirmations to establish a positive mental state (see page 199).
- Engage in a few minutes of slow, deep breathing; then visualize in fast forward the day ahead and what you plan to do and achieve.
- Review your plan for the day; decide how you can act most effectively to make steps toward your short- and long-term goals.

All-Day Mental Training

- Actively monitor and modulate your state to optimal levels for various daily activities. Alter your physiology to change how you feel (see page 108).
- Observe your thought quality. Direct self-talk and mental imagery to override negative thinking (see page 111).
- Monitor your effectiveness in all you do; consider how you could act more effectively.
- Foster awareness of potential distractions—exercise willpower in avoiding people and situations that will distract you from the day's game plan. Engage in single-tasking whenever possible.
- Strive to respond positively and productively in adverse situations. Employ the problem-solving strategies found on page 149.
- Identify limiting behaviors and determine which are most holding you back (see chapter 11).
- Use a few of the everyday brain-training techniques detailed on page 247.

Climbing Mental Training

- Use mental rehearsal and associated visualization before every climb (see page 191).
- Use brain-training practice drills to develop skills and improve technique (see page 247).
- If appropriate, use brain-training (physical) exercise strategies to increase strength, power, and endurance (see chapter 4).
- Use breathing and centering techniques, such as the ANSWER Sequence, before each climb and at each rest position (see page 107).
- Learn and employ the many techniques for improving concentration while climbing (see chapter 9).

Continued on next page

Table 12.2 *Stage Two Mental-Training Program*

Continued from previous page

- Engage in risk and fear management before every climb. Actively manage the fears and risks that you identify. Challenge unreasonable fears by climbing through them! See chapter 10 for other strategies.
- Strive to increasingly persevere in difficult and adverse situations. Develop the personal traits of mental flexibility and durability by making a game out of trying to overcome adversity (see chapter 8).

Evening/Bedtime Mental Training (10–20 minutes)

- Practice proper breathing techniques and the Progressive Relaxation Sequence (see page 106).
- Train concentration using the Second-Hand Clock Drill, Attention-Shifting Drill, and Two-Minute Breath Focus Drill (see pages 166–68).
- Practice visualizing both past and future climbs. Exercise your memory by replaying a recent great climb move by move in your mind's eye. Preprogram a project climb or prepare for a mountain ascent by visualizing preparations, strategy, and if possible the specific moves and feel of the climb (see page 192).
- Modify or erase limiting behaviors using the mental exercises and strategies described in chapter 11.

well given all the time and energy you put into climbing! While having high goals and expectations is admirable, it's an ironic fact that holding these thoughts in mind as you engage the rock makes holding on to the rock more difficult. Goal setting, visualizing a goal, and other future-oriented states of mind must be limited to periods of mental planning and never enter into mind while engaged in action. Performing your best demands that you nix outcome-oriented thinking and let go of the need to succeed. Should any thoughts of outcome enter your mind, quickly settle on the idea that it's "okay to fall" (assuming a safe fall) and that "falling won't bother me, I'll just get back up and give it another go." By willingly accepting this fate (if it should even happen), you totally dissolve the fear of falling that handcuffs so many climbers. Therefore, by being okay with falling, it's less likely you will. This simple idea is one of the most powerful in this book.

Exercising such precise and almost automatic control of your mind and body while ascending a stressful or maximal route may seem to be an unreachable goal given your current struggles with tension, distractions, and fear. Trust that you will gradually progress toward this highly distinct performance state given a consistent effort to seize control of self in stressful climbing situations. This book is packed with powerful strategies for dealing with your fears, physical tension, lack of concentration, and most other mental handicaps. Employ these strategies and make them habit, and in time you'll be climbing at a level that you can hardly imagine today.

Mental Training—Stage Three Program

This elite-level mental-training program is designed for the professional climber or anyone else who engages in climbing as a near-full-time activity. The time commitment is forty minutes or more per day, in addition to time spent training and climbing.

At the elite level, climbing becomes a deeply personal and unique pursuit. For some, the goal may be uniting with the rock in free solo ascents, while others may push their limits on sport climbs, big walls, or snow-covered mountains. Regardless of the goal, climbing at the elite level and pushing out personal—maybe even human—boundaries is an intensely mental process.

For these developing masters of rock, mental training gradually becomes a way of life—the normal way of thinking—as their thought processes on a cliff or mountain and on the flatlands are almost indistinguishable. By necessity, the elite climber's thoughts—and life—become increasingly focused on climbing. Many activities outside of climbing are abandoned in order to better focus resources of time and money, although there's usually a huge side benefit of reduced cognitive dissonance. Outwardly the elite climber exhibits a strong bias for action, as well as a preference for pragmatism; he acts with discipline, commitment, and perseverance to overcome adversity (and doubters) and to bring his vision to fruition.

Interestingly, these highly focused individuals often find ways to develop a sense of balance in their lives, for without balance they would likely burn out before reaching their mega goals. This balance is found sometimes purely in the mental world of meditation, but also often through periodic, focused engagements in other activities. Yet no matter the goal or activity at hand, common hallmarks of these maximum climbers include a desire for excellence in execution, stretching personal boundaries, and maximizing experience. Thus, the mental skills developed on the rock and for the rock are subsequently applied off the rock. Hence, maximum climbers often go on to achieve great things beyond the rock and ice of the steep.

The mental skills developed on the rock and for the rock are subsequently applied off the rock. Hence, maximum climbers often go on to achieve great things beyond the rock.

You, too, can experience maximum climbing in the mountains and beyond! The key is to maximally develop your physical abilities as well as to engage in a steady pursuit of higher and higher cognitive function. You, your goals, and the barriers between you and your goals require a highly specific mental-training program that only you can devise. Therefore you will want to use the following Stage Three program as a starting point for developing an ongoing mental-training program.

Freely add or replace exercises from throughout the book as needed. Frequently re-read the book in search of a new mental-training exercise to address any recently recognized constraints. Or perhaps your present barrier is physical, in which case you can exploit one of the cutting-edge strength- or endurance-training exercises described in part two.

Regardless of your current level of performance, remember that there is always room for improvement—you simply need to identify the limiting constraint and effectively train it up. It's not by mistake that the very best climbers tend to humbly recognize their flaws and passionately pursue improvement. After establishing *Jumbo Love*, perhaps the world's first 5.15b, Chris Sharma stated, "I'm constantly looking for ways to progress and take climbing to new places mentally and physically—taking everything I've learned up till now and trying to advance the idea of sport climbing to be more adventurous, trad, and modern at the same time."

No matter your age, goals, or current climbing level, I guarantee that you, too, can elevate performance and improve quality of experiences, almost indefinitely. The journey starts here—and for the elite climber it's largely a journey inward.

Program Goals

- Foster a personal culture of being more thoughtful and pragmatic in all you do. Strive to detach from sources of wasted energy and time, while better focusing your thoughts and energy on the top-tier activities in your hierarchy of values. Make discipline your way.

- Aspire to become a Zen master of state. Foster minute-by-minute awareness of your thoughts, emotional feelings, and physical state, striving to elevate your command of self (see chapter 6).

- Assess whether you can obtain any further gains in your physical capabilities (per chapter 4) and continue to apply the technique-training exercises in chapter 3 to improve skill and economy of movement (an area where improvement is always possible).

- Continue setting new and more challenging goals. Formulate novel achievement strategies via liberal mind experimentation. Plan your schedule weeks and months in advance to sustain a progressive course toward your goals.

- Grow your hanging-on power—the ability to persevere and press on through great adversity. Become a skilled mental gymnast by finding novel ways around and over barriers, using the powerful strategies contained in chapter 8.

- Develop an uncommon ability to concentrate and maintain single-pointed focus. Train every day with the concentration-building exercises described in chapter 9.

- Become a Zen master in managing fear and risk in the mountains and beyond. Use the fear and risk management strategies described in chapter 10 and, most important begin to trust your intuition as the ultimate source of guidance.

- Employ daily some of the mind-programming strategies detailed in chapter 11. Use these techniques to program optimal execution of climbing and nonclimbing activities.

- Regularly question whether you possess any limiting behaviors or have an activity or relationship that is a source of bad stress (as described in chapter 11). Cut yourself free from low-value activities, unnecessary possessions, or bad stress relationships that only serve to levy a "performance drag" on your life.
- Re-read this book frequently with the goal of making many of the mental exercises and strategies second nature. Use these tools daily to elevate performance, improve attitude and poise, and maximize experience in all you do.

Self-Assessment, Learning, and Planning Activities

Retake the ten-part self-assessment (see page 21) every six months to a year. Identify your three or four lowest-scoring areas and then tailor your training program to address these weaknesses. Next, mentally review some of your past struggles or failures in the steep—try to identify the root cause of the problems, since it must become the bull's-eye of your training program. Also, review the hierarchy of personal values you developed in chapter 5; then proceed to chapter 7 and perform the goal-setting and planning exercises.

Maintain a training notebook to record your daily mental training. Consider keeping a personal journal in which you record your goals, gap analysis, planning, and strategies, as well as your daily thoughts, ideas, and achievements. Someday you will view this journal as an invaluable record of your personal growth, struggles and achievements, and life experience.

Regularly peruse *Maximum Climbing* and consider what new exercises and strategies you can employ to improve your mental game. It's also helpful to read some nonfiction books on human performance, psychology, personal triumphs, and spirituality. Search for new ideas and knowledge that expand your mind and create inspiration—innovative ways to increasing performance can often be found in the pages of nonclimbing books. Freely engage in possibility thinking and thought experiments. Imagine new climbing goals and strategies, and then find a way to believe in—and act on—what you have imagined!

Daily Mental-Training Exercises

Your first few minutes of consciousness in the morning set the tone for the day, so develop the habit of exercising tight control over your waking thoughts. Begin each day with a positive affirmation and some vivid mental imagery of the exciting aspects, and key events, of the day ahead. Fight off negative thoughts, bad emotions, and physical sensations of tiredness by using the state management strategies detailed in chapter 6. Remind yourself that acute self-awareness and state control is essential for peak performance in any endeavor.

Strive for constant state awareness throughout the day—are your thoughts and actions proving to be effective in the moment? Most important, be fully aware and engaged in the moment of decision, whenever it occurs. Big or small, it's the decisions you make that often determine your effectiveness and destiny. It could be something as small as a decision on what you will do after work or school, or a big decision on how to invest your money or where to road-trip or expedition. Leverage your hierarchy of values to make the right decision rather than following the path of least resistance or the crowd.

Regularly evaluate your training and climbing plans for the days and weeks ahead. Are they properly matched to your current training strategy and future climbing goals? Be calculated and disciplined in how you spend your days—try each day to take a step toward your short- and long-term mega goals.

Similarly, you must develop acute awareness of your relationships, habits, and current belief system. Some of these fundamental and defining elements might be invisible chains that are preventing progress toward your goals. Breaking through a performance plateau and achieving an elusive goal is not only a matter of training smarter and harder, but often requires a new level of thinking in order to see what's really holding you back. In acting to simplify your life, decrease cognitive dissonance, and increase concentration and self-discipline, you spread metaphorical mental wings that elevate performance and provide a truer perspective of what really matters.

Your day should conclude with some quiet time, during which you mediate and engage in targeted mental-training exercises from this book. Dedicate the final twenty minutes or so, prior to falling asleep, to performing various mind-programming exercises—better to soak your brain with soothing and empowering thoughts than to absorb the uninspiring and perhaps even polluting drivel on TV.

Mental Training at the Climbing Gym or Crags

For the elite climber, mental training at the crags is about being fully engaged in the process of climbing, whether it's sending a V-hard boulder problem, personal-best sport climb, or multiday alpine route. Years of practice, training, and experience in the steep gradually empowers the elite climber to be aware of finer and finer distinctions of climbing effectiveness and to discriminate technical inefficiencies at a very minute level. Such remarkably acute self-awareness and masterful self-regulation facilitate extreme efficiency in movement and near-optimal use of limited physical resources.

The Stage Three elite-climber program, then, demands that you exercise your willpower to actively engage in all aspects of the climbing process from preparation, to execution, to dealing with adversity, and ending with postclimb evaluation and discovery. Furthermore, you must regularly set more challenging goals as well as raise the stakes of your commitment to climbing, thus forcibly extending your reach beyond your current grasp. As all-around master climber Steph Davis puts it, "The best climbers always take on more than seems plausible. That's how you learn."

Given extensive planning, training, and commitment, your ultimate goal in climbing is to enter the *flow state*. Flow, also referred to as *the zone,* is a distinct state of optimal experience in which your mind and body are working together harmoniously, in a challenging situation that completely engages you. Experiencing the flow state, then, is one of the ultimate goals of *Maximum Climbing*. Interestingly, flow is not something that you can learn to create on demand—it is something you must set the stage for and then let happen. World-class boulderer Lisa Rands describes experiencing the flow state on her headpoint ascent of the dangerous gritstone route, *End of the Affair* (E8 6c): "The moves flowed and I felt completely in control all the way up. It was the most amazing experience for me. My mind overcame all the fear and doubt allowing my body to move instinctively into the perfect positions."

This elite-level mental-training-at-the-crags program can be perhaps best summarized, then, as a quest to experience the flow state. Toward this end, let's examine the nine fundamental elements of flow as set forth by professor Mihaly Csikszentmihalyi, the developer of the flow concept and author of the fascinating book *Flow: The Psychology of Optimal Experience.* By learning to foster each of these elements, you set the stage to achieve optimal experience and peak performance.

1. **Match challenge with skills.** You can only achieve flow on a climb that challenges you in some way. So while doing easy climbs can be fun, experiencing flow requires that you choose a climb that will fully engage, yet not overwhelm, you.

2. **Complete absorption in the activity.** Oneness of mind and body—and a merging of you and the rock—can only happen when you are totally free of distractions. Since a distraction-free environment is unlikely, you must be able to summon a single-pointed focus (see chapter 9) that merges awareness to action.

3. **Clear goals.** Knowing what you need to do, with no ambiguity of purpose or procedure, will yield a confident, intuitive sense from which you can perform your best. Only when climbing with clear intentions—knowing where the route goes, understanding the risk and gear requirements, and a having a good sense of the moves—will you be able to achieve flow.

4. **Unambiguous feedback.** Climbing is a dynamic possess, and thus optimal performance is only possible when you correctly interpret and respond to kinesthetic and environment feedback. Possessing an acute understanding of proprioceptive and results feedback is essential for obtaining and remaining in the flow state.

5. **Total concentration on task at hand.** Dwelling on past- or future-oriented thoughts or pondering possible outcomes makes flow impossible. If you must shift into analysis mode, for purposes of route finding or risk management, make it quick and clinical and then return to a single-pointed focus on the task at hand. Using concentration techniques and preclimb rituals will help you tune out distractions and narrow your focus to the task of the moment.

6. **A sense of control.** This is not about developing a control-freak personality, but instead entering a Zen-like state of control by letting go of the controls. You do this by preparing well for a climb, and then by trusting your skills as you engage

the climb freely. The result can be a sense of floating up the rock on autopilot, courtesy of a preconscious mind programmed via repeated redpoint rehearsal, extensive associated visualization, or simply through years of climbing experience.

7. **Loss of self-consciousness.** Self-consciousness is the mental perspective of looking at yourself as others might see you. The opposite of self-consciousness is a mind-set that holds little regards for the perceptions of others and lets go of ego and the need to succeed. Achieving this mind-set requires a strong self-image and a belief in your personal mission—two traits that you can develop by applying the material of the preceding chapters.

8. **Transformation of time.** In reflecting on a flow experience, some climbers say they perceived a slowing down of time, while others feel they experienced a speeding up of events. Either way, this transformation of time is a by-product of being fully in the moment and, thus, not caring about time or speed of ascent. Entering the flow state, then, demands that you set no time constraints on your ascent—your mind is obviously not in the moment if you are evaluating your progress according to the hands of a clock.

9. **Autotelic experience is the holistic sensation of flow and the end result of the other eight elements of flow.** The pith of flow is the act of full involvement in an activity that contains within itself the purpose of its existence. The feeling of moving over stone, the intrinsic rewards of the steep, and the spirit of climbing are the reasons we all fall in love with climbing. As we improve and become conscious of the recognition and possible rewards of our successes, however, we begin to lose our connection to the reasons we began climbing in the first place. You can avoid this pitfall—which makes flow difficult—by always climbing for climbing's sake and no other reason.

Table 12.3 *Stage Three Mental-Training Program*

Elite-level mental training must be precisely goal-matched in order to produce optimal results. Therefore, use the Stage Three program simply as a template around which you develop and self-direct your mental-training program. Actively add or replace exercises from throughout the book to train up weaknesses and best prepare for upcoming climbs and long-term goal pursuit. Record your daily mental training in a notebook or journal.

Waking/Morning Mental Training (5–15 minutes)

- Use positive, goal-directed affirmations to establish a positive mental state (see page 199).
- Engage in five to ten minutes of breathing and visualization exercises. Imagine in fast forward the day ahead, the climbs you plan to do, or the training or other activities you will engage in.
- Review your plan for the day; decide how you can act most effectively to make steps toward your short- and long-term goals.

Continued on next page

Continued from previous page

All-Day Mental Training

- Actively monitor and modulate your state to optimal levels for various daily activities. Alter your physiology to change how you feel (see page 108).
- Monitor your effectiveness in all you do. Consider how you could act more effectively. Observe your thought quality; direct self-talk and mental imagery to override negative thinking.
- Vow to be exclusively a doer and possibility thinker. Disregard the criticisms of others and remain focused on taking effective action toward your goals. Stay clear of complainers and develop friendships and partnerships with like-minded individuals.
- Foster awareness of potential distractions—exercise willpower in avoiding people and situations that will distract you from your day's game plan. Engage in single-tasking and try to take a tangible step toward your goals every day.
- Strive to respond positively and productively in adverse situations. Swiftly employ the appropriate problem-solving strategies from chapter 8.
- Identify limiting behaviors and use techniques from chapter 11 to delete these habits or behaviors. Actively edit your life—eliminating low-value activities and sources of bad stress—to reduce drag and accelerate progress toward your goals.
- Whenever possible, integrate some of the brain-training exercises (see page 247) into your daily routine.

Climbing Mental Training

- Use mental rehearsal and associated visualization before every climb.
- Use brain-training practice drills to refine skills and improve climbing economy. If appropriate, use brain-training physical exercise strategies to increase strength, power, and endurance.
- Use breathing and centering techniques before every climb and at each rest position. Employ the many techniques for improving concentration while climbing.
- Engage in risk and fear management before every climb. Actively manage the fears and risks that you identify. Strive to eliminate fear of failure and embrace the fear of the unknowns relating to your goal climbs.
- Grow your hanging-on power by pressing onward through greater and greater levels of physical and mental discomfort. Expand your capacity for mental flexibility and durability by stepping it up in adverse situations and the trials of the steep.

Evening/Bedtime Mental Training (30 or more minutes)

- Practice proper breathing techniques and the Progressive Relaxation Sequence.
- Train concentration using the Second-Hand Clock Drill, Attention-Shifting Drill, and Two-Minute Breath Focus Drill.
- Engage in highly detailed visualization. Exercise your memory by replaying a recent great climb move by move in your mind's eye. Preprogram a project climb or prepare for a mountain ascent by visualizing preparations, strategy, and if possible the specific moves and feel of the climb.
- Delete bad memories to reduce the weight of past failures or criticism. Modify or erase limiting behaviors using the mental exercises and strategies described in chapter 11.

243

We live out our lives in two worlds: a physical and mental world. In the physical world, we have certain limitations based on our DNA, and perhaps due to our age or where we were born and raised. Genetically, our bodies have a finite maximum set point that determines how much strength and endurance we can develop through a long-term training program. For many climbers, these physical-world factors determine what they will do and achieve.

In the mental world, however, there are no limits. Imagination is infinite. For millennia man stared at the moon with wonder. Then one day he walked on it. The biggest step toward this achievement was President Kennedy's "moon speech" (quoted on page 128); not mere rhetoric, but a big dream expressed with resolve that would direct steady action until the dream became a material reality. This dream-fulfillment process is uniquely human—a synthesis of our endowments of imagination and willpower to physically act and persevere—and it's the very same process that has lead to all grandiose climbing achievements.

You, too, can achieve and experience grandiosity, despite the limitations of the physical world. Exceptional achievements in climbing (and beyond) are more often a matter of unbridled imagination and daring, disciplined action. As you have learned on the previous pages, there's a tremendous power to beginning each day with a mini dream (your morning visualization) and then acting with intention until the day's end. Repeating this process, day after day, and creating countless daily mini dreams that gradually built toward your big dream (the mega goal) is the secret to living a remarkable and wonder-filled life.

Sadly, many people are effective dreamers, but grossly ineffective action takers. It's my hope that your experiences as a climber, combined with the guidance of this book and the sage advice of others, will empower you to live your dream life, whatever it may be. It's my wish that you will find a unique and exciting path in climbing and, ultimately, continue on to experience a long, balanced, and fulfilling life. Toward this end, I humbly conclude this book with a look at expanding your mental skills—and transferring the power of climbing—to all that you do and all whom you meet in your remaining days on this third rock from the sun.

Find Your Own Path

There are as many different paths to take in climbing as there are climbers, so why proceed down a path already traveled? Maximum climbers, both famous and anonymous, all establish their own paths. Throughout this book I've named numerous maximum climbers of diverse backgrounds who have forged their own exciting paths through the vertical world; I hope you will, too!

If you're a beginning climber, it's natural to copy and emulate the expert climbers you know or the professionals you read about in magazines. While you may be able to successfully model some elements of their technique and climbing tactics, becoming truly competent—and someday even exceptional—demands that you explore and experiment to develop your own style and modus operandi. To continue indefinitely in the mode of copying others and climbing with the crowd is a form of self-sabotage.

After a few years in the sport, real growth requires that you form new partnerships, explore new climbing subdisciplines, and develop your own climbing style in order to launch into a totally unique and lofting personal trajectory. This is what master climbers of every generation have done, including greats such as Willi Unsoeld, Royal Robbins, Yvon Chouinard, John Gill, Pat Ament, Jim Bridwell, Wolfgang Güllich, Todd Skinner, Lynn Hill, John Bachar, Peter Croft, Steph Davis, Tommy Caldwell, Dean Potter, Rolando Garibotti, Steve House, and Chris Sharma.

The aforementioned climbers are proof that dreaming big works. All lived a rather ordinary early life, but through the power of climbing, and the will to fulfill their dreams, these individuals forged a distinctive course in the climbing world. You can, too, but beware of naysayers and also-rans who attempt to douse your fiery passion. Whenever critics sound off, take solace in knowing that at some point all great climbers are criticized or have their dreams dismissed as "unlikely" or even "foolish." It's also important to remind yourself that compulsive critics are but meager mongers of negative energy, whereas doers are believers, fulfillers, and spreaders of positive energy and big dreams.

So I implore you to find your own path and believe in it! Emancipate yourself from cultural programming and peer pressure. Unleash your imagination and live your passion, while holding little concern for image or what other people think. Be a compulsive doer, and avoid being unnecessarily critical. Persevere through adverse times, and always keep faith in a positive endgame. While no dream is guaranteed to be fulfilled, in doing all these things you are guaranteed to find uncommon success, experience, and joy in climbing.

Become a Climber for Life

Like the changing phases of the moon, everything in life waxes and wanes. While you will likely improve as a climber for many years to come, there will come a day when your physical skills begin to wane. Some climbers choose to quit climbing when improvement seems to end. Others choose to be climbers for life, as the rich experience of moving over rock and ice is as vital to their lives as the air they breathe.

As a forty-something climber, it could be that my hardest climbs are behind me—although I dream and train as if they are still before me! After more than three decades as a climber, I still find each new day in the steep to be precious and invaluable. I can't imagine life without climbing. So like many others before me, I choose to be a climber for life. Each year I aspire to travel to new areas, meet new people, and pull down on new rock. Another joy, which I hadn't anticipated in my younger days, is introducing my two boys to the adventures of the steep. As a family we spend many weekends and our summer vacations traveling to new climbing areas. One remarkable discovery is that I sometimes feel as if I am learning more from watching my boys climb—and seeing the wonder in their eyes—than they learn from watching me. Only time will tell if my boys choose to continue as climbers or decide to explore other passions; but for now my wife and I cherish each day we have with them, in the mountains and at home.

Most climbers for life have a similar story—they ultimately come to strike a balance between actual climbing and time spent on other important commitments such as school, career, and family. By avoiding the distractions of ubiquitous low-value activities and by dodging the time and financial black holes of popular culture, they continue to pursue their passion for climbing through middle age and the senior years. You, of course, can too, if you consciously choose to be a climber for life!

Set no limits for what is possible in the future—you may do your hardest climb this year or you might make your greatest ascents in your senior years, as did Yuichiro Miura summiting Mount Everest at age seventy and Stimson Bullitt leading his first 5.10 route at age seventy-eight. As detailed throughout this book, climbing is a unique activity in which skill, experience, and wisdom can often more than make up for physical declines.

Notice how many young guns try to power up routes they aren't yet ready for. Perhaps they eventually thrash to the top, but the journey is rushed, technically flawed, and perhaps even filled with angst and a lack of enjoyment. Conversely, the more mature and wiser climber takes her time, maximizes use of her physical skill and strength, and climbs when conditions are just right and the route has in some way lowered its guard to invite the ascent. Ed Viesturs has aptly summarized this concept in stating, "I've learned in climbing that you don't 'conquer' anything. Mountains are not conquered and should be treated with respect and humility. If we take what the mountain gives, have patience and desire, and are prepared, then the mountains will permit us to reach their highest peaks."

It's the journey, experience, and self-discovery in climbing that hold the greatest value.

At the very core, climbing is an experience-oriented activity, not achievement-oriented. It's not how hard or high you climb, but how much you get out of climbing. While getting to the summit may be the goal, it's the journey, experience, and self-discovery that hold the greatest value. Since you could simply walk or take a helicopter to the top of most climbs, it should be self-evident that it's the process of climbing—not the summit—that attracts you to the vertical extreme.

And so I hope that your passion for the vertical experience will make you a climber for life; ever returning to the cliffs and mountains with the wonder-filled eyes of a child and the skill and care of a wily veteran climber; always dreaming and acting on the dream; regularly rediscovering the transcendence of the maximum climbing experience; and on the most special of days perhaps even touching the sky.

Make Brain Training a Way of Life

You are not what you climb or what you possess. You are how you climb, how you live, and what you think. For "you," you can substitute your brain, since it is source of cognition and the governor of all physical activity. Hence, *Maximum Climbing* is ultimately a brain-training book disguised as a how-to climbing book.

As a final bit of instruction on how to strengthen your creative and analytical powers, I will present fifteen simple brain exercises that you can employ in just about any situation or setting. Become familiar with these fifteen exercises and then pick one to use every few hours throughout of the day, whether you are at the climbing gym, crag, work, school, out for a hike, or lying in your tent at night. These exercises are designed to improve your imagination, memory, problem-solving abilities, the use of your five senses, and much more. Such mental training literally changes your brain by forming new synapses and neuro-associations. Performing these exercises regularly will improve your mental fitness and, thus, enhance all you do!

 ### Brain-Training Exercises for Everyday Use

1. **Make a route topo from memory.** Sit down with a blank sheet of paper and draw a topo of a past project or some other favorite climb. First sketch out the macro features (cracks, corners, ledges, and such), and then try to fill in as many holds and sequences as you can remember. Climb the route again in your mind's eye and see what minute details you can recall.

2. **Say no to beta.** Being spoon-fed sequences, instead of solving them yourself, shortcuts learning and slows the brain development of an aspiring climber. Ponder the findings of a fascinating study that found that the hippocampus (the brain's storehouse and processing center of spatial information) of London cabdrivers is far more developed than that of a typical Londoner. Imagine what happens to the brain of a driver who's given a GPS unit to guide his every turn or a climber who excessively relies on beta? While short-term effectiveness will improve, brain development and skill are grossly handicapped.

3. **When in a relaxed setting, close your eyes and explore the surroundings using your other senses.** I like to do this when lying in my tent at night, but you could also do it while sitting quietly at the crags, lying in bed, or during a rest break while hiking.

4. **Mentally climb a route every day.** While your body needs rest from the rigors of climbing, you can still climb in your mind's eye and strengthen your brain in the process. Using both dissociated and associated visualization, climb a favorite past route or current project daily. Pace the mental ascent to match the rate that you would climb for real. Try to see and feel every move.

5. **Replay in your mind's eye vivid mental movies of hallmark ascents from past years.** Strive to recall minute details of the ascent including the smells, sounds, colors, and feelings of that moment. Bask in the warmth of these great memories and keep them anchored and ever-present.

6. **Memorize the faces and names of climbers you meet.** Certainly you can't remember everyone, but it's a great mental exercise to make the effort. The key is to slow down the introduction process and ask a few questions that identify something novel about the person (perhaps her hometown, favorite climb or area, profession, and the like), and then to somehow link that novel item with her name and face. Review these associations that evening and the next morning, and there's a good chance they'll pass on to long-term memory.

7. **Read more actively.** Underline key passages and pause to ponder the deeper meanings as well as how the material applies to your life. At the end of each chapter, make summary notes; review the notes after one week and again in one month. Hopefully you are already using this technique in reading *Maximum Climbing*!

8. **Challenge yourself with new activities on rest days and during your off season.** Give a try to some vastly different activities such as skiing, snowboarding, mountain biking, lifting weights, playing golf or tennis. While these activities will do nothing to enhance your climbing skills, they will exercise your brain and body in new ways, as well as provide a period for renewal of motivation.

9. **Vary your passive activities.** Read books that will challenge you in some way or learn a musical instrument. Occasionally play games that stretch cognitive abilities, such as chess, poker, or other games of strategy. Reduce time spent watching TV, movies, or absorbed in other activities that fail to challenge the brain.

10. **Each week, engage some new people at work, the gym, or outside your normal social circles.** Explore their unique beliefs, passions, and ideas by asking questions and sharing experiences. Resist rejecting beliefs that are different from yours, and instead try to understand the individual's perspective and to find common ground with your own beliefs and interests.

11. **Dedicate more time to single-tasking.** Turn off your cell phone, computer, radio, TV, or anything else that prevents you from concentrating deeply for sustained periods. Do this when reading, writing, and mentally training, as well as when talking with a friend or spending time with a loved one. By allowing your mind to quiet down and shift to a single-pointed focus, you just might discover a deeper, perhaps sublime, level of experience heretofore unknown.

12. **Laugh a lot.** Develop your talent for finding irony and humor in a wide range of situations. Search for a humorous angle to a bad situation or failure. Laugh at yourself as much as possible.

13. **Pay it forward.** Be creative in finding simple ways to help out other people. Freely share your knowledge, experiences, and positive energy with all whom you meet. Find a way to help someone who's struggling or needs uplifting—there is no better exercise than reaching down and lifting other people up.

14. **Keep a journal.** Each day or week, record your thoughts, achievements, struggles, goals, and the like. Besides creating an invaluable documentation of your life's journey, writing in a journal provides you with perspective, offers catharsis, and helps solidify lessons and accomplishments of the day.

15. **Collect beautiful moments and find wonder in the simplest aspects of life.** Too often in climbing we are so focused on the task that we forget to enjoy our surroundings. Pause occasionally, while on a ledge or when hiking, and break from your task-oriented focus in order to explore the beauty all around you. Find inspiration in the landscapes, wildlife, and weather, as well as in the successes of others. These moments of inspiration allow you to tap into the divine, whether you call it positive energy, God, the universal spirit, or whatever.

Share Your Climbing Power with the World!

Over the last thirty-three years, I've spent tens of thousands of hours climbing, thinking about climbing, training for climbing, and writing about climbing. Occasionally, I reflect on this massive life investment into what could be viewed as an exceedingly self-centered activity—has it been a wise use of my life force? Sadly, obsession with climbing has ruined the schooling, careers, and marriages of all too many people I've met over the years. Even legendary mountaineer Conrad Anker has commented on how climbing can be "a selfish and frivolous game with gravity." Perhaps you, too, have pondered whether your intense passion for climbing is a good thing.

It has been posited that climbing does nothing for anyone else and contributes nothing to humankind or the world. While this is certainly true in terms of the act of climbing, I've concluded that this assessment is absolutely false when it comes to the potential aftereffects of climbing. Here's why.

In venturing into the mountains, we become more connected with nature and the true meaning of life, sometimes even obtaining flashes of insight and a strangely powerful sense of being a part of something larger and everlasting. Furthermore, climbing can teach us more about our characters and true potential than perhaps any other life activity. Pushing ourselves in the vertical extreme teaches us to concentrate deeply, conquer fear, and persevere through adversity—all virtues that can benefit us in other aspects of our lives. Climbing therefore gifts to us a realization of the tremendous personal power with which we are endowed, but often fail to discover in other nonclimbing endeavors.

Many other climbers have come to a similar conclusion. Legendary Italian mountaineer Walter Bonatti once said, "The mountains are the means; the man is the end. The idea is to improve the man, not to reach the top of the mountains." American climbing legend Pat Ament writes, "Climbing is fairly mundane in the normal atmosphere of discourse. The more cosmic function of rock, or of climbing, might be viewed rather as bringing light to oneself or one's own light to the world." Reinhold Messner similarly concludes that "time in the mountains can change us. The useless activity of climbing mountains can be very meaningful. The meaning in me is defined through what I do, even when others consider my activities to be useless."

The real power of climbing, then, is what we discover inside ourselves and then give back to others and contribute to the world. If we use climbing only to elevate ourselves, we simply confirm that it's a selfish, frivolous game. But if we leverage our skills to excel outside of climbing, we potentially affect the lives of others and perhaps change the world in some small way.

And so it is my hope that this book helps to empower and inspire you on the rock and in all you do. I welcome your correspondence, and I am always grateful to learn of readers' unique experiences and triumphs.

In fact, one of my greatest joys as an author is hearing from climbers around the world. Recently I received two e-mails that were nearly identical in their expressed passion for climbing—one from a climber in Israel, and the other from a climber in Iran. Despite the fundamental differences in culture and ideology, I believe in my heart that these two individuals experience the same spirit of climbing. I am certain that these two climbers could share a mutually joyful experience climbing together and likely return from the mountains as lifelong friends, possessing a great mutual respect for each other's background and beliefs.

The power of climbing is indeed immense. Here's wishing that you discover the power, feel the power, and share the power!

Afterword

A Tribute to Todd Skinner

This book is dedicated to Todd Skinner, and so I wanted to tell you a bit more about this inspirational and truly exceptional individual who tragically died on October 23, 2006, while descending fixed ropes on the Leaning Tower in Yosemite.

In 1990 I traveled to Bend, Oregon, to speak at the Beyond the Rock climbing performance seminar. Little did I know I would meet a man who would soon become one of my biggest influences as a climber, author, and human being.

The event organizers booked me in a hotel suite to be shared with Todd Skinner, a rising rock star fresh off his free ascent of the *Salathe Wall* route on El Cap. It was with great anticipation that I met Todd the first evening. I knew that we had a shared interest in training for climbing and we were of similar age (Todd was five years my senior), but I wasn't prepared to meet someone who mirrored in many ways my beliefs, passions, and core values.

The first evening we talked frenetically until two or three in the morning. We shared stories and goals, discussed training strategies and influences, and revealed our bonds to our families and home regions—mine in Pennsylvania, his in Wyoming. The highlight of our first evening of conversation was the discovery that we both shared a passion for thought experiment—imagining great things that might be possible, and then mentally synthesizing and exploring a pathway that might bring it to fruition. It was during this game of mental Twister that I discovered what was perhaps Todd's greatest asset—he told me that if you could find a way to believe, even in the smallest way, that a goal was feasible, then that's all you need to start marshaling the focus and energy, and developing a strategy and team, to make it a reality.

This was an epiphanic moment for me—to act with complete belief in something that is only slightly feasible was indeed a novel approach that I'm sure I would have dismissed outside the realm of Todd's energetic influence! Instead of following a path of mild or least resistance, as is the MO of the masses, Todd would first imagine and then embark on a path of great resistance. The genius of this principle of action is that while success was never guaranteed, the arduous process would surely elevate his physical and mental abilities. (And as I would come to learn, exploring inner

Todd Skinner working a Yosemite aid line known as **The Stigma.** *Todd free climbed the thin crack in 1985, after many days of effort, making for one of the hardest crack climbs in the world at the then rare grade of 5.13b.* BILL HATCHER

251

potential was just as important to Todd as exploring a new summit.) Of course, history has shown that Todd's adamant belief in the endgame meant that a positive outcome would most often be realized—it was just a matter of sustaining belief and effort and hanging on for as long as it took.

Despite the differences in our upbringing—Todd was a cowboy climber from the Rockies and I was a suburban climber from East Coast—we shared much common ground. We both marveled at the achievements of the legendary boulderer John Gill and we each credited the Gill biography *Master of Rock* as being an early catalyst for our interest in training for climbing. As it turned out, we both enjoyed the act of training almost as much as the feeling of moving over stone. In the years that followed, Todd and I crossed paths numerous times—most memorable was training at Todd's Lucky Lane home gym and hanging out at his Hueco Training Camp—and each time it took just a few minutes before we ignited into energetic discussion of training ideas and protocols. In reflecting on those days long gone by, I now recognize them as seminal moments, and that my exchanges with Todd inspired and leavened much of what I've done as a climber and author.

Similarly, Todd influenced countless others through his unbridled passion for climbing and living. More than any other person I've met, he exuded positive energy that stuck like the sweetest honey to all who met him. His character and integrity were impeccable and likewise influential on others. Even after achieving the status of one of the world's greatest climbers, Todd remained accessible as a mentor and friend to many. You could always spot him at the crags—he was the climber with a never-ending smile and the most contagious zeal, always willing to shake a hand, tell a story, or give a young climber a tip. Befriending me and others who approached him was not some PR act of a famous climber, it was simply Todd living out one of his guiding principles. In his book *Beyond the Summit*, Todd says, "It is important for us to be mentors to someone else: a nod instead of a frown, the time spent teaching a skill, a hand held out to someone—all can make the difference in a life." He goes on, "We gain most not by reaching our destination, but by bringing others with us on the climb."

Thus, Todd's climbing achievements, as great as they are, pale in comparison with his countless simple acts of kindness and his ability to inspire all who met him. And so he lives on in those he touched and inspired—he is not gone, he has only changed form. Images of Todd live on in my dreams, and his voice rings in my ears, saying, "Live each day with enthusiasm unknown to mankind!" That's what Todd did and what he hopes you and I will do, too.

To learn more about Todd's legacy visit www.toddskinner.com.

Glossary

The following is a compilation of some of the technical terms and climbing jargon used throughout this book.

aerobic(s)—Any physical activity deriving energy from the breakdown of glycogen in the presence of oxygen, thus producing little or no lactic acid, enabling an athlete to continue exercising much longer.

afferent—Sensory feedback (to the brain) from the muscles, heart, and lungs.

anaerobic—Energy production in the muscles involving the breakdown of glycogen in the absence of oxygen; a by-product called lactic acid is formed, resulting in rapid fatigue and cessation of physical activity.

anaerobic endurance—The ability to continue moderate- to high-intensity activity over a period of time; commonly called power endurance or power stamina by climbers, though these terms are scientifically incorrect.

anaerobic threshold—The workload or level of oxygen consumption where lactate production by the working muscles exceeds the rate of lactate removal by the liver; typically at 50 to 80 percent of maximum intensity of exercise, and in proportion to one's level of anaerobic endurance conditioning.

antagonist—A muscle providing an opposing force to the primary muscles of action (agonist).

anxiety—Nervousness or distress about uncertainties and future outcomes.

arousal—An internal state of alertness or excitement.

beta—Any prior information about a route, including hold location, sequence, rests, gear, clips, et cetera.

blocked practice—A practice routine in which a specific task is practiced repeatedly, as in working a crux move or sequence.

campus (or campusing)—Climbing an overhanging section of rock or artificial wall with no feet, usually in a dynamic left-hand, right-hand, left-hand (and so forth) sequence.

campus training—A climbing-specific form of reactive training, developed by Wolfgang Güllich at the Campus Center, a weight-lifting facility at the University of Nürnberg, Germany.

center of gravity—The theoretical point on which the total effect of gravity acts on the body.

contact strength—Initial grip strength upon touching a handhold; directly related to the speed at which the muscular motor units are called into play.

crux—The hardest move, or sequence of moves, on a route.

dynamic move—An explosive leap for a hold otherwise out of reach.

efferent—Neural signals the brain directs to the skeletal muscles.

endurance—The ability to perform physical work for an extended period of time. Cardiovascular endurance is directly related to VO2 max, whereas muscular endurance is influenced by circulation and available oxygen.

exteroception—Sensory information from sources outside the body.

flash—To climb a route first try without ever having touched it, but with the aid of beta.

glycemic index (GI)—A scale that classifies how the ingestion of various foods affects blood sugar levels in comparison with the ingestion of straight glucose.

Golgi tendon organ—Sensory receptors located between the muscle and its tendon that are sensitive to the stretch of the muscle tendon produced during muscular contraction.

hangdogging—Climbing a route, usually bolt-to-bolt, with the aid of a rope to hang and rest while practicing the sequence.

headpoint—Leading or soloing a climb after toprope rehearsal.

homeostasis—The body's tendency to maintain a steady state despite external changes.

Hypergravity Isolation Training (HIT)—A highly refined and specific method of training maximum finger strength by climbing on identical finger holds (isolation) with greater than body weight (hypergravity). Also known as Hörst Isolation Training.

interval training—A method of anaerobic endurance training that involves brief periods of intense training interspaced with periods of rest or low-intensity training.

interoception—Sensory information from sources within the body.

lactic acid—An acid by-product of the anaerobic metabolism of glucose during intense muscular exercise.

maximum strength—The peak force of a muscular contraction, irrespective of the time element.

metacognition—Awareness of one's thoughts, and use of this self-awareness to regulate one's thoughts.

modeling—A learning technique in which an individual watches, then attempts, a skill as performed properly by another person.

motor learning—A set of internal processes associated with practice or experience leading to a relatively permanent gain in performance capability.

motor skill—A skill where the primary determinant of success is the movement component itself.

motor unit—A motor neuron, together with a group of muscle cells, stimulated in an all-or-nothing response.

muscular endurance—The length of time a given level of power can be maintained.

neuron—Conductive cells of the nervous system; the core component of the brain, spinal cord, and peripheral nerves.

neuroplasticity—Refers to changes that occur within the brain as a result of experience.

on-sight—When a route is climbed first try and with absolutely no prior information of any kind.

power—A measure of both the force and the speed (speed = distance x time) of a muscular contraction through a given range of motion. Power is the explosive aspect of strength.

proprioception—Sensory information from within the body arising from the sensory receptors found in muscles, tendons, joints, and the inner ear that detect the motion or position of the limbs and body. Also known as kinesthesis.

random practice—A practice sequence in which tasks from several classes are experienced in random order over consecutive trials.

reactive training—A power-building exercise that couples, in rapid succession, a forceful eccentric contraction with an explosive concentric contraction.

redpoint—Lead climbing a route bottom-to-top in one push.

schema—A set of rules, developed and applied unconsciously by the motor system in the brain and spinal cord, relating how to move and adjust muscle forces, body positions, et cetera, given the parameters at hand, such as steepness of the rock, friction qualities, holds being used, and type of terrain.

skill—The capability to bring about an end result with maximum certainty, minimum energy, and minimum time.

strength—The amount of muscle force that can be exerted; speed and distance are not factors of strength.

synapse—Functional connections, mediated by chemical neurotransmitters, between neurons and other non-neuronal cells that provide perception, thought, and memory, as well as facilitating motor control and more.

Tabata—A grueling interval-training protocol involving twenty seconds of maximum-intensity exercise followed by ten seconds of rest, usually repeated up to eight times. Named after its developer, Izumi Tabata.

Valsalva Maneuver—Forced exhalation of air against a closed mouth to increase chest and abdominal pressure (core tension) during a hard climbing move.

variable practice—Practice in which many variations on a class of actions are performed; the opposite of blocked practice.

visualization—Controlled and directed imagery that can be used for awareness building, monitoring and self-regulation, healing, and, most important, as mental programming for good performances.

VO2 max—Maximal oxygen uptake, as in the measurement of maximum aerobic power.

wired—Known well, as in a wired route.

working—Practicing the moves on a difficult route via toprope or hangdogging.

References
and Reading List

Ament, Pat. John Gill: *Master of Rock*. Mechanicsburg, PA: Stackpole Books, 1998.

———. *How to Be a Master Climber*. Boulder, CO: Two Lights, 1997.

Boga, Steven. *Climbers: Scaling the Heights with the Sports Elite*. Mechanicsburg, PA: Stackpole Books, 1994.

Brown, Katie. *Vertical World*. Guilford, CT: FalconGuides, 2007.

———. *Girl on the Rocks*. Guilford, CT: FalconGuides, 2009.

Buzan, Tony. *Use Both Sides of Your Brain*. New York: Plume, 1991.

Child, Greg. *Over the Edge*. New York: Villard, 2002.

Csikszentmihalyi, Mihaly. *Flow: The Psychology of Optimal Experience*. New York: Harper Perennial, 1990.

Davis, Steph. *High Infatuation*. Seattle: The Mountaineers Books, 2007.

Doidge, Norman. *The Brain That Changes Itself*. New York: Penguin Books, 2007.

Florine, Hans, and Bill Wright. *Speed Climbing*. Guilford, CT: FalconGuides, 2005.

Garfield, Charles A. *Peak Performance*. New York: Warner Books, 1984.

Harris, Dorothy V., and Bette L. Harris. *Sports Psychology: Mental Skills for Physical People*. New York: Leisure Press, 1984.

Hepp, Tillman. *Wolfgang Güllich: A Life in the Vertical*. Stuttgart, Germany: Boulder Ed., 1994.

Hill, Lynn. *Free Climbing: My Life in the Vertical*. New York: Norton, 2002.

Hörst, Eric. *Training for Climbing*. Guilford, CT: FalconGuides, 2008.

———. *How to Climb 5.12*. Guilford, CT: FalconGuides, 2003.

———. *Mental Wings: A Seven-Step, Life-Elevating Program for Uncommon Success*. www.mentalwings.com, 2003.

Ilgner, Arno. *The Rock Warrior's Way*. La Vergne, TN: Desiderata Institute, 2003.

Jackson, Susan A. *Flow in Sports*. Champaign, IL: Human Kinetics, 1999.

Livingston, Michael K. *Mental Discipline*. Champaign, IL: Human Kinetics, 1989.

Messner, Reinhold. *Moving Mountains*. Provo, UT: Executive Excellence Publishing, 2001.

O'Connell, Nichols. *Beyond Risk*. Seattle: The Mountaineers Books, 1993.

O'Connor, Joseph, and Ian McDermott. *Principles of NLP*. San Francisco: Thorsons, 1996.

Peale, Norman Vincent. *Positive Imaging*. New York: Ballantine Books, 1982.

Schmidt, Richard A., and Craig A. Wrisberg. *Motor Learning and Performance*. Champaign, IL: Human Kinetics, 2004.

Skinner, Todd. *Beyond the Summit*. New York: Portfolio, 2003.

Tutko, Thomas. *Sports Psyching*. New York: Perigee Books, 1976.

Twight, Mark. *Extreme Alpinism*. Seattle: The Mountaineers Books, 1999.

Ungerleider, Steven. *Mental Training for Peak Performance*. Emmaus, PA: Rodale Press, 1996.

Viesturs, Ed. *No Shortcuts to the Top*. New York: Broadway Books, 2006.

Weinberg, Robert S. *Foundations of Sport and Exercise Psychology*. Champaign, IL: Human Kinetics, 2003.

Zak, Heinz. *Rock Stars: The World's Best Free Climbers*. Munich, Germany: Rother, 1997.

Index

M

Mandela, Nelson, 21
Master of Rock: Biography of John Gill
   (Ament), 252
maximum climbing. *See also* specific
   aspects of, 244–49
   definition of, 9–11
meditation, 39, 113, 115, 218
   daily, 229–30
   effect on brain structure, 37
   and focus, 164
medium-term goals. *See also* goal setting,
   128–29, 130
mega goals. *See also* goal setting, 125,
   128, 137, 233
   strategy for, 130–33
Meltdown route
memory. *See also* mind, 9, 43–45
   negative memories, 208–9
mental imagery. *See also* mental training;
   visualization, 111, 113
   guided imagery, 192
   mental rehearsal, 190–91, 230, 231
mental training, 3, 5, 47, 155, 189–90,
   221–49
   affirmations, 199–200
   behavior modification, 201–18
   brain skills and mental skills, 13, 14
   and brain structure, 36, 37
   developing willpower, 19–21
   development in levels of climbers,
      13–15
   guided imagery, 192
   history of, 11–12
   improvement curve, 223–25
   maintaining concentration, 155, 156
   mental rehearsal, 190, 191–92,
      230, 231
   optimal training, 222–23
   physical simulation, 198–99
   positive spin on adversity, 142–43
   problem solving strategies, 149–53
   self-assessment, 26, 27, 28
   self-awareness, 85–97
   seven absolutes of, 226

smart training, 225–27
stage one program, 228–31
stage three program, 237–43
stage two program, 232–37
summary of benefits and
   methods, 14
visualization, 192–98
Merzenich, Michael, 34–35, 221
Messner, Reinhold, 124, 197
   ascent of Everest, 18, 70
   climbing's purpose, 249
   on criticism, 183
   on fear, 171
metacognition. *See also* mind; thoughts,
   17, 87–88, 97, 201, 229
midbrain, 32
mind. *See also* mental training; brain, 3,
   5, 7, 31, 38–45
   awareness, 38–39
   conscious mind, 39–40
   controlling thoughts, 110–18
   directing with self-talk, 162, 165
   memory, 43–45
   mind/body/emotions interaction,
      100, 101
   and neurons, 34
   preconscious, 40–41
   programming strategies, 189, 190
   taking mental inventory, 120, 121
   unconscious, 41–43
Miura, Yuichiro, 246
Model, Bobby, 140
modeling, 61, 66
moment. *See* present, staying in
monthly goals. *See also* goal setting,
   128–29
moods. *See also* emotions, 99
   and posture, 108
motivation, 125–26, 127
   and adversity, 140
   increasing, 204–6, 218
motor learning. *See* motor skills
motor skills, 47, 48–49
   and brain, 3, 8, 9, 14
   development in beginners, 13

About the Author

An accomplished climber of more than thirty years, Eric J. Hörst (pronounced hurst) has climbed extensively across the United States and has established hundreds of first ascents on his home crags in the eastern United States. A student and teacher of climbing performance, Eric has personally helped train hundreds of climbers, and his training books and concepts have spread to climbers in more than fifty countries. He is widely recognized for his innovative practice methods and training techniques, and since 1994 he has served as a training products design consultant and online Training Center editor for Nicros, Inc., a leading manufacturer of climbing walls and handholds.

Eric is author of *Training for Climbing, Conditioning for Climbers, How to Climb 5.12,* and *Learning to Climb Indoors,* all of which have foreign translations. His articles and photos have been published in many outdoor and fitness magazines including *Climbing, Rock and Ice, Dead Point, Urban Climber, Outside, National Geographic Adventure, Men's Health, Muscle and Fitness, Experience Life,* and *Men's Journal.* He has appeared on numerous TV broadcasts and produces Training Tip podcasts for PodClimber.com. Visit Eric's Web site, TrainingForClimbing.com, for training articles and information on all his books, or to schedule a training seminar, an editorial interview, or a speaking engagement.

Eric currently lives in Lancaster, Pennsylvania, with his wife, Lisa Ann, and his sons, Cameron and Jonathan.

Other FalconGuides
by Eric J. Hörst

Training for Climbing is a comprehensive, science-based tome that covers all aspects of climbing performance including training strength, technique, and the mind, as well as in-depth chapters on nutrition, accelerating recovery, and preventing/treating injuries. *TFC* is the definitive climbers' resource, and it's the training text of choice by climbers in more than fifty countries!

Conditioning for Climbers is the ultimate manual for climbers who are looking to improve their physical capabilities. The book follows a logical progression of self-assessment, goal setting, general conditioning and weight loss, core conditioning, and climbing-specific training to develop strength, power, and endurance. Regardless of your age, ability, or sports background, this book will empower you to develop and engage in a supremely effective conditioning program.

How to Climb 5.12 is a performance guidebook to attaining the most rapid gains in climbing ability possible. It provides streamlined instruction on vital topics such as accelerating learning of skills, training your mind and body, and becoming an effective on-sight and redpoint climber.

Learning to Climb Indoors is the most complete book available on indoor climbing. Topics covered include beginner and advanced climbing techniques, tactics, strategy, basic gear, safety techniques, self-assessment, and a primer on mental training and physical conditioning. This guide includes everything you need to know from day one as a climber through your first year or two in the sport.

ACCESS: IT'S EVERYONE'S CONCERN

The Access Fund is a national nonprofit climbers' organization working to keep climbing areas open and conserve the climbing environment. Need help with a climbing related issue? Call us and please consider these principles when climbing.

- **ASPIRE TO CLIMB WITHOUT LEAVING A TRACE:** Especially in environmentally sensitive areas like caves. Chalk can be a significant impact. Pick up litter and leave trees and plants intact.
- **MAINTAIN A LOW PROFILE:** Minimize noise and yelling at the crag.
- **DISPOSE OF HUMAN WASTE PROPERLY:** Use toilets whenever possible. If toilets are not available, dig a "cat hole" at least six inches deep and 200 feet from any water, trails, campsites or the base of climbs. Always pack out toilet paper. Use a "poop tube" on big wall routes.
- **USE EXISTING TRAILS:** Cutting switchbacks causes erosion. When walking off-trail, tread lightly, especially in the desert on cryptogamic soils.
- **BE DISCRETE WITH FIXED ANCHORS:** Bolts are controversial and are not a convenience. Avoid placing unless they are absolutely necessary. Camouflage all anchors and remove unsightly slings from rappel stations.
- **RESPECT THE RULES:** Speak up when other climbers do not. Expect restrictions in designated wilderness areas, rock art sites and caves. Power drills are illegal in wilderness and all national parks.
- **PARK AND CAMP IN DESIGNATED AREAS:** Some climbing areas require a permit for overnight camping.
- **RESPECT PRIVATE PROPERTY:** Be courteous to landowners.
- **JOIN THE ACCESS FUND:** To become a member, make a tax-deductible donation of $35.

P.O. Box 17010
Boulder, CO 80308
303.545.6772

ACCESS FUND
your climbing future
www.accessfund.org